Defiant Publics

Also Written or Edited By Daniel Drache (and Others)

La ilusión continental seguridad fronteriza y búsqueda de una identidad norteamericana, (Siglo XXI Editores: México, 2007).

L'illusion continentale: Sécurité et nord-américanité (editions Athéna, 2006)

Borders Matter: Homeland Security and the Search for North America (Fernwood Publishing, 2004)

The Market or the Public Domain: Global Governance and the Asymmetry of Power (Routledge, 2001)

Health Reform: Public Success, Private Failure, with Terry Sullivan (Routledge, 1999)

States Against Markets: The Limits of Globalization, with Robert Boyer, (Routledge, 1996)

Warm Heart, Cold Country: Fiscal and Social Policy Reform in Canada, with Andrew Ranachan (Caledon Institute, 1995)

Staples, Markets and Cultural Change: The Centenary Edition of Harold Innis' Collected Essays (McGill-Queen's, 1995)

Canada and the Global Economy (University of Athabasca, 1994)

The Changing Workplace: Reshaping Canada's Industrial Relations System, with Harry Glasbeek (James Lorimer, 1992)

Getting On Track: Social Democratic Strategies for Ontario, with John O'Grady (McGill-Queen's, 1992)

Negotiating with a Sovereign Quebec, with R. Perin (James Lorimer, 1992)

The New Era of Global Competition: State Policy and Market Power, with Meric Gertler (McGill-Queen's, 1991)

Politique et régulation modèle de développement et trajectoire canadienne, with Gérard Boismenu (Méridien/L'Harmattan, 1990)

DEFIANT PUBLICS

The Unprecedented Reach of the Global Citizen

Daniel Drache

with Marc D. Froese

polity

First published in 2008 by Polity Press

Polity Press
65 Bridge Street
Cambridge CB2 1UR, UK

Polity Press
350 Main Street
Malden, MA 02148, USA

ISBN-13: 978-0-7456-3178-3
ISBN-13: 978-0-7456-3179-0(pb)

Typeset in 11 on 13 pt Berling
by Servis Filmsetting Ltd, Stockport, Cheshire
Printed and bound in the UK by MPG Books Ltd, Bodmin, Cornwall

The publisher has used its best endeavors to ensure that the URLs for external websites referred to in this book are correct and active at the time of going to press. However, the publisher has no responsibility for the websites and can make no guarantee that a site will remain live or that the content is or will remain appropriate.

Every effort has been made to trace all copyright holders, but if any have been inadvertently overlooked the publishers will be pleased to include any necessary credits in any subsequent reprint or edition.

For further information on Polity, visit our website: www.polity.co.uk

Contents

List of figures   vii
Acknowledgements   viii

Introduction: Goals and Values that are   1
Inescapably Public

1   The Crowded Public Sphere and its Discontents   24

2   Market Fundamentalism and the Worried Public   54

3   Digital Publics and the Culture of Dissent   89

4   Nixers, Fixers, and the Axes of Conformity   115

5   Infinite Varieties of the Modern Public: 144
    Novelty, Surprise, and Uncertainty

    Appendix: Critical Human Rights   172
    Conventions of the Global Public Domain

    A Note on Sources   179
    Select Bibliography   184
    Index   187

If a man sets out to hate all the miserable creatures he meets, he will not have much energy left for anything else.
Arthur Schopenhauer, *Studies in Pessimism*

Figures

1   Declining support for the new   5
      "Pax Americana": popular approval ratings
      for Bush and Blair
1.1   Unweighted international inequality,   39
      1950–98 (measured by the Gini coefficient)
2.1   The resurgent anti-market vote, 1995–2006   64
2.2   Taxes as a collective sharing of resources   73
      in the public interest
3.1   A surfer's guide to the 1 billion-strong   103
      e-public universe
4.1   The compass of post-modern dissent: reinforcing   124
      social inclusion
4.2   The embedded axes of conformity: me individualism   132

Acknowledgements

David Held holds a special place in the festival of thank yous. He proposed that I extend my ideas about the public domain in a time of intense globalization and volatility. I particularly wanted to explore this seminal concept from the standpoint of agency rather than structure. The challenge appeared to be simple but turned out to be much more complex and demanding than ever imagined. I owe him a special debt of thanks.

In preparing *Defiant Publics*, I have received equal amounts of encouragement and critical feedback. Among those who were positive skeptics about this project are: Jules Duchastel, Robert Cox, Stephen McBride, Marjorie Cohen, Warren Crichlow, William Coleman, Harry Arthurs, Hazel Ipp, Robert O'Brien, Donna Bobier, Randy Germain, Ute Lehrer, Bob Kellermann, Andy Cooper, Janet Conway, Roger Keil, Duncan Cameron, Claude Serfati, Jan Arte Scholte, Mel Watkins, Isidoro Cheresky, Inés Pousadela, Stephen Clarkson, Marie-Josée Massicot, and Gilles Allaire. Michael Adams pitched in to help rethink the title and I am appreciative of his support.

Marc Froese played a key role in the final preparation of the manuscript. He has been brilliant in crafting words, clarifying ideas, and bringing his own special insights to the final preparation of the manuscript. A special thanks to him.

Many ideas were work-shopped at a number of conference settings including the Centre of Globalization, McMaster University (2005), the University of Ottawa's Department of Political Science (2006), the École CNRS, CIRAD INRA Thématique in La Rochelle, France (2005), the Seminario Internacional Ciudadanía,

"Sociedad civil y participación política," at the University of Buenos Aires (2005), the Political Studies Students' Conference "The State of the State: New Challenges in the 21st Century" at the University of Manitoba (2005), and at the University of Warwick's Centre for the Study of Globalization and Regionalization, "Regionalization and the Taming of Globalization" (2005).

Daniel Salée, Concordia University, was generous with his time and thoughts about the dynamics of power and its central theoretical importance for my examination of the culture of dissent. He also gave the manuscript a critical read in the final stages. Imre Szeman, McMaster University, and Peer Zumbansen, Osgood Hall Law School, York University, also read the final manuscript and their critical comments made a difference. Justice Marion Cohen brought to my attention Hannah Arendt's powerful essay "Personal Responsibility under Dictatorship," which helped shape my thinking about micro-activism. Finally, George Baird, Dean of Architecture at the University of Toronto and a prolific writer on things public from an architectural perspective, let me read his important manuscript, "Public Space: Political Theory; Street Photography; An Interpretation," which helped sharpen my own thoughts about Walter Benjamin, Jürgen Habermas, Nancy Fraser, and Hannah Arendt.

A group of graduate students has had a very positive role in the critical development of my ideas. Greg Smith worked closely with the idea of false majorities and prepared the tables and charts that shed light on my arguments. David Clifton has been an important mainstay throughout and helped with the modeling of global e-publics and also with preparing different tables and charts on the e-universe. Alex Samur and I shared a common project on the semiotics of disobedience which is available at Canadian Cultural Observatory (www.culturescope.ca). Jean-François Crépeault showed me the link between my own work and social values and media activism. He also helped in the earlier stages of the draft. Jaigris Hodson has been very useful in discussing the role of public reason in the making of the global citizen and helped prepare the appendix on human rights conventions. Our many discussions on the multifaceted articulation of public reason in an Internet age helped clarify my thinking.

Laura Taman played a critical role in reading multiple drafts and in editing the text throughout. I am much indebted to her sharp pencil and smart editorial judgment. I have been fortunate to work at the Robarts Centre for Canadian Studies at York University for the past fifteen years first as Director and now as its Associate Director. Seth Feldman, the current Director, has offered a lot of moral support throughout the many drafts.

Polity Press has been very kind and supportive as well as patient. Emma Hutchinson and Sarah Lambert, both editorial assistants at Polity, have offered much encouragement throughout.

It is convention to acknowledge support from those closest to the author. As always, family matters in my case, and loads of appreciation are due to Marilyn and Charlotte who have been tolerant, obliging, and kind to a fault. Very special thanks indeed!

Daniel Drache, Toronto, January 2008

Introduction: Goals and Values that are Inescapably Public

The decisive turning point

In the aftermath of the Allied victory in the Second World War, values and goals that were inescapably public captured people's attentive imaginations. "Things public" was a highly evocative, catch-all phrase that covered everything from new citizenship rights to state regulation of the modern capitalist economy. To speak of the public had an authentic, highly optimistic ring of pluralism to it and seemed the perfect choice of words for a democratic age. No one who had experienced the cataclysmic war had any doubt that a greatly expanded public domain embodied hope for a better life. It evoked the collective power of entitlement and the longing for a fair and just international order. Collective action became a core responsibility of the public, just as the ideal of citizenship would constitute the postwar framework for many postcolonial countries. As for the heart of economic policy, the seamless functioning of markets seemed to be banished forever from the modern repertoire of public policy.

In a more cynical time when Western liberal democracies regrouped to manage the perceived danger of Soviet communism, right-of-center governments enthusiastically embraced these same virtuous sounding policies that promised stability because it made for good politics that won elections, kept the Left out of power, and also protected governments from the harshest criticisms of their own citizens. With the fall of the Berlin Wall in 1989, a new era of international politics began. It consecrated an improbable marriage between the economic triumphalism of technocratic elites and the political optimism of easily led global publics that expected their governments would continue to build strong cohesive societies and foster the public interest through generous government spending. This book is about their violent and chaotic divorce.

At first during the Cold War period, elites everywhere were convinced that they had tamed the shrew of public dissent. Capitalism was to be the basis for all social life, and market fundamentalism was to be the religion that gave us domestic bliss at home and peaceful prosperity abroad. In his bestseller *The End of History*, Francis Fukuyama saw no reason to alter this convenient arrangement. Millions agreed with him that this was the most pessimistic of ages, a period in which the public saw few possibilities beyond the paternalism of global capitalism.[1]

Today, coordinated and defiant activists are standing up to market fundamentalism and testing the conservative belief in a narrowly defined technocratic process of politics. These diverse publics in Australia, Brazil, and South Africa have challenged the command and control structures of undemocratic state authority and the new property rights created by global neo-liberalism's agenda of privatization, deregulation, and global free trade.[2] How could the high priests of supply-side economics, who preached the power of low taxes, freewheeling entrepreneurs, and liquid capital for global growth, have missed the other side of globalization – the rise of social movements, micro-activists, and networks of oppositional publics? How could Fukuyama, like many elites before him, have failed to learn Hegel's biggest history lesson?

Hegel, like the classical scholars he studied, understood well that history is a process of evolution and change. Social change is a foundational element of human society and the best efforts of the political class to maintain social structures that facilitate hierarchy and protect political privilege are ultimately self-defeating. What should we make of these angry, defiant, self-organizing publics as they reshape the sphere of interactive communication and affect the landscape of electoral politics? How should we think about this new geography of power with its disorderly voices, opposing interests, and virulent claims?

These are only a few of the pressing questions we must consider. Whether or not neo-conservatives are prepared to face it, their defining moment is over. Global politics and US hegemony have dramatically changed over the two presidential terms of George W. Bush. Signs of imperial overstretch are visible everywhere, and US expenditure on armed forces has placed new stresses on the American economy. The Bush revolution's attempt at engineering regime change has organized new forms of resistance that challenge American bullying in managing the global economy.

In the 1990s, it was fashionable to define global neo-liberal reforms with such phrases as "macro-economic stabilization," "structural reform," and "deficit cutting." The respective crises in Mexico, Russia, Brazil, and Asia owe a lot to the rigid template thinking associated with the Washington Consensus. The new discourse is no longer framed by accommodating the market but by taming it. "Governance," "transparency," "institutions," "democratic policy," and "accountability" reflect the deep shift away from American leadership. Moises Naim got it right when he wrote that: "concerns about states that were too strong has now given way to concerns about states that are too weak."[3] The single-minded obsession with crushing inflation has been substituted by a much more immediate need to regulate chaotic financial markets following the collapse of the US subprime housing market A new global order is taking shape, and there is very little Clinton, Obama, or McCain can do to restore American hegemony to its former glory.

Polarized global publics and electoral volatility

Global elites and many publics still have not come to terms with the new politics of the age and the growing role of parliaments, courts, non-governmental organizations (NGOs), and the engaged angry citizen qua voter. What has changed is that the structure and system of global economic neo-liberalism are under siege from both the progressive left and the populist right. In 2007, a majority of angry French voters cast their ballots for Nicolas Sarkozy rather than Ségolène Royal; the Right garnered a larger share of the protest vote than the Left. In neighboring Belgium, the center-left Christian Democrats bloodied the nose of the Flemish socialist coalition. The ideological splintering of liberal values and economic principles has introduced new uncertainties for ruling parties everywhere. Elites are divided about how much to spend on public services and how much the social market needs to be strengthened. For more than a decade, voter loyalty has become flux increasingly unpredictable as disgruntled publics shift votes to fit their volatile mood swings.

Presently angry voters have opted for Bolivarian alternatives in Chile, Bolivia, Argentina, Brazil, and Venezuela. They not only want a change of government but more fundamentally a different model of development. In Spain, Sweden, Norway, New Zealand, and even Canada, voters are looking for alternatives to market democracy that so far have eluded them. They want governmental reform and a major policy overhaul. After more than a decade of unprecedented wealth creation, the issue of building more equitable societies is now on the agenda. In Germany, almost two-thirds of voters voted against Angela Merckel and the Right. In 2007 Australian voters finally turned with a fury against John Howard, the last Bush proconsul, to defeat his coalition government. They voted Labour into office with a massive majority more than doubling their seats in parliament. Even George W. Bush and Tony Blair, who once enjoyed popular support levels that verged on a cult of personality, have plummeted in public esteem following their tragic invasion of Iraq. In March 2003, public opinion formed a general consensus that Bush and Blair should be allowed to implement their vision of collective security. By December 2004, cautious support had turned to strong public opprobrium, and indeed a tidal wave of disgust was triggered by the images of Abu Ghraib prison (see figure 1). No one could have predicted this global electoral realignment that would polarize public opinion and shake up the electoral map.

The new IT model of social relations

Foucault's star has never shone more brightly in academic circles and he is the undisputed authority to discuss state governance practices, where panoptic authority disciplines citizens, punishes dissent, and ratchets up the grip of elites on the levers of power.[4] As valuable as Foucault's ideas are for a penetrating analysis of the exercise of power in modern societies, this frame tells us surprisingly little about the current changes underway in the

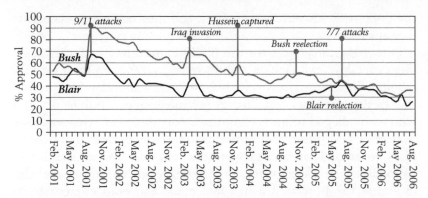

Figure 1 Declining support for the new "Pax Americana": popular approval ratings for Bush and Blair

Sources: Robarts Centre, 2007, adapted from NYT/CBS polls; Ben Schott, "Five Years of Consequence," *New York Times*, September 7, 2006

public domain. Anger over the heavy-handed tactics of elites has reached new levels, and publics are giving vent to their frustration. The "decline in deference," to employ Neil Nevitte's astute phrase, is challenging the core institutions of liberal society.[5] In the family, father no longer knows best; in politics, presidents and prime ministers are magnets of distrust, in organized religion a majority of the faithful no longer practice rite or ritual.

Suddenly it would appear that people have acquired a new vantage point. Social movement activists today are in possession of the organizational and informational tools required to rescue the idea of the public from the instrumental economic rationality of the market and return it to its original roots in individual action, collective achievement, and public reason. The signing of the Land Mine Treaty in 1999 against the use, stockpiling, and production of land mines is perhaps the most iconic example of a success story of transnational protest helped by a small army of diplomats. The creation of the International Court of Justice in 2002 to prosecute any government or national citizen from a signatory state for crimes against humanity is another milestone that could not have happened without the support of millions of activists worldwide. Their cumulative impact has registered at the United Nations in the dozens of conventions, treaties, and international agreements (see appendix).

One important boost for the NGO community is that government officials can no longer claim sovereign impunity for gross violations of human rights ever since an American judge accepted in the 1980s universal jurisdiction lawsuits against public officials who were alleged to have committed torture – war crimes against humanity – outside the United States. The near extradition of Pinochet rattled American governments as they realized that international law and foreign courts could have such legal muscle. The idea that the power of a national court can hold citizens from another country accountable for crimes against humanity and other extreme human rights abuses has given new legitimacy to the influence and role of non-state actors.[6]

We need to find an objective way of assessing the effectiveness and impact of all this micro global activism so varied and geographically disparate for imagining the future. There are tens of millions of micro-activists organizing their neighborhoods, protesting the abuse of power in their city, demanding clean water, better teachers, and a modern school system. Political scientists have not paid a lot of attention to these atom-like civic actors who operate under the radar screen and are not part of any formal social movement. No news network covers what they are demanding or reports on their successes or failures. They are cursed with anonymity but are important nonetheless. They connect people and frame issues like the environment, AIDS, and poverty when no one else cares. Some experts are dismissive of this innovative churning substratum of free-floating global activism that lacks organizational structure and a full blown ideological identity, but this too is a mistake.

Micro-activism and the dynamics of power

Inglehart's empirical research for the last decade has found that activities that challenge hierarchy and elitism are on the upswing in virtually all postindustrial societies ever since thousands of anti-globalization protesters stopped the World Trade Organization (WTO) Seattle Ministerial dead in its tracks in 1999. People are not "bowling alone" as Putnam insisted in his classic article by the same name. Publics have become highly critical of institutionalized authority in general "and are less likely to become members of bureaucratized organizations." [7] While traditional clubs and organizations, from mass political parties to the Elks and the Masons, have experienced falling memberships, more people are active in public than ever before, signing petitions, holding boycotts, and joining online communities. Inglehart discovered no widespread pattern of citizen disengagement in the Americas, Europe, or Asia. People are shifting their loyalties, not switching off. They are getting their heads into the game.

The second signal condition is that publics are increasingly better informed and better educated about the world around them. Many decades ago the great American scholars Paul Lazarsfeld and Robert Merton wrote about the social impact of the mass media, at that time print, radio, and television. They were deep pessimists about its "narcotizing dysfunctionality" and the information overload that the free flow of information has had on the world of the citizen. [8] Two generations later citizen democracies no longer conform to this stereotype, if indeed they ever did.

Today massive social change in the structure of power is intimately related to the remarkable evolution of the structure of communication. In previous times the technology of communication was highly centralized along with the mechanism of governance and public authority. We live in a very different world that is defined by the globalization dynamic in which the technology of communication and structures of public authority are highly decentralized, networked, and driven by a model of social relations rooted in a complex culture of consumption. When this occurs, society becomes destabilized by the intense diffusion of new information technology, new ideas and the anti-democratic top-down command-control model of social organization. Like the rapid and massive introduction of the radio in the early twentieth century and the telegraph decades earlier, new forms of communication and political activism require us to rethink the dynamics of power and the way that digital technology reallocates power and authority downwards from the elite few towards the many. [9]

This is a radical idea perhaps, but one that has always been firmly grasped by those who understand the power of words, ideas, visual images, and texts. Sixty years ago, Harold Innis described the "bias of communication," a phenomenon by which technology transfers a great deal of social power to those with the ability to use it.[10] The strategies of new social movements seem to validate this Innisian hypothesis. The central idea that this book sets out to explore is that new communication technologies of text-messaging, blogging, and going on line, when coupled with grassroots organizing strategies, offer citizens a unique set of opportunities to engage in public participation and advocate bold strategies for social change. The public is no longer constituted of individuals meeting face to face; more than ever it is a complex network of many engaged individuals who come together around large and small issues that consume their time and interest in spite of geographic distance. Why is all of this happening?

The individual in public: reasoning together

At the heart of every dissent movement is a struggle with elite authority over how societies allocate public and private goods. Establishing the boundary line for rights and responsibilities between private interest and public purpose has always been intensely important, but is particularly so at a time when states, markets, and publics are negotiating the rules of economic integration and political interdependence. Societies need rules, and when political power is no longer contained within the nation-state, finding new ways to address transnational issues, from poverty eradication to climate change, becomes a primary focus point for publics. If there are to be clear sites of national authority and a stable international community, the public domain, in which consensus, cooperation, and public discourse figure predominately, has a compelling role to play as one of the coordinates that will "rebundle" identity and territory, in John Ruggie's evocative words.[11]

Terms such as "the public domain" and "public reason" constitute the new vocabulary of global dissent.[12] But it is this exercise of reason in public for defined social ends that has been pushed to the front of the agenda by new information technologies. These differently constituted discursive arenas should not be confused with the commonly accepted definition of the public sector. Nor should the public domain be limited to the provision of public goods, a staple of modern liberal economic theory. The public domain is a sphere of political agency, first and foremost, in which individuals work together to meet collective needs and overcome complex political and economic challenges. *The public domain, above all else, is a forum in which to be heard.* This is a very different insight on what it means to be in public, but it is hardly radical. This definition of the public can be found in the political writings of Enlightenment philosophers and more recently, in the theoretical contributions of the aptly named and loosely defined recognitionist school of citizenship founded by Hannah Arendt and led today by Charles Taylor, Arjun Appadurai, and David Held.[13]

Recognitionism has become the dominant current in social science for thinking about the public domain. Even the term is new and its ideas reflect the need to transcend narrow academic disciplines such as law, economics, and political science. The irreversible trend toward the growth of democratic rights and the rule of law at the international level has gone hand in hand with a more inclusive approach to pluralism. Through this rights-based discourse the international community empowers governments to take collective responsibility for all their citizens. The urgent need to create pluralistic, diverse societies was born out of the catastrophic world wars of the twentieth century and the Holocaust. The colonial legacy of racism and social exclusion has been amply documented by anthropologists, historians, and cultural theorists. After 1945 societies began to rededicate themselves to humanist ideals best reflected in the growth of international human rights law. Philosophers have long argued that rights rest on a foundation of tolerance and social recognition. Without recognition of the uniqueness not only of individuals, but also religions, ethnicity, and cultures, there can be no strong system of human rights.

Recognitionism has struck a deep cord with researchers worldwide. Its theoretical contributions range from a deep study of the transcendent ethic of human rights, to the power of public reason as one of the motors of transformative social change. It also presents a powerful explanation of collectively-minded individuals who form discursive communities of choice. The common thread that runs through the recognitionist school is plainly seen in the work of Charles Taylor, who declares that:

> our identity is partly shaped by recognition or its absence, often by the *mis*recognition of others, and so a person or group of people can suffer real damage, real distortion, if the people or society around them mirror back to them a confining or demeaning or contemptible picture of themselves . . . due recognition is not just a courtesy we owe people, it is a vital human need.[14]

This penetrating read of recognition draws directly on Hannah Arendt's theorization of the public as the primary site of recognition and the terrain of individual achievement. Hannah Arendt was one of the great postwar theorists of the twentieth century. She believed that a liberal society in a social democratic age was rooted in public transparency and individual actions performed in public.

The right to have rights: the wide-angled vision of the Recognitionist school

David Held explored the implications of this vital collective need. His key contribution is a sophisticated theorization of how the transfer of power from national to international levels has shifted the locus of citizenship. The cosmopolitan citizen does not need to choose between the community and identity that they were born into and the communities of choice that they belong to outside the traditional boundaries of their states and societies. At any time they may belong in multiple spheres of political interaction maintaining overlapping ideas and identities. Other schools of thought in this vein include the neo-Gramscians such as Michael Hardt and Antonio Negri who have gained a large following in cultural studies.[15] Also the Network Society thesis of Manuel Castells has been influential among those scholars who are interested in mapping the shifting sands of structuralism.[16]

Uniquely Arjun Appadurai stands apart as a theorist of misrecognition. He shows how new forms of wealth generated by electronic markets have increased the gap between the rich and the poor. This phenomenon, coupled with fast-moving technologies of communication and highly unstable financial markets, produces anxieties about people's identities. And these anxieties hold new potential for violence.[17]

No matter the school of thought, much attention has been focused on "things public" and the way we think about them because the one thing that all scholars now agree upon is that the public domain will be the defining arena of conflict and progress in the twenty-first century. The modern and multidimensional public domain has expanded beyond the bounds of elites and the control of the political class. As a body of public opinion, the sphere of interactive communication has lost its social exclusivity. You don't have to attain a high level of education to be part of it. You can be a teenager at a cyber-café, a tenant renter in Bombay, a soccer mom, a boomer retiree, or from any of the inner cities of the world. The 1 billion person e-universe has not yet reached its limits. It keeps on expanding at the blistering pace of more than 10 percent annually. And many of the issues debated and discussed, such as the rights of children, once exclusively the prerogative of the private sphere of the family, are now subject to the public's scrutiny.

In an era of globally connected networks of communicative interaction, the personal is not only political, it is also public. Whereas Habermas thought that the institutions of modern society and government frequently attempted a refeudalization of the public sphere, in which bureaucratic interests trap the public in a clientelistic relationship with public authority, we think that modern communication technologies, which blur the lines between public and private, citizen and client, have widened the access points into public discourse and offer a phenomenal opportunity to democratize the public domain. Over the past three decades, the public domain has become more diverse, conflictual, and internally differentiated. More than ever, it is a sphere where theory, possibility, and the virtual can become real.

The early modern conception of the public was rooted in a complex understanding of what it means to be an individual – a person with many different values, goals, aspirations, and motivations. If liberalism in political theory has given us a robust view of the individual living in society, then economic liberalism offers a one-dimensional caricature of the individual. Economic theory simplifies the concept of the socially embedded individual. The economic individual is a rational maximizer, a person who sees the world in terms of self-interest, economic utility, and scarcity. For the economic individual, the public does not exist as a significant category. Society is the totality of all individuals and is rooted in market activity. Those goods that individuals are unable to produce are produced through collective effort. These "public goods," such as national defense, are the rationale for a public sector. But there is no room in this view for a notion of public goods and the public good that is separate from economic need and the self-interest of individuals. When Margaret Thatcher pronounced in her famous 1987 interview with *Woman's Own* magazine that "there is no such thing" as society, she was simply reducing liberal economic theory to its foundational assumption.

The search for theoretical clarity about the modern idea of the public

Most people intuitively understand a concept of the "public" that sharply contrasts the understanding of Baroness Thatcher and other neo-liberal thinkers. For nineteenth-century liberals and twenty-first-century social conservatives the public stands in contrast to the private world of the family and the everyday experience of work. In the present we tend to define the public in terms of openness and inclusiveness with regards to the actions performed in public spaces as well as the attitudes and values that define "public" values. When we think of the public as an ideal institution, we think of the Keynesian welfare state as a step up from the watchman liberal state. When we think of the kinetic energy of crowds and the revolutionary potential of the public, we think of the *citoyens sans culottes*. When we imagine the capacity of the public to reason about the common good, we think of the American founding fathers who came together to throw off the yoke of colonialism and build the first modern democracy. Public reason, for James Madison, Thomas Jefferson, and Alexander Hamilton, was an active process of thinking about the possibilities for a collective future, not the passive process of public opinion polling that passes for the general will today. All of these are part of what it means to be in public, yet we need to find our way out of the definitional morass that holds us back from thinking of the public today as an interactive environment in which we, as individuals, play a valuable autonomous role just as citizens have repeatedly done in the past.[18]

What is the relationship between the public as an institution, the public as a force for change, and the public as a body capable of thought and reason? Can our knowledge of the public even hold all of these concepts at once? The answers lie in the way we define the noun "public." In common parlance the public refers to space that is owned or supervised by the state, or the people who gather together in such a space. In this usage, people in public have little in common except their wish to experience some aspect of social life together, such as a speech, concert, or political protest. But this is not always what has been meant by "public."

Hannah Arendt reminds us that in classical antiquity the public was a space of appearance and recognition, a space where individuals were recognized and actions could be judged. A person was affirmed in their individuality and recognized for their achievements in public. This idea dovetails nicely with Habermas's idea that public acts of assembly and speech have the power to change the ways in which we are governed and the policies pursued by our governments. Public debate sets the rules by which society is governed. Every controversial action on the part of government is debated first in the public sphere. In this way we can understand the notion of the public to have yet another critical dimension. It is a sphere of uniquely endowed communicative action in which citizens can reach consensus on divisive and complex issues. From these definitions, we can imagine the public to be the decisive space for recognition as well as the sphere of choice for individuals whose action is informed by the process of reasoning together.

Our common belief of what it means to be in public is not far off this mark, but we have been misled as to the capacity of the public for collective action because our definition of what it means to be an individual has been so thoroughly informed by economic theory. The classical appreciation of individualism emphasized the ability to reason with other people and the capacity to be recognized in public. Before economic liberalism claimed a monopoly on the concept of individualism and Marxism claimed the realm of collective action, classical political theory imagined that individuals need the public and that the public needs individuals. Contemporary citizen practice has reclaimed this older tradition of the individual and the public – a symbiotic relationship that was never properly understood by thinkers in the conservative and radical traditions.

The great reversal: devolving power downwards

So far the "great reversal" consists of *three constant and cyclical phases*. First, in the beginning period of globalization, political and regulatory powers were transferred away from the state and into the command and control structures of global financial corporations. In the early 1980s, markets for money were deregulated in the United States and corporate financiers were given new powers to redirect massive flows of capital as they saw fit. The value of derivatives markets and hedge funds skyrocketed into the trillions of dollars. New rights, and the attendant wealth and privilege, were given to the few; countless workers with well-paying jobs were stripped of economic security. In the words of Martin Wolf, the lead economic reporter for the *Financial Times*, "there has been a big income shift from labour to capital – managers can earn vast multiples of employees' wages."[19] The shocking extent to which this power transfer had taken place without the public being the wiser was first revealed by the spectacular collapses of Enron in 2001, Worldcom in 2002, and the Hollinger newspaper empire in 2005.

At the same time, technological change drove the other side of this double movement in which communicative power funneled downward from the few toward the many. In every historical epoch, the Innisian bias of communication has had the potential to topple hierarchies and facilitate the radical transfer of political power. This does not happen the way that Marx imagined, with workers seizing control of the commanding heights of the economy. Rather it happens because information becomes a currency of exchange, and technological change democratizes access to information. Ironically, Marx was partially right. When the production of information becomes the highest goal of societies, digital technology and the Internet allow anyone to control their own means of information production. New technology encourages opportunities for social action and amplifies the voice of the activist.

Second, just as printed text was instrumental to the birth of modern forms of national identity, so hypertext has given birth to the powerful idea of the global citizen connected to other citizens through the networked public. Print capitalism presaged nationalism, national community, and state sovereignty as Benedict Anderson has shown.[20] The printing press, the map, and the museum constructed the ideal of the nation even as people's lived experience remained firmly rooted in the local with no real identity beyond the village gate. At the time of the French Revolution only 11 percent of the population spoke French. Information moved at a snail's pace and even as late as the 1860s a quarter of French army recruits only knew patois. The same is true today of the Internet, the satellite, and the news broadcast, which construct the possibility of an idealized global village, a term coined by Marshall McLuhan, even as most people remain local actors.

The dominant feature of globalization has been a slow bleeding of power from the national level, toward regional organizations, international institutions, and non-governmental actors. Information flows are behind this structural transformation, and Manuel Castells demonstrates the way in which new informational processes create a new form of consciousness today in the global "network society."[21] A pessimistic reading of this process is that national sovereignty has been subverted, and the nation-state is being hollowed out by multinational corporations. A more optimistic reading focuses on the way that citizens are developing new forms of engagement to achieve their goals at a time when the old templates of authority and loyalty no longer fit the contours of social life.

Finally, these new citizenship practices have become the motivating ethos for emergent forms of transnational public action. Micro-activism is the idea that individuals can make a difference through their actions wherever they live, work, or meet. Micro-activism is entrepreneurial in the Schumpterian sense because it creates new political forms where none existed before; projects are undertaken in an ad hoc way, with individuals rising to take action on an issue that they feel strongly about and disengaging after they have made a contribution. Micro-activists recognize that they can participate in the public sphere without devoting decades to gaining credentials and developing the legitimacy of a specialist. In a very real way, micro-activists recognize there can be no individuality without being in public, and there can be no public without a concrete understanding of others as individuals with their own hopes, dreams, and desires. None of this is to suggest that the act of being in public or the reasoning of micro-activists is necessarily enlightened or progressive. Publics are often just as reactionary as the worst dictators. Activists can be informed and forward-looking, or biased and prejudiced. They can be autonomous, independent-minded, and contrarian. Or they can be moulded, manipulated, and kept on a short leash by elites.

Pessimism about 'things public' and the need for dissent

Today, more than at any other time in the recent past, the public domain has to be understood and defined as an arena of activism, with its own rules, norms, and practices, which cut across the state and market and other public-private agencies.[22] The public domain's values are those of citizenship, activism, and the notion of the public interest. It has long furnished civil society with the much needed resources to function effectively by creating sanctuaries where the price mechanism does not operate. The public domain was "ring-fenced from the pressures of the market place, in which citizenship rights rather than market power governed the allocation of social goods."[23]

The popular perception has been that the public domain beyond the state is troubled and in decline after a long period of studied neglect. Following the Second World War, there was strong support among academics and policy makers on both sides of the Atlantic for a more robust sharing of power between state and international institutions. While realists argued that peace would be maintained by a nuclear balance of power, the institution building of idealists promised a more equitable world order than that which had given birth to the bloody twentieth century. Several long decades later, during the Washington Consensus era, it was accepted as self-evident truth that the most important regulatory and economic management processes occurred beyond the territorial boundaries of the nation-state – an idea lifted from the idealist traditions, but twisted by the rhetoric of market triumphalism to suit the needs of ambitious multinational corporations. Now, more than ever, the public domain has been reinvigorated by the great debate between those who see the international public domain as a space of discourse and public reason and those who see it as primarily an arena for market exchange.

The fact is that this notion of neo-liberal international regulation has been increasingly challenged because the nation-state has not crumbled as the seat of public authority as once predicted by experts of all stripes. This is the third dimension of the discourse. Markets and publics are not clashing in outer space. Publics draw upon the authority of the state in their attempt to counter the overreach of market actors – and it appears that this strategy may yet bear fruit. Public spending has risen steadily throughout the neo-liberal era. The state has not been hollowed out though it is leaner than it once was. Elites are divided on which model of the public is relevant to national needs and priorities. State spending in Germany, France, Sweden, and Italy is well above the 40 percent mark of gross domestic product (GDP). In the global south too, no one would claim that the declinist theory applies to India, China, Brazil, or Argentina.[24]

Amartya Sen rightly notes that dissent and criticism are now widely perceived to be legitimate alternatives to deference, paternalism, and autocratic authority.[25] The process of doubting and questioning that began at the height of Western market triumphalism has climaxed in a great U-turn of political power. Dissenters, activists, and new social movements have begun to rescue the idea of the public from the economic determinism of the Washington Consensus world order. Its market-oriented policies framed public policy in the 1980s and 1990s and were synonymous with structural adjustment, aggressive privatization, public deregulation, and the cutting of social programs to meet strict deficit targets. The theology of market fundamentalism rejected the concept of a public sphere to promote equity, democracy, and transparency; yet the return of the public domain is undoubtedly the watershed event of our times.

The observant reader will not overlook the two defining moments that provide the context and focus of the current cycle of dissent. The first was a decision at the summit of the European Union's leaders in July 2007 to take the unprecedented step to remove from its constitution a commitment to "free and undistorted competition," the core idea of global neo-liberalism. This will potentially have far-reaching implications for the rebalancing of the European Union's priorities. EU ministers are beginning to see the need to get right the balance between public and private in the modern mixed economy. The new skepticism about neo-liberal policy goals is represented, paradoxically, in the dynamic leadership of new French president Nicolas Sarkozy, whose right-wing populism has captivated French voters. He has emerged as the leader of the hour, who is symbolically committed to reducing the EU's total commitment to liberalization.

The Sarkozy backlash against globalization and his demand that the EU reorder its priorities is in part a response to a large and growing majority who want governments to distance themselves from the free-market theology. European governments are seeking "more flexibility" – the code words for moving away from the strict letter of the old dictates that outlawed public sector cost overruns, wantonly privatized hundreds of state enterprises, and weakened the regulatory clout of public authority. It now appears that France will not meet the European Union's stability pact through 2012, a fact that barely produces a ripple in Brussels or the leading financial centers of the EU. Evidently the tide of privatization has long crested and governments see the need for smart interventionist strategies to address structural adjustment and brutal competitive pressures.

Second, the dramatic collapse of the Doha round of WTO trade negotiations provides a companion bookend to this time of upheaval. The international order has entered into a new political cycle. Developing countries are no longer willing to be bullied into making trade deals they regret. Equally, northern governments are less enthusiastic about trade liberalization at a time when voters are angry over globalization's social costs. The creativity and hard work of global micro-activists has had a major impact on this shift in global attitude. The great free-trade machine no longer rules the international community unchallenged.

The structure of the argument

The first chapter examines one of the most prominent arenas in the battle between public and private – the World Trade Organization. Originally conceived as simply an extension of the legal rules for trade governance, the WTO now is the most contentious governance institution in the world. Its elite, technocratic mode of operation drew the wrath of activists and public intellectuals who saw it as an antidemocratic tool of capitalist expansion. The great theoretical debates of public policy have always been about managing the delicate relationship between public and private. Karl Polanyi captured this push-pull dynamic in his classic work, *The Great Transformation*.[26] He and many others have remarked on how the international financial institutions developed at the end of the Second World War provided an institutional safety net for fragile economies and troubled markets. The WTO was the next logical step in the growth of the institutional architecture for global trade, but liberal internationalism has become a battleground for competing theoretical approaches for balancing private interest and the public good. The WTO is a prescient example of how the organizing know-how of activists and the galvanizing power of public anger are transforming the international public domain in important new directions with respect to international jurisprudence.

The second chapter argues that it is critically important to track and map the contested existence of "things public." There is no one public for everyone, and we need to come to terms with the modern idea and ideal of the public domain in which our purposes, values, and goals are inescapably *public*. What is new today is that the once state-centered public domain has splintered into many different spheres; the sphere of interactive communication has extended its frontiers and provided organizing capacity to those who did not possess it in the past. Micro-activism is about

challenging the power of elites for democratic ends; it has different motivations, agendas, and influences, but remains starkly
populist and anti-authoritarian. Voting patterns reflect this mood
swing and uncertainty. The young, urban, educated voter is
showing a preference for coalition governments and unorthodox
right-left coalitions.

The third and fourth chapters show how powerful, internationally-minded publics have learned to use worldwide information flows as a discursive weapon. There are still doubts among
many academics and policy elites as to the efficacy of public
activism. They see the public as people who are dumbed down by
mass culture and rendered voiceless by the tandem command and
control models of state and market power. But the public has
never been phantom-like, the trivializing term Walter Lippman
coined to explain its alleged disinterest in public issues.[27] Modern
publics in different regions of the planet have shed their perceived
docility.

How can we understand the modern notion of publicness as collective voice and strategy? Micro-activism has created a unique
global political culture that challenges the mainstream ideals of
social and political conformity. Furthermore, civil society and social
movements are developing their capacity to innovate and create
new political forms and practices, a fact that has become strikingly
apparent since the "battle in Seattle" in 1999. We examine the
reasons why the decline of deference has produced an almost
perfect storm of popular activism worldwide. Hypertext, disgruntled publics, and micro-activism have triggered the improbable
U-turn of our times.

The rebels and activists of today are nothing like the global
protest movements of 1968. The radical movements of that time
culminated in factory occupations, millions of anti-war protesters
marching in the streets, Paris under siege, and America's inner cities
burning. The fourth chapter argues that we need to think beyond
the constructed legacy of the golden age of anti-Vietnam protest
that shook the political order of capitalism to its core and instead
look at the possibility for citizen engagement today and down the
road. This fixation with the anti-war Vietnam protest movement is
now a strategic obstacle to finding a way to see beyond our con-

temporary present-mindedness. Nostalgia for this former age locks the cynic-observer into a mind-set where capitalism can only be victorious.

The fifth and final chapter examines how the forces of space, place, and citizenship are creating infinite varieties of the public. Triumphant liberalism, far from being a universal program for all, is on a collision course with surly and informed global publics. The growth of new state practices and growing institutional divergence across jurisdictions needs to be examined, interrogated, and put into perspective. The globalization mythology is being recast for a new era; and in the process, citizens have loosened economic integration from its deterministic moorings. Are these in reality significant markers of a new political chapter in the offing? Or is it only a cyclical dip in public thinking? We argue that social diversity and new models of citizenship have become constituent elements in explaining the return of the public domain at the state and global levels. The filters and frames that once kept the public largely disaggregated and out of harm's way are less and less effective. New modes of communication, and the organizations they help create, are fundamentally transforming the way that politics happens. The question is now, who will rule the future?

Notes

1. Francis Fukuyama, *The End of History and the Last Man* (Toronto: Free Press and Macmillan Canada, 1992).
2. John Williamson, "What Should the Bank Think About the Washington Consensus?" Prepared as a background to the World Bank's *World Development Report 2000* (Washington, D.C.: Institute for International Economics, 1999) at www.iie.com/TESTIMONY/ Bankwc.htm; John Williamson, ed., *The Political Economy of Policy Reform* (Washington, D.C.: Institute for International Economics, 1990).
3. Moises Naim, "Facts and Fashion in Economic Reform: Washington Consensus or Washington Confusion?" at www.info.org/external. pubs.ft/seminar/1999/reforms/Naim.
4. Michel Foucault, *The Archaeology of Knowledge and the Discourse on Language*, trans. A. M. Sheridan (New York: Pantheon, 1972).

5. Neil Nevitte, *The Decline of Deference: Canadian Value Change in Cross National Perspective* (Peterborough, ON: Broadview Press, 1996).

6. Jack Goldsmith, *The Terror Presidency: Law and Judgement Inside the Bush Administration* (New York: W. W. Norton, 2007), pp. 56–63.

7. Ronald Inglehart and Christian Welzel, *Modernization, Cultural Change and Democracy* (Cambridge, UK: Cambridge University Press, 2005), p. 117.

8. Paul F. Lazarsfeld and Robert K. Merton, "Mass Communication, Popular Taste and Organized Social Action" in *Media Studies: A Reader*, ed. Paul Marris and Sue Thornham, 2nd edn (New York: New York University Press, 2002), pp. 22–23.

9. Robert Cox, "Civil Society at the Turn of the Millennium: Prospects for an Alternative World Order," *Review of International Studies* 25:1 (1999), pp. 3–28.

10. Harold Innis, *Markets and Cultural Change: Selected Essays*, ed. Daniel Drache (Montreal: McGill-Queen's University Press, 1995).

11. John Ruggie, "Territoriality and Beyond: Problematizing Modernity in International Relations," *International Organization* 47:1 (1993), pp. 139–74.

12. Tony Bennett, Lawrence Grossberg, and Meagan Morris, *New Keywords: A Revised Vocabulary of Culture and Society* (Malden, Mass.: Blackwell, 2005).

13. Hannah Arendt, *The Human Condition* (Chicago: University of Chicago Press, 1958); Charles Taylor, *Multiculturalism and the Politics of Recognition: An Essay* (Princeton, N.J.: Princeton University Press, 1992); Arjun Appadurai, "Disjuncture and Difference in the Global Cultural Economy" in *The Phantom Public*, ed. Bruce Robbins (Minneapolis, Minn.: University of Minnesota, 1993); David Held, "Cosmopolitan Democracy and the Global Order: A New Agenda" in *Perpetual Peace: Essays on Kant's Cosmopolitan Ideal*, ed. James Bohman and Matthias Lutz-Bachmann (Cambridge, Mass.: MIT Press, 1997).

14. Charles Taylor, *Multiculturalism: Examining the Politics of Recognition*, ed. Amy Gutmann (Princeton, N.J.: Princeton University Press, 1994), pp. 25–6.

15. Michael Hardt and Antonio Negri, *Multitude: War and Democracy in the Age of Empire* (New York: The Penguin Press, 2004).

16. Manuel Castells, "Materials for an Exploratory Theory of the Network Society," *British Journal of Sociology* 51:1 (2000), pp. 5–24.

17. Arjun Appadurai, *Fear of Small Numbers: An Essay on the Geography of Anger* (Durham, N.C.: Duke University Press, 2006).
18. Engin Isin, *Being Political: Genealogies of Citizenship* (Minneapolis, Minn.: University of Minneapolis Press, 2002).
19. Martin Wolf, "The New Capitalism," *Financial Times*, June 19, 2007.
20. Benedict Anderson, *Imagined Communities: Reflections on the Origin and Spread of Nationalism* (London: Verso Press, 1991).
21. David Held, *Democracy and the Global Order: From the Modern State to Cosmopolitan Governance* (Stanford, Calif.: Stanford University Press, 1995); Manuel Castells, *The Rise of the Network Society* (Cambridge, Mass.: Blackwell, 1996).
22. Daniel Drache, *The Market or the Public Domain: Global Governance and the Asymmetry of Power* (London: Routledge, 2001).
23. David Marquand, *Decline of the Public* (London: Polity, 2004), p. 5.
24. Organization for Economic Cooperation and Development, *State Spending* (Paris: OECD, 2007).
25. Amartya Sen, *The Argumentative Indian: Writings on Indian Culture, History and Identity* (New Delhi: Penguin Books, 2005).
26. Karl Polanyi, *The Great Transformation: The Political and Economic Origins of Our Time*, new edn (Boston, Mass.: Beacon Press, 2001).
27. Walter Lippman, *Public Opinion* (New York: Macmillan, 1961).

1

The Crowded Public Sphere and its Discontents

Modern liberalism and the realist challenge

Our understanding of what it means to be in public has always been embedded within historical and legal theories of territorial citizenship. Modern liberalism traces the lineage of citizenship through the feudal bond to land and lords, what Michael Ignatieff in another context calls blood and belonging. Today citizenship is most frequently described in constitutional terms, as the legal bond between you and the state. Constitutions have become, over the past century, the sine qua non of modern citizenship with their focus on rights and duties. It is impossible to imagine a group of people acting together, as citizens, who are not bound by the legal authority of a constitution. What's more, it is legally and politically unfeasible to give up your passport and be a free-floating "citizen of the world." Those without passports are most often refugees fleeing from a desperate past to a precarious future.

Being stateless is to be in peril, the equivalent to being homeless. It leaves the individual without a set of firm rights and without meaningful recourse to the law. And yet today, an increasing number of individuals and organizations are navigating the chaotic waters of international civil society – so many in fact that some scholars have begun to ask whether we are entering an era of the global citizen.[1] The busy international realm is populated by many actors: cosmopolitan elites looking to slip the bonds of state sovereignty, market actors looking for new investment opportunities, social activists looking to internationalize their values or beliefs, and states themselves, the only legitimate actors in the eyes of realist legal theorists. The question that continues to nag at the corner of scholarly consciousness is: is it even possible to draw a distinction between the public and private at the international level? The answer depends upon whom you ask.

Realist international relations scholars are skeptical of the idea of a public domain outside of state authority. For the classical realist, the international level was a lawless universe in which sovereign states obeyed no higher authority. The godfather of idealist institutionalism was Princeton professor and later American president Woodrow Wilson, who argued that the organization of the space beyond the state is not only possible, it is essential to an orderly and peaceful world. He considered that a domain of Things Public has always existed beyond the state, sometimes a space of debate, discussion, and compromise, at other times a Hobbesian state of near-sighted self-interest.[2.]

Early idealists hoped that thicker bonds of interdependency would lessen the possibility that supposedly civilized nations would slip into the vicious anarchy of global war again. There was little in the Anglo-American legal tradition about the concept of common property and interdependence. Instead they looked to Roman law with its rich legal tradition of public goods and property: *res nullius, res communes, res publicae, res universitatis*, and *res divini juris*. All these things "unownable" or shared collectively corresponded to the world of human affairs that James Doyle argues in his seminal article on the public domain supported "a set of claims about justice and utility."[3]

For the idealist, the institutionalization of a public domain was the prerogative of states. Most of the categories of things publicly owned and made open to the public by law stood against the powerful claim of exclusive rights and the dangers from overuse and depletion. Things public operated as an intellectual and legal check against absolute sovereignty. Anarchy was both a political danger and a tool of socialization that forced states to cooperate, as the great English scholar of international relations, Hedley Bull, argued so convincingly.[4] Both of these views of state authority were highly abstract and have been subject to intense scrutiny over the past decades. Not only are they criticized because they do not adequately represent the state of the international public domain (that is, they provide an unsatisfactory account of the myriad agreements, institutions, diplomatic understandings, and international norms that have been developed over the past several hundred years to bring order to political interaction), but they also hold little predictive value because they only theorize the processes and pathways of state power – what we term "structural power." They do not adequately recognize the growing potential of public power – what we call "relational power." Ideas, ideologies, and identities are forms of relational power.[5] The most prominent example is the markedly diverse anti-globalization movement that expects to tame globalization from below by demanding accountability and imposing constraints on global capitalism.

The transformative dynamics of relational power

The rise to prominence of relational power alerts us to the fact that social goods of all kinds, from human security to sustainable environmental practices, can and do override entrenched private property rights in specific circumstances. The imperative associated with these collective necessities is compelling because it is both direct and democratic. As well, it speaks to the concern that the goods owned in common should remain with us – the public – and not be monopolized by private interests. The rallying of collective goods in the service of the public is the fundamental idea behind the modern notion of the public domain. It is about the sustainability of the public interest and the social bond in the broadest senses of the terms.

In the postwar period, international interdependencies have grown and become primary sites of political life, democratic values, and legal norms of social justice. International organizations, from the WTO to the United Nations, were designed to constrain aggression, promote cooperation, and defend the global public interest as it has evolved over the past sixty years. Idealist thinkers have tended to harbour a more expansive belief in the transformative power of international institutions than have realists. Yet, as thinkers such as Jürgen Habermas and Hannah Arendt have shown, the public domain may be protected and promoted by public authority, but it grows through the action of the citizen, not the edict of the bureaucrat.

Nevertheless, a formal, rules-based system is necessary at the international level because, in Henri Lefebvre's terms, public space has to strike and maintain a proper balance between its use value for citizens and its exchange or commercial value for business.[6] This is why public space is never solely public but is always a mix of public and private use, a mix of formal need and informal custom, used by elites and appropriated for popular and democratic action. This unique mix of characteristics and mentalities protects the public from the destructiveness of ruthless commercialism. Modern liberalism envisions an international public domain that conforms to its theoretical notion that freedom and individual autonomy are guaranteed by the market, not the public. It leaves a large amount of space for property rights, a modest role for regulation, and relegates publics to gadfly status.

This way of thinking has led to a rules-based order that is upheld and legitimized by powerful states and maintained through the Westphalian norms of sovereignty, autonomy, and self-help. Even the trading order has not been immune from hard power politics. Not surprisingly, over the past couple of decades the things we share in common have begun to shrink. Governments around the world have sold off state enterprises, privatized public utilities such as water, and imposed user fees on public space. In many jurisdictions, health care systems have been dismantled and unemployment benefits cut. The attack on "things public" is without recent precedent. The primary challenge for activist publics lies in extending these goods once held in common.

For globalization to be seen as a fair and equitable process, publics agreed that the market needed a watchdog to enforce the rules-based system and defend the global public interest against short-term corporate rent-seeking and selfish governments. International society wants public institutions with the capacity to police market actors and ensure that they maintain a reasonable and a high standard of conduct. The launch of the WTO in 1995 provided the global economy with the first fully realized institution of international trade governance. Economic rule making from a supranational trade authority was supposed to create an institutional framework to help growing markets function more efficiently and build a stable interstate global order. Ultimately, this naive position would never fully address the asymmetries of power in the world trading system. Nor would its emphasis on procedural equality provide an adequate political framework in which to address the social impacts of globalization. The clash between liberal institutionalism and public power would reframe multilateral trade governance and bring the concerns of developing countries to the front of many national foreign policy agendas.

Interdependence and economic rulemaking

How did the World Trade Organization, the badly understood institution of international trade, become a source of heightened public anxiety by the turn of the millennium? In the public's mind, the WTO has become a symbol for the extreme economism, policy fatalism, and ideology of market fundamentalism.[7] The creation of the WTO brought together the many disparate agreements that comprised the international network of trade treaties. Agreements on trade in intellectual property, services, agricultural goods, industrial products, trade-related investment measures, and even sanitary standards for exports were all gathered under one umbrella. Originally, the concept of a one-stop shop for trade regulation seemed to be a good idea because it would reduce the numbers of trade officials that small countries would need to employ, and it would harmonize the many different standards used to govern the global flow of goods and services. When the WTO took its place in the pantheon of international financial institutions, trade analysts and member countries believed that the multilateral system for the management of the global economy was largely complete.[8] Today, that initial optimism has evaporated.

Negotiations in the Doha round of trade talks had largely ground to a halt by 2006. During the final days of the Bush administration's Trade Promotion Authority, in the summer of 2007, talks among the G4 – the United States, European Union, Brazil, and India – also reached a standstill. So far it is unclear what impact, if any, the lack of forward movement in the Doha round will have on the global economy. Certainly there is no system meltdown despite the breakdown in trade negotiations. Global merchandise trade is growing at a robust 6 percent annually and services trade at a phenomenal 10 percent annually.[9] This is more than twice the average rate of growth in OECD (Organization for Economic Cooperation and Development) countries. In China, India, and Brazil, an emerging middle class is driving domestic growth at rates that challenge the economic superiority of North America and Europe.[10] In 2006, *The Economist* reported that half of the world's industrial products are now produced in the global south. According to the newest research, within a decade, 20 percent of Fortune 500 firms will be southern multinationals.[11] Neither Marxian dependency theory nor neo-liberal economic theory foretold such a large-scale transformation. A new balance of power is emerging at the heart of the World Trade Organization.[12]

In many countries, unfettered liberalization unleashes a large and uncertain structural adjustment process. The expectation is that trade will stimulate economic performance, driving up wages and productivity. But stiff global competition frequently forces firms to shed labour and cut wages. The human cost of adjustment is not factored into the neo-liberal trade model, and this is one of the main reasons that the international trade regime will never replace domestic governance in many key areas of public policy. States are reluctant to share their responsibility for the protection of the public domain. Indeed, governments understand their political potency and recognize their centrality to the maintenance of national identity, cultural cohesiveness, and social belonging.

The WTO as a pint-sized liberal public domain

In hindsight it can be seen that the WTO provides us with a highly informative case study in the issues associated with the implementation of a top-down, legally intrusive, liberal model of public space rather than a self-organized public domain of debate, discussion, and reason. Superficially, the WTO seems to meet Robert Keohane's definition of democracy at the international level as "voluntary pluralism under conditions of maximum transparency."[13] How can any country be against this vision of the rule of law? Or turn its back against a legal system in which everyone is to be treated procedurally equally? How can a country not favor an arbitration process that is supposed to neutralize state power in the Westphalian system? To be part of the WTO is to say to the world that you are open for business, and you have modern market regulations in place. A decade ago this powerful logic appeared unstoppable. Every country wanted to get inside the big tent of global free trade. But at present small countries in the global south remember with a certain distaste the American and European arm-twisting rhetoric used by free-traders in the Uruguay round to pummel their reservations into dust.

The big picture reality that the public never grasped in its entirety is that first and foremost the WTO was created with a very large mandate and a bold vision of the international order. It was to be a harmonizer of public policy with respect to subsidies, state spending, and social services. In particular, intellectual property rights and the privatization of public services were to be an engine for muscular and progressive trade liberalization. It was also supposed to embody the public values of transparency, comprehensive rules, and legally binding dispute settlement.

Global governance and the attack on the cultural commons

Most important for this discussion are its newest regulatory frames for trade in services and intellectual property. The General Agreement for Trade in Services divides services trade into four modalities, covering everything from the provision of financial services to the movement of service providers.[14] Civil society activists are concerned that the liberalization of services such as finance and insurance as well as intellectual property rights will lock in the current unequal division of labor in the global economy.

The Trade-Related Intellectual Property Rights Agreement is highly controversial because it creates strict standards for the treatment of intellectual property rights.[15] Intellectual property is one of the largest growth areas in the global cultural economy, and activists are furious that northern media and entertainment multinationals would attempt to fence in creativity in order to protect corporate profits. The present intellectual property regime is unlikely to enforce compliance. Global publics when habitually downloading music, photos' and files are indifferent to the protestations of transnational corporations. Without exclusive property rights these titans of the global cultural economy are being boarded and scuttled by southern pirates.[16]

The other major network of intergovernmental regulation is centered at the United Nations. The concerns of activists, publics, and governments about the subordination of cultural trade to WTO discipline have been taken to the United Nations Educational, Scientific, and Cultural Organization (UNESCO). One of its mandates is to promote cultural diversity and pluralism in artistic expression. Ongoing negotiations at UNESCO are aiming to remove the trade in cultural goods from under the WTO's direct supervision because of national concerns that culture should not be treated like other commodities. This concern stems from the fact that cultural goods and services are not like other commodities. They have multiple values for informational, entertainment, and identity purposes.[17]

Earlier research exaggerated the determining role of corporations on consumers and audiences and overstated the passivity of consumer networks. In his influential book on Latinity, Americanness, and global consumption, Nestor Canclini's central proposition was that consumption has been transformed into "an arena of competing claims" and "ways of using it."[18] Flows of media text and critical ideas help reconstitute a social bond that has been sundered by neoliberal cultural funding cutbacks and mind-numbing appeals to consumer materialism.

Cultural protection is not necessarily the same as patent protection as it is conventionally understood. In the realm of culture, rights to the fruit of creativity do not necessarily impinge upon rights to access knowledge.[19] Furthermore, rights are not commodities themselves; rather they simply guarantee that creators may enjoy the fruits of their labor. In the global cultural economy, the most striking fact is that the WTO has established no set standards for diversity and accessibility.[20] Only UNESCO has a framework agreement in place supported by all countries except the US. In the real world the "center of the trade universe" has aggressively let public space be encroached upon by omnipresent property rights and aggressive corporate branding.

Simply put the WTO's regulatory model views diversity as a function of competition and not the other way round. Consumers choose their cultural diet from a buffet of options, and just like many real-world buffets, portion size is more important than quality and breadth of choice. The Anglo-American model requires super-size profits and relies on regulators to create an environment conducive to corporate growth. Media conglomerates in the US are aggressively promoting the US State Department's objectives to broaden copyright law and deepen trade liberalization. In contrast, policy makers in the EU understand that the culture/trade interface cannot be one-dimensional and trade must accommodate diversity

A public domain of commercial interaction requires a set of rules that are comprehensive in scope, comprehensible to all, and in the interest of everyone. It has to provide a legal order that holds individuals and organizations accountable before the bar of international justice, and it must have the institutional capacity to address the social dimension of international society.

The crisis of trade multilateralism

Free-trade multilateralism has not been able to meet this high standard. Three-quarters of the WTO's membership are developing countries, and this fact goes a long way toward explaining the current changes underway in the liberalization dynamic and the creation of a commercial public domain beyond the state. The new southern centers of market power agree with the United States on one thing – a bad deal is worse than no deal at all. Susan Schwab, the US trade representative hit the nail on the head when she said that "if you do one of these once every generation, and your objective is to liberalize trade, why would you settle for something that doesn't do a whole lot to liberalize trade?"[21]

With the collapse of the Doha round, it is now clear to all that the WTO has not become the constitutional capstone of a global economic community, much less a participative example of international public-mindedness.[22] Its bureaucracy and political assemblages do not have the touch necessary to steer a tight course between the interests of states, the goals of multilateral trade governance itself, and the public imperative for an inclusive global economy.[23]

The WTO has done so little for global development that its troubled amendment of the intellectual property rights agreement to allow for generic drug exports to Africa is all that it can claim as a win on the development file. When members eventually agreed to change the export rules for medicines, many spectators eagerly waited for cheap drugs to flow into Africa, but this was not to be. The rules are so byzantine and strict that generic producers are not able to use them. Of course, this is what branded pharmaceutical manufacturers wanted. They were afraid of a global marketplace where low drug prices in poor regions drove down global prices. Publics were disgusted with this weak-kneed variety of liberalism, nations were nervous about the potential weakness of the WTO's newfound humanitarianism, and branded pharmaceutical corporations were delighted that their monopolies remained unharmed.

In the past several years three lines of criticism have risen to the top of the critics' lists. Judith Goldstein of Stanford University argues that the WTO's legal system is too complex and too rigid to conclude future trade rounds. In the rush to legalize everything in the Uruguay round, negotiators created a legal straightjacket for themselves and future generations for two reasons.[24] First, the all or nothing approach to agreement building makes consensus an increasingly rare commodity in the international trade regime. Second, the devaluing of informal arrangements such as the type that flourished under the General Agreement on Tariffs and Trade (GATT) has put in place an adversarial system that is antithetical to effective liberalization talks.

Adding a layer of legal adversarialism onto the existing state mercantilism is a recipe for cardiac arrest. This is an implicit criticism of Tom Friedman's view of globalization as a golden straightjacket that binds nations to a prosperous but narrow range of options.[25] Goldstein argues that this sort of rigid thinking is actually harmful to the economic prospects of states because it takes the firm resolve and fine motor skills of national authority to maneuver the lumbering ship of government – not to mention a healthy dose of creativity and lateral thinking to navigate the shoals of globalization. Diplomats and policy analysts are the poorer for operating in the WTO's constricting environment.

Sylvia Ostry, a former high-level Canadian diplomat and a pioneering trade scholar, argues that even though the WTO appears to be a well-designed liberal organization, it does not have the capacity to function globally in the interest of all its members. Its engineering is fundamentally flawed. It is, in her words, "a Mercedes Benz sedan with the engine of a Volkswagen," by which she means that it has a remarkably effective dispute settlement arm but little else going for it.[26] This is an apt metaphor because the WTO is advertised to prospective buyers as the latest in institutional engineering and performance. In reality, however, it is a knowledge-based institution designed for elite drivers such as trade lawyers and economists, but powered by governmental bureaucrats enarmoured its profile and presence in order to intimidate other motorists. At the end of the day, the WTO is a disappointing ride for countries such as the United States, who can afford to drive it. Yet the allure of prosperity and comfort continues to beguile members who are too poor to put the pedal to the metal.

The most damning critique comes from Nobel prize–winning economist Joseph Stiglitz who argues that initially the WTO was timely and innovative, but nobody had stopped to parse its meaning for the social dimension of globalization. Stiglitz's research dives into the complex theories that attempt to explain how the information you have shapes the economic decisions you make.[27] He argues that because international trade takes place under conditions of incomplete information and therefore imperfect competition, traders with more information make better decisions and get better outcomes. In the current system, the United States, Japan, and the European Union are very good at using their superior information-gathering skills to optimize economic decision making.

Regrettably, small countries do not have an information processing advantage. Without a decent vantage point from which to survey the action, they are at the mercy of more powerful states and must take on faith their analyses of the state of play in the global economy. It comes as no surprise then that the current form of trade regulation, founded in econometric analysis and ruled by trade lawyers – the Western equivalent to philosopher kings – does not benefit the poor. Global free-trade rules have turned out to be very blunt instruments indeed, wielded by the wealthy in the interests of the elite.

Given these criticisms, how can we understand the WTO's liberal public domain position at the crossroads of the international system? Stiglitz demonstrates how law can be a weapon for bullying and punishment when organizations are not designed with the public interest in mind. This is the antithesis of a sphere of inclusive interaction. Goldstein lets us see that public reason and adversarial legalism cannot comfortably coexist. Ostry agrees, noting that the refinement of process cannot replace reasoned discourse at the global level. The WTO remains a sphere of elite interaction, resembling Habermas's early public sphere of ritual and formalized procedural freedoms. It is a heavy, top-down, bureaucratic, unaccountable, and clientelistic organization – the perfect example of the liberal internationalism captured by bureaucratic interests and subordinated to the will of the powerful core member states.

Challenging extreme economism

By the 1980s something totally unexpected had occurred that was to change the dynamics of citizen–state relations. Global publics had become a permanent feature of the political landscape in North America and Europe, but also micro civil society organizations and individuals were on the move in the Soviet Union and communist East Asia. It seemed as if dissent had become the default position of a growing number of intellectuals, scholars, and the creative class worldwide.

Public opinion leaders and busybody activists in many countries are now fully convinced that free trade is no longer a compelling explanation for national growth because it assumes that business, rather than good governance, shapes the well-being of citizens. The neo-liberal theoretical model stressed the importance of exports for national economic development. In nations such as Canada this explanation made a certain amount of sense but it has become trapped by its resource dependency. Heterodox economists were quick to point out that nations are more likely to liberalize their markets as they grow, rather than grow through free trade. To this historically grounded critique trade theorists had no answer. Nor could they offer a compelling argument for trade in terms of its impact upon public goods and public infrastructure.[28] By the late 1990s, it was becoming apparent that the social costs of unregulated markets were too high for any nation to bear alone.

The answer in the global north was to pressure southern countries to open their borders while simultaneously putting in place non-tariff barriers at home to protect domestic producers. The best-known example of this "organized hypocrisy" was the Continued Dumping and Subsidy Offset Act of 2000 passed by the US Government and informally known as the Byrd Amendment after Democratic senator Robert Byrd of West Virginia who sponsored the legislation. The Byrd Amendment allowed the funds raised by duties applied to foreign goods that the United States considered to be subsidized, to be distributed annually to the American businesses that were affected by the low-price product in question. Subsidization in this sense meant producing a product through means that American officials at the International Trade Commission determined to be unfair or anticompetitive. This included the use of government support in the form of grants, targeted tax breaks, and subsidized factor inputs to name just a few of the ways that governments give domestic businesses a leg up in the busy global marketplace.

Of course, there is a basic conflict of interest in allowing American firms to materially benefit from denouncing foreign products as anticompetitive. But US legislators in the Bush administration considered the Byrd Amendment to be a reasonable compromise between the needs of domestic producers for a home market and their demands for open markets around the globe. The Byrd Amendment raised the hackles of the world's trading nations and was used by their policy makers to point out American intransigence on the trade file. This legislation was one of the poisoned chalices that seemed to vindicate the growing disillusionment with the future prospects of trade multilateralism. But the real lesson to be taken from Byrd is that every country, even the world's most successful trader, takes measures to protect its social bond from the unequal outcomes of globalization.

When the theory of free trade points in the wrong direction

Clearly, the concept of global free trade needs to be revisited. In fact, Columbia University economist Jagdish Bhagwati, an icon amongst free-trade proponents, has become much more circumspect about the possible benefits of free trade. He has argued recently that in the absence of effective public regulation the invisible hand is likely to point in the wrong direction.[29] Governments have learned quickly that, by themselves, markets tend toward monopoly. Only through the active regulatory intervention of public authority are we able to benefit from open markets and trade liberalization. Theoretically this leads to two important insights.

First government has an important role to play in addressing market failure – especially failures relating to rent-seeking and imperfect competition. In their quest for low production costs and high profit margins, firms sometimes resort to any number of questionable and borderline legal practices, from the unethical use of child labor in factories in the global south, to the aggressive enforcement of patent protections, trademarks, and copyrights to keep competitors out of the market. Regulating unfair and unethical practices is critically important because countries today rely on exports for jobs and domestic growth more than ever before. In the postwar Keynesian period, most industrial countries relied on their exports as only one component of wealth and job creation.[30] Collective bargaining kept wages high, and it was not uncommon for family incomes to double each decade. Today, exports have become the dominant driver of the economy.[31] Especially in the global south where structural adjustment replaced import substitution policies, exports are the determining factor in the growth equation. As a result, governments require a regulatory model that deals effectively with competition issues that arise from the new global interdependency.

Second, domestic economic well-being is increasingly determined by international market conditions, rather than by the economic environment at home. In the past, trade was perceived as an export-enhancing activity that reinforced a system of mass production and mass consumption. Lower tariffs, longer production runs, and cheaper goods were seen to generate an endless stream of high-paying jobs. Now trade is increasingly job destructive for many industries as firms have to cut costs, trim payrolls, shorten commodity cycles, and shift production offshore to China, Brazil, or India.[32] When market stabilization measures are beyond the reach of any one nation, governments have a duty to protect their citizens from the international business cycle. This requires that they reinvest in state assistance programs, job training centers, and post-secondary education. In a world of increasing economic complexity and volatility, governments recognize that the primary means of stabilization is a renewed commitment to the welfare state, what the European Commission has recently termed "flexicurity" – a combination of labor flexibility and worker security.

Traditionally, modern liberalism has been blind to the social externalities of trade and to the problem of basing public solidarity on an economistic foundation. That something was dreadfully wrong became apparent as a number of the poorest countries in Africa began to slide down the Human Development Index in the late 1990s – a troubling reality for those who believed that open markets could save the poor from the ravages of political neglect and governmental mismanagement. It didn't. To be sure, there have been important gains made by leading southern countries. India has emerged as a powerful trader and multilateral leader, as have Brazil and Mexico. Unquestionably, the biggest winner of the competition sweepstakes is China.

Business consultants have shown that China is fast on the way to replacing the United States as the "world's workshop," contributing one-third of global economic growth in 2004. But China also bears the dubious distinction of being the most unequal nation in the world, a worrying development to its single-party technocracy who, it now appears, has not managed globalization as much as it has managed them.[33] The costly trade-off between social welfare and efficiency that is the hallmark and chief policy aim of market fundamentalism has fueled a cycle of skepticism among informed publics who now see the profit-maximizing strategies of international competition as posing a danger to the stability of societies in both the north and south.[34] Branko Milanovic shows in figure 1.1 that income inequality continues to be a marked feature of the world economy. Even though poverty levels have been reduced in some areas of China and India, distribution has been

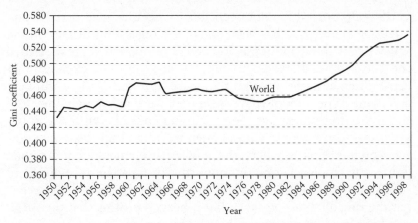

Figure 1.1 Unweighted international inequality, 1950–98 (measured by the Gini coefficient)

Source: Branko Milanovic, 2001. *Worlds Apart: Measuring International and Global Income Inequality*. Princeton, N.Y.: Princeton University Press, at www.networkideas.org

skewed to the global rich and emerging urban elite in the megacities of Asia, the Middle East, and Latin America.[35]

The market or the public domain?

In the early 1990s, modern liberalism assumed that the social concerns of modern publics could be relegated to the back burner of public policy because the gains from the new system would more than offset the criticism it would face. Judged on its success, publics would rally to the WTO, or at the very least, outspoken critics would be silenced by the bottom-line gains of the poor. This did not happen. It has taken the policy community the better part of a decade to realize that gains from trade are the result of a successful mix of transparent market regulation and redistributive social institutions. Of course, there are still many dyed-in-the-wool policy experts who refuse to acknowledge the redistributive role of public authority and the prominence of the public domain in economic capacity building.

This is all the more depressing given the fact that the United Nations has full-spectrum support for its Millennium Development

Goals – although it has not been able to meet its poverty reduction targets. Amartya Sen has been one of the biggest influences on the way we now think about poverty and development.[36] He described the causal links between material well-being, the expansion of capabilities, and the freedom to choose different ways of thinking and living. When people have been poor for long enough, they lose the ability to think about the means and ends of well-being in the same way as do people with enough to eat and the material comforts of life. This is where the educative element of the public domain is crucial. Economic opportunity must be recognized as such in order for it to play a role in poverty reduction. This insight has the ring of common sense, but it bears repeating that the social bond is a product of the public, not the market.

The major economic success stories also offer cautionary tales about the visible limits of private provision for social necessities. Private expenditures on health care in India and China have grown dramatically in the last decade. In China since 1998, private spending has jumped from 2.75 percent of GDP to 3.6 percent according to the latest data from the World Health Organization. For the 1.3 billion people in China, health care is no longer universally available and private hospitals increasingly supply top-quality care only to those who can afford it. In India public health care expenditure has declined steadily since 1998. The privatization of health services is even more dramatic with over 80 percent of health expenditures now paid by individuals, families, and businesses. In New Delhi, dozens of modern private hospitals have opened their doors, yet almost no new public health care facilities have been built over the past two decades. This seemingly unsolvable public crisis is not uncommon as private health care has exploded from Rio to Shanghai.

The incentive to put a price tag on public health is very strong where state spending on health care is low and taxation levels are nowhere near OECD levels. We who live in material comfort in the developed north believe that we are insulated from the horrors of an underdeveloped health care system. Yet by default and often by design, private delivery fills a vacuum when the social bond is broken and the public domain abdicates its responsibility for the poor and the vulnerable. When the public sector does not consistently create and implement redistributive social policies, inequality inevitably inches upward.[37]

The ballooning costs of open markets – another broken promise

The biggest challenge to the liberal model of Malthusian markets and Darwinian individualism has been in the unanticipated *reversal* of public support for economic globalization. Around the turn of the millennium, a Harvard-led social values survey showed that almost 20 percent of adults born after the Second World War saw themselves as cosmopolitan citizens of the world, identifying with their continents or the larger human condition, rather than a particular culture or creed. Another 20 percent identified as localist in orientation and were only concerned with their own particular communities.[38] The cosmopolitans had great confidence in global governance and thought that in the future more and more of the world would think like them. Today, publics are unsure of how to respond to the globalization phenomenon and are increasingly unwilling to allow elites to guide them through the complex minefield of trade-offs that separate the beleaguered welfare state from the promised land of global prosperity.

The marketization of Western capitalist democracies was sold to the public as a cost-effective alternative to the expensive and bureaucratic welfare state. The argument was that open markets cost the public very little. With the invisible hand of the market doing the heavy lifting, the overall rise in economic well-being would allow governments to claw back expensive social programs. The end result would be prosperity, smaller government, and greater economic freedom. The reality was that open markets cost about as much as did the welfare state. With the money channeled into emergency social spending, corporate competitiveness programs, the reengineering of regulatory institutions, and new state security measures to deal with the rise in violence that comes with soaring inequality government spending has risen persistently in most jurisdictions.

In the United States taxes for middle America remain constant and stable, except for the large and generous tax cuts given to the rich by President Bush as a reward to his electoral base. They are able to purchase any public good such as education, health care, and security privately. Consequently the dismantling of the welfare state by Clinton in the mid-1990s has left the US social bond highly exposed as it has been downsized and deprived of much needed reinvestment. Some would say that the polarized rhetoric of state spending in an era of globalization is Reaganomics redux, cutting taxes to reduce the size of government that never happened; indeed, thanks to Reagan's increased military expenditures, government became bigger and more costly.

Of course, it is difficult, and perhaps impossible for a democratically elected leader to cut the social entitlements that voters pay for with their own tax dollars and have come to expect from government. Belatedly, many economists have come to realize that free trade and small government are incompatible ideas because efficient markets require a robust public system for regulation and redistribution. They failed to factor in the social expense of globalization, and it has been higher, especially in the developed world, than anyone could have anticipated.

Globescan, one of the largest transnational polling firms, has been tracking public opinion in key issue areas for about seven years.[39] They have discovered a marked trend towards a self-conscious distancing of public opinion from the ideas of modern liberalism. For the entire G7 as well as South Korea, India, Brazil, Russia, and China, support for globalization fell from 62 percent to 54 percent between 2002 and 2006. That is a decline in confidence similar to that experienced by Bush and Blair in the bloody aftermath of "victory" in Iraq. At the same time, support has risen for what Globescan pollsters refer to as "protect me globalization," evidenced in indignation about the social costs of globalization, accompanied by a cautious optimism about the future of social integration.

According to recent polls, the average person is not a xenophobe. They are supportive of multiculturalism while they also want to preserve their jobs, neighborhoods, and communities. They want their governments to draft policies that protect their way of life while allowing them to remain open to new experiences. In the past five years, support for social-market protectionism has grown from 68 percent to 76 percent amongst more than 20,000 people polled in thirteen countries. This is a massive reversal in global public opinion.[40] Public opinion now indicates a preference for a gradual opening of global markets that balances the expectations of citizens with possibilities for deeper social integration.

The transformative power of information

Many experts have made much of the transformative power of fast-flowing information. The linkage between the activist and the new global sphere of interactive communication could never have taken place without the technological revolution that gave rise to what Appadurai has termed "global cultural flows." These are flows of information and ideas that "generate acute problems of well-being and encourage an emancipatory politics of globalization."[41] Global cultural flows carry with them the promise of freedom through knowledge even as they erode the regulatory apparatus of authoritarian public policy. Even those people in the poorest nations know that global flows of information are the new currency of exchange. What's more, they hope that these information flows will transform their own conditions of poverty and want. For the poorest in the global south, learning to read can make the difference between subsistence and security. The most recent evidence shows that the digital divide is shrinking, and the rural poor, long thought to be unreachable by aid and education, are gaining access to new forms of communication that they did not imagine possible in previous generations. It is a well-known fact that the microprocessor is already more ubiquitous than the telephone.[42]

Literacy is largely taken for granted in the developed world, but teaching all children to read in the poorest nations has been a nearly insurmountable challenge to full and substantive citizenship in the past. It is no accident that at a time when children in the most impoverished places on earth are learning to read, entrepreneurs and activists in the global north are working to make a laptop computer a reality for every child in the global south. An ambitious project to be sure, but one that will shift the power of communication further down the social pyramid in the coming decade. Computers are the ideal literacy-building tools because they are so

intimately linked with economic well-being and social improve-
ment – even more so than books. With the closing of the last great
intellectual divide, people in the poorest countries are developing
new capabilities, and this has major implications for the growth of
the global public domain.

According to Emmanuel Todd, this bottom-up, flow-intensive
redistribution of power may be the most significant trend of our
times, transforming the poorest states from "least-developed" to
developing nations and at the same time raising social, political,
and economic expectations around the world.[43] Over the past
twenty years, fertility rates, the number of children born per
woman, have fallen in almost every country across the globe.[44] As
societies redefine gender roles, corresponding values, rules, institutions, and family practices are transformed.

Literacy has become a strategic resource to facilitate the active
participation of both genders in the public life of southern societies. Even in places such as Afghanistan, torn by poverty, civil
war, and violent religious oppression, literacy rates have more than
doubled (from 18 percent to 47 percent).[45] Rising literacy and
falling fertility rates create a demographic condition in which information flows play an increasingly central role both in the enhancement of social well-being and also, invariably, in the fostering of
public identity. A literate and empowered underclass is one of the
most dangerous forces known to transnational economic elites.

Micro-activists strike back

The explosion of micro-activism has taken experts by surprise. In
1995, there were only about 150 NGOs present when the WTO
came into being.[46] Close to 1,000 NGOs were registered at the
WTO's Cancún Ministerial in 2003, a figure only slightly smaller
than the roughly 1,300 official delegates. Post 9/11, the global
public's defiance and questioning of authority has intensified and
deepened, especially in the context of suspended civil liberties,
restrictive transportation policies, and the revelations of the Abu
Ghraib prison torture scandal. Governments have had to pay
attention to the unexpected appearance of globally-minded and
politically savvy activists. Public Citizen, Corporate Watch,

ATTAC, the Corporate European Observatory, CIVICUS, the Third World Network, and the World Social Forum are some of the better-known and most effective transnational dissent networks.

Refining the early work of scholars of cosmopolitan citizenship, Sidney Tarrow, the distinguished American sociologist, gives us two unique insights.[47] First, political empowerment does not lift citizens out of their territorial context. They remain rooted in the local and legally bound to the national. Second, he shows that many, many people are being empowered, not just northern NGOs, and the educated elite of southern anti-globalizers. He understands citizens to be actors rooted in national contexts "who engage in regular activities that require their involvement in transnational networks of contacts and conflicts." This includes immigrants who are part of transnational diasporic production and distribution networks, firms that segment parts of their production process to subcontractors in cheap-labor countries, labor activists who link northern and southern NGOs, activists in advocacy networks that link local concerns with international institutions, and scholars who utilize international contacts to link with sites of international conflict. It also includes journalists who bridge economies and cultures as professional witnesses and spectators. Each of these groups, and many more besides, make up the growing realm of citizens who work, play, and organize themselves in a domain beyond the state.

The notion of citizenship is still deeply rooted in national territory and Westphalian public authority. Yet there has been a massive movement by activist publics to create networks of individuals and organizations that span the globe. Nevertheless, the concept of a public domain beyond the state remains problematic because it raises a key definitional challenge – is it possible to ascribe a citizenship ethos to activism beyond state boundaries? In strictly realist terms it is not. In the absence of an overarching authority, both state and non-state actors are on their own in a "self-help" system. But can we really say that Médecins Sans Frontières is pursuing its material interests in the same way that Microsoft is? Is the activism of Greenpeace on the same agential footing as the expansion plans of Shell Oil? As citizens we draw a qualitative distinction between action in the service of wealth creation and those actions that are specifically directed toward the public good.

We understand that self-interest, properly harnessed, serves the public good. More people are willing to pay higher taxes, for example, if they know that they are getting high-quality health care and well-paved roads in return. Beyond the basic wisdom of enlightened self-interest, few buy into the "greed is good" ethos on a fundamental level. Conceivably it is a legacy of the short twentieth century – this ingrained understanding that short-sighted self-interest has a vastly destructive potential.

The greatest legacy of postwar development in the global north has been the expansion of individual capabilities to the point where children today grow up knowing that as individuals, they can and must make a difference in the world they live in. Not surprisingly, the dream of a citizen-centered public domain continues to tenaciously grip the popular imagination. The WTO model of public organization has never fired the imaginations of activists. Who could rhapsodize about its closed-door deliberations, irreversible decision-making mechanisms, and all or nothing approach to membership? All of these policies were designed to enhance the efficiency of the institution at the expense of democratic deliberation.

Instead liberal institutionalism has been fixated by a single idea. Traditionally it tried to solve the problem of citizenship at the international level by designating a highly restrictive theorization of the global system as an intergovernmental arena where states remain the only legal subjects of international law of significance and therefore the only citizens of any note. The problem with this conceptualization of citizenship is that the world has moved on. We have entered an age of systemic interdependency in which the traditional concepts of state sovereignty, hard boundaries, and territorial citizenship are being challenged from all sides. The emergence of international human rights norms is the most vivid example of this shift. Seyla Benhabib is right when she notes that "treatment by states of citizen-residents within their boundaries is no longer an unchecked prerogative."[48] Our understanding of what is legitimately the choice of states and what is properly overseen by watchdogs outside the state is radically different than it was even fifty years ago.

Scholars used to think that the hard power of arms and money was the only form of influence that mattered. But there are too many powerful non-governmental actors and too few viably effective states for anyone to seriously imagine that statehood is the only route to formal recognition at the international level. More than a decade ago Susan Strange wrote that one has to distinguish between structural power – the power to affect the framework in which decisions are made – and relational power, which is the influence that one organization or individual can bring upon another.[49] Today we see that both forms of power are in play in the domain beyond the state. The organization of international relations has evolved to reflect the shifting balance between structural and relational power. More to the point, the relational power of networked activism provides the lens through which to understand the emergence of a reconstituted global public domain beyond the state.

Citizenship and belonging

In an age of unparalleled interdependency, citizenship may be territorially and culturally rooted for now, but there exists an increasing discourse around the right to choose the community to which we give our commitment and creative endeavors. Clan, kin, and constitution continue to loom large in our expression of belonging, but the relational bond of our collective humanity is strengthened when we share our hopes, fears, beliefs, and uncertainties with those who exist outside our immediate national contexts.

More than forty years ago Peter Berger, the eminent sociologist, observed that:

[T]he discontents engendered by the structures of modernity in the public sphere have a disconcerting way of reappearing in the private sphere. In their private lives, individuals keep on constructing and reconstructing refuges (that they experience as home) but over and over again the cold winds of homelessness threaten these fragile constructions.[50]

His words were more prescient than he could have known. The most fundamental function of home is to protect the individual from the terror of anonymity. As the carapace of our hierarchical and bureaucratic societies hardened in this hyper-commercial age, belonging at the state level became an either-or proposition. This strengthened the feeling of home for some, but drove others to seek their identity beyond the reach of state control. These political refugees and self-styled cosmopolitans, destitute wanderers, and wealthy expatriates colonized the public domain beyond the state.

In ways unforeseen even at the height of the welfare state, the micro-activist has recreated her identity touchstones through a web of social relations that extends downward into communities of fate into which we were born and upwards into communities of choice with whom the active citizen chooses to engage. The digital do-it-yourself universe re-engineers our expectation of belonging even as it reconfigures the sphere of activism. Yet the network is more than a virtual refuge. In fact it has become a highly resourced sanctuary from the dysfunctional family relations of the neo-liberal state and a means for social engagement, but not the end result of political struggle. Like the revolutionary activists of the nineteenth century who struggled for a better life for all citizens, activists today want to make things political that have been removed from the public eye by cynical politicians whose sole concern is the wealth of their nation. They are intent on repoliticizing and extending the public sphere after two decades of its persistent hollowing out.

The two defining issues on its agenda are war-making and the prosecution of the "war on terror". First the Bush administration's illegal invasion of Iraq did not undermine the power of the postwar legal order as some commentators have suggested. If anything, it made democratic nations even more aware of the dangers associated with bypassing the UN Charter. Bush has adopted the right to pre-emptive self-defense without Security Council authorization. Such a stance makes the world a more dangerous place. Far from securing the well-being of US citizens the Bush doctrine places them on the offensive at a time when international diplomacy requires a muscular return to multilateralism. In one of the most important books on the topic, *War Law*, Michael Byers astutely writes that the US is a "single super power that hardly seems to care" about the integrity of international law.[51] For global anxious and angered publics cowboy diplomacy has unintentionally made international law more important than ever.

Secondly the Bush administration has shown nothing but contempt for the limit civilized nations have placed on the use of force and torture. "Rule twisting megalomanics . . . have corrupted US and global politics since 11 September 2001."[52] These atrocities at Guantanamo and secret prisons in the name of the US "war on terror" have galvanized public opinion worldwide. Global public opinion does not know how the global system of justice and human rights will be achieved. But it is the issue more than any other that has taken on a force of its own in providing the big picture framework of democratic dissent.[53]

Despite the positive vision of the public presented here, the public domain beyond the state is in many ways still an ideal type, a representation of what a community based upon the right to choose might look like. In important areas that regulate state violence we know that the public domain beyond the state lacks teeth and its weakness has allowed it to be co-opted by a number of ruthless world leaders who place expediency and national self-interest before human rights. A mountain of social research teaches us that publics are infinitely capricious, often progressive, and sometimes reactionary – choosing demagogues over democrats especially in times of insecurity and upheaval. Public opinion has never been more powerful, yet in the information age micro-publics in vast numbers frequently appear to be less certain of their goals and operate under the radar screen. They are often the last to march and protest. Globalization, market fundamentalism, unilateral militarism, and terrorism in the name of faith have shaken their vision of a more inclusive form of society. As the democratic public grows by inches and feet, it is an inconvenient truth that the visceral, antisocial public also increases in influence in yards. It is this second imposing duality that marks the return of the public domain after the triumph of markets. In the public domain, activists and despots, citizens and anarchists struggle inevitably to give definitive articulation to very different visions for our global future.

Notes

1. Claire Cutler, *Private Power and Global Authority: Transnational Merchant Law in the Global Political Economy* (Cambridge, UK: Cambridge University Press, 2003).

2. Margaret Macmillan, *Paris 1919: Six Months That Changed the World* (New York: Random House, 2001).

3. James Doyle, "The Opposite of Property?" *Law and Contemporary Problems* 66:1, 2 (Winter/Spring) 2003, p. 6.

4. Hedley Bull, *The Anarchical Society: A Study of Order in World Politics* (London: Macmillan, 1977).

5. Susan Strange, *States and Markets* (London: Blackwell, 1988).

6. Henri Lefebvre, *Writings on Cities*, trans. and ed. Eleanor Kofman and Elizabeth Lebas (London: Blackwell, 1996).

7. John Ralston Saul, *The Collapse of Globalism and the Reinvention of the World* (Toronto: Penguin Books, 2005).

8. Douglas A. Irwin, "The GATT in Historical Perspective," *The American Economic Review* 85:2 (1995), pp. 323–8.

9. Statistics represent the growth in trade in goods and services for 2005. See the WTO's International Trade Statistics, 2006, at www.wto.org/english/res_e/statis_e/its2006_e/its06_overview_e.htm.

10. Branko Milanovic, *Worlds Apart: Measuring International and Global Inequality* (Princeton, N.J.: Princeton University Press, 2005).

11. Antoine van Agtmael, *The Emerging Markets Century: How a New Breed of World-Class Companies Is Overtaking the World* (Chicago, Ill.: The Free Press, 2007).

12. Sylvia Ostry, "The Post Doha Trading System," paper presented at the Pre-G8 Academic Conference, University of Glasgow, June 29–30, 2005.

13. Quoted in Richard Devetak and Richard Higgott, "Saving the Social Bond" in *The Market or the Public Domain: Global Governance and the Asymmetry of Power*, ed. Daniel Drache (London: Routledge, 2004), p. 374.

14. For complete texts of WTO agreements, see www.wto.org.

15. Bryan C. Mercurio, "TRIPS, Patents, and Access to Life Saving Drugs in the Developing World," *Marquette Intellectual Property Law Review*, 8:2 (2004), pp. 211–50.

16. Mickey Kantor, "Film Pirates Are Robbing Us All," *Financial Times*, March 18, 2004.

17. United Nations Educational, Scientific, and Cultural Organization, "Universal Declaration on Cultural Diversity" (Paris: UNESCO, 2001).

18. Nestor Garcia Canclini, *Consumers and Citizens: Globalization and Multicultural Conflicts* (Minneapolis, Minn., and London: University of Minnesota Press, 2001).
19. Lawrence Lessig, *Free Culture: How Big Media Uses Technology and the Law to Lock Down Culture and Control Creativity* (New York: Penguin Press, 2004).
20. Michael P. Ryan, *Knowledge Diplomacy: Global Competition and the Politics of Intellectual Property* (Washington, D.C.: The Brookings Institute Press, 1998).
21. Edward Alden and Alan Beattie, "Schwab to 'Think Big' on Market Access," *Financial Times*, June 12, 2006.
22. Even as the Doha Round falters, the value of merchandise and service exports continues to grow. In 2005, world merchandise exports were worth approximately $9 trillion, and the export of services topped $2 trillion. And yet the realities of global politics have roughly intruded on the theory of trade liberalization. See Robert Wolfe, "Decision-Making and Transparency in the 'Medieval' WTO: Does the Sutherland Report Have the Right Prescription?" *Journal of International Economic Law* 8:3 (2005), pp. 631–45; and Jagdish Bhagwati, "Don't Cry for Cancun," *Foreign Affairs* (January/February 2004), pp. 52–63.
23. Daniel Drache and Marc Froese, "Deadlock in the Doha Round: The Visibly Slow and Steady Decline of Trade Multilateralism" (June 2007), at www.robarts.yorku.ca/projects/wto/pdf/deadlock_at_doha.pdf, June 2007.
24. John Barton et al., *The Evolution of the Trade Regime: Politics, Law, and the Economics of the GATT and the WTO* (Princeton, N.J.: Princeton University Press, 2006).
25. Thomas L. Friedman, *Winner Takes All. The Lexus and the Olive Tree: Understanding Globalization* (New York: Farrar, Straus and Giroux, 1989).
26. Sylvia Ostry, "Making Sense of It All: A Post-Mortem on the Meaning of Seattle" in *Seattle, the WTO and the Future of the Multilateral Trading System*, ed. Roger B. Porter and Pierre Sauve (Boston, Mass.: Harvard University Press, 2000).
27. Joseph E. Stiglitz, *Towards a New Paradigm for Development* (Geneva: United Nations Conference on Trade and Development, 1998).
28. Richard Cornes and Todd Sandler, "Are Public Goods Myths?" *Journal of Theoretical Politics* 6:3 (1994), pp. 369–85.
29. Jadish Bhagwati, *Free Trade Today* (Princeton, N.J.: Princeton University Press, 2002).

30. David Held et al., *Global Transformations: Politics, Economics and Culture* (Stanford, Calif.: Stanford University Press, 1999).

31. Sylvia Ostry, "Globalization and the Nation-State: Erosion from Above" (Timlin Lecture, University of Saskatchewan, Regina, 1998).

32. Dani Rodrik, *Has Globalization Gone Too Far?* (Washington, D.C.: Institute for International Economics, 1997).

33· Dominic Wilson and Roopa Purushothaman, *Dreaming with BRICs: The Path to 2050*, Global Economics Paper: 99 Goldman Sachs, October 1, 2003, at www.gs.com.

34. UN Millennium Project, *Investing in Development: A Practical Plan to Achieve the Millennium Development Goals* (New York: UNDP, 2005), at www.unmillenniumproject.org/reports/fullreport.htm.

35. Milanovic talks about two "concepts" of inequality when comparing inequality across countries: concept one is unweighted international inequality, and concept two weighted global inequality. Concept one inequality, the weight of each country is 1/n (n being the number of countries); in other words, all countries are afforded the same weight in the comparison regardless of their population. In concept two, each country's Gini coefficient value is weighted according to that country's share of the world's population.

36. Amartya Sen, *Development as Freedom* (New York: Knopf, 1999).

37. International Monetary Fund, *IMF Bulletin* (November 20, 2006).

38. Pipa Norris, "Global Governance and Cosmopolitan Citizens" in *Globalization and Governance*, ed. Joseph S. Nye Jr and Eliane Kamarck (Boulder, Colo.: Lynne Rienner, 2001).

39. Doug Miller, "Globalization in Decline," *Ottawa Citizen*, May 16, 2007, at www.globescan.com/new_archives/miller_citizen/.

40. BBC World Service Poll, "Israel and Iran Share Most Negative Ratings in Global Poll," BBC World Service poll, at http://globescan.com/news_archives/bbcntryview/.

41. Arjun Appadurai, "Grassroots Globalization and the Research Imagination" in *Globalization*, ed. Arun Appadurai (Durham, N.C., and London: Duke University Press, 2001), p. 6.

42. Daniel Drache and David Clifton, "The Shrinking of the Digital Divide" (unpublished study, Robarts Centre, York University, December 2006).

43. Appadurai, "Grassroots Globalization," p. 6.

44. Emmanuel Todd, *After the Empire: The Breakdown of the American Order* (New York: Columbia University Press, 2003).

45. Todd, *After the Empire*.

46. Jan Scholte, *Democratizing the Global Economy: The Role of Civil Society* (Warwick, UK: Centre for the Study of Globalization and Regionalization, 2003).

47. Sidney Tarrow, "Rooted Cosmpolitans: Transnational Activists in a World of State" (working paper, Workshop on Transnational Contention, Cornell University, 2001), p. 24, at http://falcon.arts.cornell.edu/sgt2/contention/default.htm.

48. Seyla Benhabib, *The Rights of Others: Aliens, Residents, and Citizens* (Cambridge, UK: Cambridge University Press, 2004), p. 12.

49. Susan Strange, *The Retreat of the State: The Diffusion of Power in the World Economy* (Cambridge, UK: Cambridge University Press, 1996).

50. Peter Berger, Brigitte Berger, and Hansfield Kellner, *The Homeless Mind: Modernization and Consciousness* (New York: Random House, 1973), p. 188.

51. Michael Byers, *War Law: Understanding International Law and Armed Conflict* (New York: Grove Press, 2005), p. 146.

52. Byers, *War Law*, p. 155.

53. "On Torture and American Values: Editorial," *New York Times*, October 7, 2007.

2

Market Fundamentalism and the Worried Public

The inevitability of things public

Is it possible to tame globalization and develop a more equitable global order? This is not an abstract question. The liberalization of worldwide markets has brought everyone on this planet closer together. The world would be a simpler place if markets were stable and the processes of production and distribution functioned equitably. Perhaps, if capitalism worked the way it should in theory, there would be no need to make a distinction between the competitive world of markets and the collective world of "things public." But markets are not equitable. As Polanyi demonstrated fifty years ago, without the public, our societies as we know them could not exist. They would be torn apart by market forces, destroyed by the self-interest of the few. Today, our understanding of what it takes to live together is undergoing a profound shift. Most importantly, the current processes of economic integration cut both ways. Markets have grown in size and strength and so has the public.[1]

In the primary sense of the term, the public domain is about the processes, structures, and resources such as the environment, cultural commons, or something as simple as the local park, all of which have been carved out from the terrain of the market and the domain of state authority. Its collective features provide us with the social necessities that make living together democratically bearable.[2] Public culture always has a convergent point. It is the wild zone of participation, debate, discussion, mobilization, negotiation, and autonomy. While elites want to dominate and be in command, activist, non-conforming publics are constantly pushing to break down the barriers and pry open the closed circle of power. In this information age, the sphere of interactive communication has been strengthened, broadened, and deepened by new information technologies to a degree Jürgen Habermas, one of the best-known twentieth-century theorists of citizenship, never envisioned. Democratic, public "busybodies" are everywhere visible and are demanding accountability from public authority. They want to be consulted, acknowledged, recognized, and listened to.

The public domain is best understood as a large multidimensional area of social life, which overlaps with the market and the state, yet operates according to its own norms and values. The overarching principles that govern the market are contained in the laws of supply and demand. Likewise, governments operate within the fixed parameters of their constitutions, with a division of powers that is in theory strictly observed and which cannot be easily altered and modified except in exceptional circumstances and through judicial review. The public is not so well delineated, but David Marquand captures its essential social character as "the values of citizenship, equity, and service and the notion of public interest, distinct from private interests. In it, citizenship rights trump both market power and kinship bonds."[3]

The concept of the public has a long and illustrious pedigree, with roots in modern economic, political, social, and legal thought. Adam Smith understood the over-arching public interest to be quite different and separate from the private interests that governed economic transactions. Likewise, the great political theorists of the seventeenth century, Thomas Hobbes and John Locke, knew that the public was more than its individual actors – it represented collective social interests. Hobbes and Locke considered the primary interest of publics to be security, although Hobbes located the Leviathan's concern in human security – the fear of others – and Locke located it in the security of property rights and the attendant privileges for the fortunate few.

Perhaps the greatest Enlightenment thinker to take up the cause of the public was Jean-Jacques Rousseau. He understood perfectly the delicate balance required to maintain the viability of the public in the midst of private interests. He said that:

in a well conducted city, everyone rushes to the assemblies. Under a
bad government . . . no one takes an interest in what is done there,
since it is predictable that the general will won't prevail, and so
finally domestic concerns absorb everything.[4]

This portrayal of the slide from action into distraction could have
been written about our societies today, but it was first penned in
1762. Classical social theorists from the nineteenth century, such
as Émile Durkheim and Max Weber, were also struck by the tensions and dynamics between things public and things private.[5] And
certainly in the study of the law, the differentiation between public
law, which governs the relationship between individuals and public
authority, and the private law of commercial transactions has been
entrenched for centuries.

A zone of exclusion and coercion

Much of the time though, the public has not been the idealized
space imagined by social theorists where disgruntled people can
mount a "collective response against the principle of established
authority."[6] For most of its history, capitalism has valued property
rights over social need and things public were pushed into the
corner of a large and hostile political world. Democracy has coex-
isted uneasily with markets as deeply entrenched property rights
have slowed the spread of equality. This is the salient point – that
the public did not appear spontaneously. Only with maximum
political will, and then not always, has the public sphere become a
place of inclusivity. Furthermore, to maintain the public domain as
the primary site of political life, democratic values, institutions, and
debate has required a great investment in upkeep.[7] Without nour-
ishment and custodial care, "things public" inevitably begin to dete-
riorate under the corrosive pressure of markets.[8]

Harry Arthurs, one of Canada's foremost critical legal scholars,
makes the fundamental point that private domains are constituted
and legitimated by a distinctive ideology and belief system. The
universe of the public is divided from the world of the private by
shifting, permeable, and sharply contested boundaries of private
property rights.[9] We have to pay special attention to the highly

contested boundary disputes that occur where the public overlaps with the private. Historically, the profit imperative of the private domain has created a situation in which market actors view the public domain as an unequalled opportunity for expansion into non-market life. They want to supplant the state as the principal provider of many services. They will spare no expense to own what is shared in common. They have both the resources and the will to use the full weight and authority of the law to weaken the idea of a freestanding public domain. This pressure in large dosages can only erode the ideals of community and citizenship. Private property rights persistently encroached upon civil liberties and political participation in earlier periods because homo economicus was allowed unfettered access to the non-market sanctuaries set aside by society.

The defining features of the modern public domain include public goods, public regulatory authority, and the public sector. Public goods such as access to an education, the right of assembly, and free speech benefit everyone and cannot be considered private property – public space is one example. In society today, public space is a by-product of social and state activity.[10] We can think of public space in terms of social activity such as a street festival, or as the space allocated to a particular public endeavor by the state, such as a museum. The public authority of government to be an effective manager of markets includes the capacity to regulate the economic activity of market actors as well as the authority to limit the intrusion of markets into the public domain.[11]

There is also the intergenerational responsibility for the protection and conservation of the planet's environment, including ground water, fisheries, the atmosphere, and the oceans. Stewardship of our environmental resources is increasingly central to our understanding of what it means to be a publicly-minded citizen. And although the environment is our common inheritance, it does not fall strictly into the public domain because while the air we breathe and the water we drink belongs to everyone, the land that industry uses to grow our food and harvest resources is often privately owned.[12]

Of course, there are other aspects of the public domain that overlap with the private sphere such as networks of engagement between citizens. Robert Putnam terms this "social capital" and noted the way that these networks facilitate cooperation and coordination of the *civitas* particularly in the interface between the local and the global.[13] It is important not to forget the sphere of interactive communication as a final critical aspect of the public domain. It is formed by new communication technologies such as the Internet. The flow of new communication technologies is governed by the market, yet they facilitate debate, discussion, mobilization, and the building of discursive communities.[14]

The bias of communication: a pivotal concept

Scholars have successfully argued that the ability to communicate is crucial to the well-being of the public. Literacy movements, an informed and free press, and the growth of public opinion independent of the state and powerful vested interests have been historical markers of a growing public domain. The growth of the popular, penny newspaper, both sensational and informative, and its much later electronic reincarnation, the "blog," are part of the progressive evolution of modern practices of public communication.[15] A Habermasian reading of the current stage of globalization highlights the way that new forms of communication unleash the radical innovative potential of the public.[16]

Habermas theorized that public communication and the formation of public opinion originally relied on face-to-face engagement.[17] But communication technology allowed for a decentralization of the opinion-formation process, as newsprint and later the television allowed for the faster dissemination of ideas. Today, he notes, this process of political engagement and public reason is no longer confined to the agora as it was in ancient times, but rather takes place through digital means in the global polis.[18] The particular modality of this process within the global interactive sphere of communication was foreseen by Harold Innis, Canada's first internationally recognized cultural theorist.[19]

Taking the case of the print revolution, Innis demonstrated how the invention of the printing press was integral to the popularization of new forms of public communication. The printing press brought new ways of doing politics to a larger audience than ever before. Yet its most important consequence was in relation to the exercise of power, for the invention concentrated influence in the hands of the few who owned presses. The pattern, which Innis deduced, is evidenced in the way elites cultivate each wave of new technology to enhance their authority and prestige by denying others access to knowledge-intensive technologies. The newspaper industry that arose around the printing press was quickly monop- olized and nurtured by elites, a fact evidenced by an especially subtle form of political control exerted over the dissemination of "public" information. "Freedom of the press had been an essential ingredient of the monopoly for it obscured monopolistic charac- teristics."[20]

The nineteenth-century press remained both a mediator and intensifier of public discussion at the same time as it was a vehicle for profit and elite opinion. The specialized power that came with the ownership of the means of public communication was used as an economic weapon and as an instrument of power for empires, nations, and states seeking to impose their control over other people and territories. Innis puts the situation in its starkest terms when he observes that "[T]echnological innovations were devel- oped and adapted to the conservative traditions of monopolies of communication with consequent disturbances to public opinion and to political organization."[21]

It was in this period of industrialism and the rapid growth of international markets that grassroots organizing and popular dissent became effective tools for political change. Socialist move- ments, populist organizations, and cultural activists used the new print technologies to get their messages out to eager and receptive publics. Elites in every industrial country controlled the powerful bodies of communication such as the mass circulation dailies, as they continue to do today. But as print technology advanced, so did small presses, subversive newspapers, and the spread of radical ideas. Critical thought and rational dissent existed independent of formal organizations. Even as print media concentrated political power in the hands of a few, the technology itself created new pos- sibilities for public dissent.

Innis's groundbreaking research into the origins and possible futures of public communication suggested that in an era of unprecedented technological change, the bias of communication shifts political power downward and towards the margins of societies.[22] This process has destabilizing effects on traditional patterns of authority even as elites harness new communication technologies for their own ends. The kind of socio-economic change it triggers can be tracked as it follows predictable and relatively coherent patterns. He believed that culture, politics, and communication were closely linked but causality was rarely linear.

Significantly, Innis concentrated on the most visible and complex side of the relationship between empire and communication, the bias of communication and the owners of communication. Unlike Habermas and Arendt, he never focused on the sphere of communication itself. From his colonial vantage point, it was taken for granted that elites would control the pathways and technologies of communication to the best of their abilities. The most striking convergence between Habermas and Innis is their belief in the decentralization of communication that takes place through technological advancement. It counteracts the clientelistic aspects of modern citizenship in which the citizen is subordinated to supplicant status by the manipulative use of political semiotics – the signs and symbols of authority. In Habermasian terms, decentralization limits the process of feudalization of the public sphere by which elites use their control of the organs of communication in order to subordinate the public to mere rubber stamp status.

Taken together, Habermas and Innis provide a compelling account of the processes currently underway in the public domain. Critical theorists of the same period imagined citizens to be incapable of organized protest on the scale seen today, or even if capable, distracted from their purpose by the entertainment industry. As it turns out, with the arrival of the 1 billion-strong Internet universe and another 2 billion individuals text-messaging and talking on their cell phones, more people have a voice in the public domain, and citizens are able to speak with whoever they want and have the capacity to organize social networks nationally and transnationally more than ever before. How does one fit together the explosion of the global public sphere to meta-shifts in world public opinion? Is there a deeper trend that needs to be interrogated and theorized?

The worried global public: defending the best interests of society

As citizens have become more independent-minded they are increasingly critical of the institutions that govern the world. Global surveys of public opinion have uncovered the existence of a vast worried public since 2001, and these poll results about their lack of confidence in governments, corporations, and global institutions paint a very clear picture of the harm people believe is caused by their elected authorities.[23] The question asked of 20,000 respondents in sixteen countries between 2001 and 2005 was how much the major institutions "operated in the best interests of society" at a time of intense globalization. Trust in global companies was at its lowest levels since the survey began in 2001. The sharpest drop in trust occurred in Spain, the USA, Argentina, Germany, and Brazil. China and India stood against the trend.

These deeper changes in the dynamics of power make feasible new forms of social activism and the public sphere is again a contested space. The emancipatory vision of Max Horkheimer and Theodore Adorno advanced in their masterful volume *Dialectic of Enlightenment* and Herbert Marcuse's incendiary criticism of Western society's overweening obsession with consumption in *One Dimensional Man* have deeply influenced the public domain today. No longer dependent on mass media for their information publics have acted on the "trust deficit" and the low esteem they have for elites around the world. The decline in deference towards "dad" in the family, presidents and prime ministers in politics, generals in the military, and chief executive officers of the world's most powerful corporations has given rise to all kinds of elite-challenging mass action.

Global Citizens are signing petitions, starting boycotts, creating art, breaking copyright laws, filesharing, blogging, and engaging in elite challenging activities just as Englehart, Castells, and Wellman, the foremost experts on global networking and values, predicted. Above all, they are no longer living in their self-constructed silos. Instead *they are talking to one another.* They are vocally anti-authoritarian toward elites and their institutional authority and unafraid to voice their opposition to the policy platitudes and pessimistic worldviews of both the left and the right. They are better informed than the anti-war movement of the sixties and the new information technology skills have given them the capacity to have staying power. Anthony Downs once predicted that the attention span of modern dissenters was short and would easily be distracted. How mistaken he was. [24] The high quality of contemporary discursive participation reflects communications skills that have migrated down the pyramid. The information technology (IT) revolution is a mass phenomenon driven by the consumer at the bottom of the pyramid hungry for information, distraction, and talk as well as the accessibility opened up by falling prices. The Global Citizen can be found in coffee shops, when she discusses the issues that matter to her with members of her community. The Global Citizen can be found at the mall, when she chooses to support certain businesses over others by "voting with her wallet". . .She can be found online at election time and between elections blogging, chatting, questioning.

At a deeper level, to be a social actor today one needs to patch into the worldwide digital communications network. Do-it-yourself techno-gurus, bloggers, musicians, writers, public intellectuals, counterculture activists, and even knowledge caretakers such as universities, archives, and museums contribute new ideas about what it means to be a citizen in the transnational cultural context. Benedict Anderson has argued that in the nineteenth century, print capitalism created the modern citizen and nationalism as the mainstays of the nation-state. In the twenty-first century, hypertext is recreating the modern concept of global citizenship through access to new collective identities and new ways of understanding the relationship between local and global. [25]

The text-messaging phenomenon sweeping Asia, Europe, North America, and Africa is a striking example of Anderson's primary insight. Today digital technology is available to those who have never had access to it in the past, including the poor, children, and the disabled, particularly in the global south. E-mail and text-messaging technology were also used to orchestrate mass demonstrations of dissent, such as the "battle in Seattle" in 1999 and those in response to the Madrid bombings in 2004. [26] "Texting" has been an ideal instrument for organizing spontaneous public demonstrations in

Asia's megacities as well. The anti-Japan demonstrations of 2005 in China were facilitated by text-messaging, which was used to mobilize thousands of urban Chinese in Beijing and Shanghai.[27] The instantaneous transmission of photos from Rwanda, the former Yugoslavia, and Iraq alerted global publics to human rights abuse and galvanized international condemnation against American imperial ambitions.

The spread of mobile technology, like any other new technology, has initially occurred unevenly. Just reflect on the past decade or so. In North America the diffusion of computers and broadband was intense and spectacular in the nineties but Mexico was not part of the first wave. Then the Internet and the cell phone grew at double digit numbers in the EU but not Asia. By 2000, the Internet revolution had arrived in China and India and tens of millions of people went online and bought the latest IT phone. Still Africa seemed lost "in translation" without a developed infrastructure and landlines, the costly legacy of its colonial past. There is, however, reason for cautious optimism. By 2005 Africans bought 80 million cell phones annually, roughly the population of France and Portugal. The digital divide is shrinking and will contract yet again when the One Laptop per Child program takes off and millions of laptops will be distributed to schools, universities, and community centers. The cumulative effect has been an exponential democratization of communication.

The traditional left-right worldview imagines that power begets power and that new information technology empowers corporate intellectual property proprietors. Ownership of the means of communication brings wealth and the ability to control the social agenda, but with the digital communications revolution, the reverse is true. Civil society uses information and communication technologies (ICTs) to strengthen a bottom-up approach to mobilization of the sort necessary for the democratization of the information society.[28] Since the mid-1990s, digital technology has been a lynchpin of popular protest and mass dissent. Now, at the dawn of the twenty-first century, it has entered the mainstream of local and regional cultures alongside the other revolutionary media of mass communication, radio and television.[29]

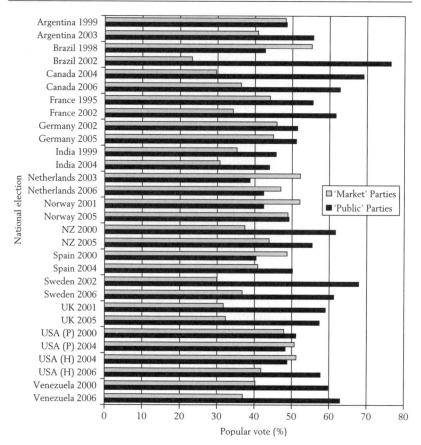

Figure 2.1 The resurgent anti-market vote, 1995–2006
Source: Daniel Drache, unpublished study, Robarts Centre, 2007

The anti-market vote and value-added of micro-activism

As in the nineteenth-century era of the printing press, the dominant trend today is toward an intensification of elite control of politics, the economy, and society. Yet at the same time, new opportunities for activism and the strategies of grassroots organizers confer legitimacy on collective action. Since 1995, voters in fourteen major national jurisdictions have begun to reject the neoliberal agenda. In twenty-three of the past thirty elections in the sample shown above, public-oriented parties took a larger share of the popular vote than did market-oriented parties (see figure 2.1). After two decades when every election revolved around cutting budgets and reordering priorities to make society more competitive and less sheltered from the global business cycle, the modern voter has learned from firsthand experience a lot about the goals and outcomes of neo-liberalism.

Modern globalization has been a great educator of people for the past two decades or longer. Contemporary public opinion experts remind us that voters are glued to their television sets when the thousands of candidates from the Left and Right repeatedly clash at election time. The leaders debates focus the mind: how deep should welfare benefits be cut? Are unions too powerful? Taxes too high? The economy not competitive enough? These debates are rarely decisive as a one-off event, but strategists are unanimous in their view of their critical cumulative role in shaping public opinion. Angela Merckel, the current German chancellor, lost the televised debate to Gerhard Schröder but narrowly won a plurality. Her party barely held its own, winning only 1 percent more of the vote. In 2007 in Mexico, Felipe Calderón and Andrés Manuel López Obrador battled to a draw, but Calderón squeaked through in the bitterly contested election. Mexico remains deeply divided despite Calderón's disputed narrow victory. Silvio Berlusconi, the Italian media czar and one of the iconic leaders of the global Right, was hammered by Romano Prodi in front of Italian viewers. Prodi went on to defeat Berlusconi.

These elections, as well as dozens of others fought over very similar issues, have had a cumulative impact on the minds of voters. The backlash against right-wing parties cannot be judged strictly by who wins the elections. The swing to a skeptical mind-set contains an important insight about cumulative shifts in public opinion. Voting analysis reveals a much more dynamic picture of the average skeptical citizen. It is someone that learns through experience, is not immobilized by cynicism, and can acquire a level of literacy. Literacy is the most critical element as it enables the modern voter to sift fear from fact, form from substance, and ideological goals from empirical outcomes. Is this not the learning curve of public reason and debate that confronts every movement from below as they fight for the hearts and minds of the vast middle? Keynesians did this in the 1930s as postmodern feminists and environmentalists have had to engage in the same process to fight to defend their ideas in the public sphere. There is no puzzle here. Ideas have to be put into play by every means available and pushed into the mainstream by surly in-your-face counterpublics if the public agenda is ever to change in a substantive way.

The countries shown in figure 2.1 represent a sample of developed and developing countries with multiple political parties, a universal franchise, and vigorously contested elections. The fact that in more than 88 percent of the elections held over the past decade public-oriented parties have won a majority of the votes is quite simply stunning. It reveals how deep the disenchantment with global neo-liberalism is and how effective is the diffusion of the message of the anti-globalization movement to those who have never marched or militated. The backlash against the neo-liberal Right with its programs of less taxes, more competitive labor markets, and fresh support for private industry has defeated incumbent governments wedded to template governance. But voters are not necessarily voting for left-oriented parties in the traditional sense. The center of the political spectrum, once a dead zone of mind-numbing conformity, has been transformed into a site of debate and new thinking about public policy. The voter is faced with conflicting claims about doing more for welfare, immigration, and public social policy.

The most striking illustration of this point is Nicolas Sarkozy's success in capturing the French protest vote in the presidential election of 2007. As a candidate he was, by the standards of French political life, an unconventional figure whose views crossed the left-right spectrum. A supporter of the European framework, a defender of national industrial champions, a believer in lower taxes, and an advocate of a new social consensus on working hours and global warming, Sarkozy represents an impossible, contradictory, and mercurial mix of pro-market and pro-public ideas all premised on an essential optimism that the center can drive political change. This is the surreal nature of modern electoral politics where publics vote for populists and the institutional Left is shut out of the electoral prize of winning office.

Modern discerning voters are no longer wedded to ideological preferences once cast in stone and the choice between the Left and Right. There is good reason for disenchantment. Many Left voters have never forgiven Tony Blair, François Mitterand, and Gerhard Schröder for betraying socialist core values and ideals. These communities joined by political fate, class, and values have moved on, freed of their generational loyalty to one party and a singular set of beliefs. If ideology is not a sure predictor of how defiant publics will vote, what is?

The modern rebellious elector increasingly looks to an array of political parties that best reflects their growing disenchantment with the culture of entitlement, political parties that dominate political life for decades in many countries with little prospect that an alternate party will form a national government. This is the most visible sign of a vast electoral realignment underway. This may be the social democratic alternative, some kind of hybrid of left values and right pragmatism. Or it may be the populist right-wing party that offers a circle-the-wagons answer to the discontents of globalization and centralization of power in modern society. Or it may be a coalition of smaller center and left of center parties that promise action on the environment, an end to corruption and crony politics.

The hybrid, unstable center

Modern voters are spurning the old left-right conventional markers and instead are ready to cast their ballot for parties that promise more effective public authority and institutional reform, as Finnish voters recently did when they chose a center-right coalition to be the next government. In Quebec's provincial election in 2007 voters created a minor political tsunami on Canada's political landscape. Fed up with the broken promises and an incompetent Liberal provincial leader they parked their votes with a right-wing provincialist federalist party. Apply the same logic in the case of Italy where voters kicked out Berlusconi when worries about job loss and corruption finally persuaded a plurality of electors that Prodi was the only alternative. In Northern Europe, conservative parties in countries with a strong social democratic culture have painfully learned that they cannot afford to be subservient to market forces American-style. The majority of Scandinavians are voting for center and often center-right parties that promise to tame globalization, do more with less public spending, and only fine-tune the high-skill, high-tax model of public life.

In Sweden the center-right conservatives, known as Moderates, won the election of 2007 by arguing that the average Swede is actually becoming poorer. They argued that the Scandinavian welfare model needed to be maintained with an eye to the value of the services offered and the cost of these services to citizens. These new right-centrists speak of caring, diversity, and rising above old ideological divides – a stark rhetorical shift from the slash and burn policies of previous neo-liberal governments. In Denmark the 2007 election reduced the center-Right's parliamentary majority and the conservative government will have to rely on the center-Left to govern in a number of key policy areas. Today, not many centrist voters still believe that residual Keynesianism is the main obstacle to domestic growth and economic well-being.[30] Instead new coalitions offer voters electoral systems that are badly in need of realignment. Elections are more fractious, polarized, and often attention-grabbing in Europe and Latin America.

In the same vein, where does the US fit into this new model of politics? The organized anger of middle America has returned to mainstream US politics with a vengeance by demonstrating a newfound interest in political change. It appears that even so-called "Evangelical voters" have shed their ideological skins and are looking for answers to pressing public policy issues. A recent poll from the liberal Center for American Values in Public Life asked 2,500 respondents to rank the eight major issues of the election: gay marriage and abortion came dead last. Ending the Iraq war and Republican corruption were the top-of-mind election issues across the US. Health care was the other priority. A strategic part of middle America, once the heartland of Bush's moral conservatism, has changed its primary colors.

In 2006, US voters gave control of both the House and the Senate to the Democrats for the first time in over a decade. Experts had not predicted the extent of the landslide victory, the most polarized mid-term election since the Vietnam era, which saw the Democrats winning thirty-four seats in the House and six in the Senate in a very hard fought campaign.[31] In the 2007 presidential primaries the fluidity and uncertainty of the voter have derailed the campaign strategies of the leading Democratic and Republican contenders. Despite raising more than a billion dollars the establishment candidates of Hillary Clinton, Barack Obama, and Rudy Giuliani are losing ground to wildcard last-minute entrants into the race like Huckabee. The well of voter anger has left the race in late 2007 in a state of turmoil in the primaries. Clinton's lead has been narrowed and challenged by Obama who won an upset victory in Iowa. The volatility of the voter's mood-swing took experts by surprise a week later when Clinton defeated Obama in New Hampshire. No expert understands or can predict what will be the final outcome given the near dead tie in votes and primary delegates after super-Tuesday.

The American primaries have done more to shatter the idea that North Americans are destined to row together towards a common goal and a set of understandings. This hard fought race has caught the cynic off guard and demonstrated that US political renewal is under way on a scale no one could have predicted a year ago. It is disheartening to a degree unimaginable that Mitt Romney, one of the leading Republican contenders, actively campaigned on removing twelve million illegal, mostly Mexican, immigrants from the United States within ninety days. None of his opponents saw anything wrong with wholesale removals but have a different strategy, one of style not substance. How does one factor in the equal impulse of reaction and reform in comparing the Democratic and Republican primaries? What portents does the future hold for a world post-Bush/Cheney?

The rebalancing of deep integration with democratic politics and the nation-state is well advanced in North America, but it is uneven and uncertain as the burden falls on the vagaries, spin of the candidates themselves and short-run needs of US electoral politics. It may be that global neo-liberalism in its present complex configuration is unravelling at the end of the Bush presidency, but it may also be regrouping in more lethal directions.

No one person, government, or expert has a ready-made answer to the multidimensional nature of political regime change globally. It remains the perennial million dollar question. The best minds of researchers and analysts across the globe are now focusing their efforts to shape the future direction of the global economy and democratic politics through research on institutional and other kinds of long-term systemic change. This interface between international organization, political economy, law, and political science is one of the most complex and important; for it is here that we see the coalescence of options and forces that are shaping the future not only in a theoretical and analytical sense, but engendering and encouraging new actors and supporting diverse cultures and geographies of agency.

The modern free-floating voter: looking right, looking left

We are in a difficult and unpredictable transition period, and what happens next will be socially significant. In many instances voters are heading to the high ground of anti-market politics; in others they are looking at positively contrarian unpredictable kinds of voting alternatives. This readiness to try new voting patterns is an anathema to the hard Right and traditional Left. Academic experts haven't come to terms with the fluidity and cross-voting pattern it entails. The vote against a ruling party is the logic that drives the voting system almost everywhere. In an era where few political parties campaign on the "vision thing," the most radical step to take is to create a political hybrid and hope it will create a "brake on the traditional pedal of power." In dozens of elections around the world this new strategy of building local coalitions has pushed political resistance beyond the traditional arrangements of the past decade. This movement is important for three reasons.

First, disgruntled voters are punishing neo-liberal ideologues for implementing programs that sound good in theory, but do not work in practice, as the recent elections in Spain and Brazil confirm. Second, they show a marked preference for coalition governments that function as a brake on more privatization and deregulation. This is what led to the defeat of the BJP (Bharatiya Janata Party) in India. Third, voters are critical of template politics from both the Left and the Right. They are drawn to political parties who campaign on principle and present alternative ideas about the environment, redistribution, and big-picture political reform.

Support for third parties has grown in almost every jurisdiction. Centrist voters are becoming much more activist and unpredictable. Doug Saunders writes that "parties across the spectrum have had to become more flexible to keep hold of this wily, mercurial, activist new kind of vote in the middle."[32]

It would be naive to claim that the failure of template neo-liberalism is due entirely to the intervention of activists and social movements. It is more accurate to state that the biggest proponent of neo-liberal orthodoxy is the United States, and the Bush administration has had to abandon its rhetoric of extreme economism in order to prosecute its ill-fated war in Iraq. The US no longer represents a gold standard of fiscal probity. With ballooning double-figure deficits, the US cannot point to its fiscal and trade performance as a policy framework for all countries to follow. As for unemployment, Germany and France have seen their unemployment fall to the lowest levels in twenty-four years. Their high-wage, high-tax economies are creating hundreds of thousands of new jobs. Social Europe is going head to head with liberal America and proving to be a tough competitor.

Second, deficit cutting freed up a lot of public money, and G8 governments are awash in cash. Dozens of governments have money to spend after years of cutting social welfare programs and reducing benefits. These factors, coupled with the rise of dissenting publics, explain the trend toward more generous government programs and reinvestment in the public.[33] When one examines where governments are spending in industrial countries as a group, public spending fell in only one category – that of public investment – from an average of 3 percent of GDP to 2 percent. By contrast, income support benefits to the unemployed, the disabled, single parents, and the elderly represent the most important area of state expansion. Also, spending on interest and debt doubled by the late 1990s; although these payments still represent less than 5 percent of GDP.

In the European Union, Japan, and the United States, tax rates as a percentage of GDP are higher today than they were in 1980 – this too is a paradoxical feature of neo-liberalism. Even as governments hacked and slashed at the public sector, they recognized its strategic importance for the delivery of public goods. In particular, the Scandinavian countries, with their high-tax and high-wage economies, continue to be large spenders – almost 60 percent of GDP is driven by government. At the opposite end are Ireland, the UK, and the US, low-spending governments in efficiency-driven societies. Yet even in the UK by the end of the Blair years, social spending approached EU averages. [34] Also in the southern hemisphere where neo-liberal policies made the deepest inroads due to World Bank and International Monetary Fund (IMF) conditional loans, state spending and its public regulatory function are back with a vengeance in Argentina, Chile, and Venezuela.

The state is being reshaped in myriad jurisdictions, and there is no single trend toward convergence. In Europe, tax rates have been marginally lowered. In Germany and France, the VAT is being raised. In other European countries, corporate tax loopholes are being closed, which effectively raises taxes on business. In Germany, a minimum wage for the service industry has been implemented, and in France, the SMIG (Salaire minimum inter-professionnel garanti) covers more than 40 percent of service workers. The fact that unemployment is at record lows across the OECD is proof positive that neo-liberal discipline and export-led demand have worked, albeit in a crude and vicious way. Welfare rolls have been slashed and entitlements pruned. Nevertheless, the big picture numbers show that the tide is changing. The idea of collective sharing has returned to the policy table. In the neo-liberal worldview taxes are seen as carrots and sticks that governments use to reward and punish anti-competitive rule-breakers (see figure 2.2). But the political economy of public spending today shows us that governments are once again taking seriously the concept of taxation as a resource to be used in the public interest.

The three narratives of globalization

So while elites are having second thoughts about hollowing out the public sphere, at the grassroots level the changes are equally dramatic. When Habermas talked about the refeudalization of the public sphere that resulted from the capture of the public sphere by bureaucratic interests, he did not envisage a phenomenal democratization of entry into the public sphere by millions of

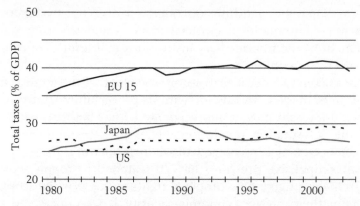

Figure 2.2 Taxes as a collective sharing of resources in the public interest
Sources: European Commission,2004; OECD

engaged micro-activists. The public sphere for communication is less exclusive today and more internally differentiated and accessible than ever before. Many of the issues that were once relegated to the private sphere of the family are now part of the public domain. In an era of globally connected networks of interaction, the personal is not only political, it has also acquired a resiliency and novelty not evident since the last great wave of dissent in the 1960s when anti-war publics poured into the streets in the days of rage and revolution.

It is axiomatic that society has always needed well-constructed institutions where the rules and principles of contending interests can reconcile conflict without giving any single group the power to make their views and interests prevail over others. The Cold War and the anti-communist policies of Western governments cultivated the social values of the silent majority's belief in law and order and national pride. Richard Nixon, Ronald Reagan, and Margaret Thatcher drove a deep wedge between dissenting and conforming publics. By contrast, the information revolution and the associated belief that the public has a central role to play have raised the expectation that public information and space should exist outside of the market. In a way that should surprise no one, global publics increasingly look to their own governments to exercise their fiduciary responsibilities when it comes to maintaining national public spheres. They are rightfully disconcerted over the dysfunctional behavior of international financial markets and advocate a reinforcement of the intermediary institutions that limit the power of markets over people.

It has taken two decades to absorb the fact that the intense globalization of markets worldwide with its powerful integrative pressures is not totally new or unprecedented. Long before the Internet and the information revolution, belief in a triumphant world market occupied a privileged place in modernity. In every age, global competitive pressures have threatened to topple existing hierarchies and give new property rights to some while stripping others of their meager economic security. If we understand anything, it is that the globalization narrative possesses an endless capacity to reinvent itself when conditions demand it, and today is one of those redefining moments.

When policy makers, academics, and activists began to preach the gospel of globalization in the 1980s, their first reflex was to both fear and champion only the triumphalism of markets. Shrinking the public sphere and downsizing the welfare state were the goals. The earliest narrative of globalization in the 1980s swept into public prominence and initially told a deterministic story of markets and conquering global corporations in which the public played no part. It invoked a vision of expansive economic freedom where anyone could place their money anywhere in the world. This freedom would come at a cost to state sovereignty, but the payout would be enormous – unprecedented wealth for the corporations and states that were willing to put their faith in the invisible hand of the market. Strangely, the rhetoric of the first-wave globalization narrative sounded extremely pessimistic – "the end of state authority," "the end of economic geography," "the demise of the nation-state," and other images and language of catastrophic structural transformation.

This narrative was a product of the deregulation of financial markets and increased capital mobility set in motion by American legislators and the privatization of UK state enterprises in the early 1980s. Massive cross-border flows of investment and "hot money" – the foreign cash that drives up the value of stock markets – promised prosperity for all if only governments would give the market a free rein. And it appeared as if governments could do little else. Seemingly no government could or would stand in the way of progress and prosperity – no matter what the price of many so-called efficiency measures. Public space in the form of buildings, programs, parks, and new development initiatives – all critical components of "things public" – was sold off and privatized by governments. They needed to pay for the increasingly expensive tax cuts and incentives that free-marketeers blithely assured them were necessary in order to create more efficient markets.

Anti-globalization activists were reviled as Luddites, communists, and naive xenophobes. Thomas Friedman put the issue most starkly when he declared that countries had to make a choice between the "Lexus" of prosperity and the "olive tree" of social solidarity and parochial identity. Firms and countries who chose the Lexus understood that "nobody is in charge," and that market forces were unstoppable and global commerce triumphant. Getting on the globalization boat was not just good business sense, it was the only way for countries, whatever their stage of development and however different their aspirations, to stay afloat in the most turbulent of waters. Individuals and nations who desired the olive tree were cautioned to pause and think long and hard about letting anti-market claims of identity cloud their judgment. It was no accident that Friedman's chosen olive tree motif is also a potent symbol of place and lineage in the strife-torn Middle East. The market, not people, was at the center of the first globalization narrative.

Nevertheless, the paradox of modern sovereignty is that the less it appears to matter in global affairs, the more it matters in practice for social well-being. Globalization did not render state sovereignty irrelevant, as Fukuyama and Friedman confidently and wrongly asserted; rather state sovereignty has been revealed as the porous and incomplete condition it has always been. The autonomy accorded to sovereign states has become more important to national authority. And the idea that states have the power to set their own political agendas has been central to the activist strategies of engaged citizens everywhere. Fast-flowing information has not undermined the autonomy of states so much as it has enhanced their interdependency with other states and non-state actors. As Joseph Nye has demonstrated, the revolution in information technology makes soft power – the power to attract and persuade rather than dictate and compel – all the more important for modern governments. Social groups and individuals play an expanded role in world politics, an arena that used to be the exclusive preserve of state authorities.[35]

The globalized digerati

The second narrative of globalization was a starkly dissimilar story. It was about unstoppable information flows, unstable levels of foreign investment, and the possibilities afforded by new information and production technology. Towards the end of the 1980s, the first globalization narrative of free markets and deregulation had begun to affect state strategy. As a result, the second globalization story emphasized the possibilities afforded by technological progress and the rise of the "digerati" – an elite class of young, entrepreneurial, creative types who would engineer the transformation of work, taking the old Fordist, industrial economy and creating from it a lean, mean, postindustrial service economy. It was a world of brash individualism where the public domain was to be the handmaiden to world-class information entrepreneurs and skilled middle-class professionals. Jeremy Rifkin promised "the end of work," and even skeptics looked forward to leaving the office and setting up their base of operations in the local Starbucks thanks to micro-digital processors. Indeed, millions of professionals are no longer bound to their desks today, but carry with them the panoptic presence of the iconic BlackBerry. Canada's Research In Motion, its inventor, alone expects to have 10 million online subscribers worldwide by 2010.

The rise of new information technologies also radically cut transportation costs, making offshoring an attractive and cost-effective answer to the perceived problem of high wages in the industrialized north. A smaller state and benign enlightened capitalists would redefine the public interest for those equipped for the information age. New telecommunications industries promised further efficiencies to make the global economy more inclusive. Why pay top dollar to back-office staff in North America, when the same thing can be purchased in India at a fraction of the cost? The off-shoring of good jobs in the manufacturing and administrative sectors created a windfall for private investors in the telecommunications industries, but it left workers in the global north with a sour taste in their mouths.

Restructuring played a big part in the phasing out of organized labour, which had been crucial to postwar prosperity for so many families. The cost of making a transatlantic telephone call had fallen to a price approaching zero, but the promise of technological efficiency had become a reality for the contingently employed and the once secure mass-production workers who saw their jobs shipped out to China or any of the other low-cost manufacturing jurisdictions. Their incomes went south along with production. Walmart became the icon of the dispossessed. Cheap goods from China became a kind of wage subsidy for low-income earners whose real wages actually long ceased to raise with the end of the US postwar boom. Low-priced consumer goods were a symbol of prosperity in the 1950s, but by the 1990s, pundits had begun to chatter about "the high cost of low prices." Robert Greenwald's documentary by the same name became a rallying cry for the public incensed by the structural transformation of work in the United States.[36] Even CNN's Lou Dobbs got into the act, proclaiming that offshoring amounted to a "war on the middle class" in America.

For publics worldwide, globalization had been first seen as an inexorable industrial force that was incompatible with the social entitlements and a robust public domain that had sheltered the public throughout most of the twentieth century. Next, it had been sold to them as a postindustrial transformation of work. Older institutions of public participation, such as the trade union, were no longer thought to be relevant. There had been a massive transfer of power from the public to the private, but now financial globalization was seen for the experiment that it actually was. Nevertheless, while the transformation of work was largely illusory, the transformation of communication was not.

In the first globalization narrative, the Internet was thought to be the next frontier of the retail sector. While there were some early successes, it turned out that the only consistently reliable "e-tail" products were the age-old vices of gambling, prostitution, and porn. Early retailing experiments failed because the technology was not advanced enough to replace the social experience of shopping. In the second narrative, the Internet was the essential link between people and the workplace. Web 2.0 technology delivered faster transfer of information and at the same time it popularized instant messaging. New forms of social networking ballooned and "texting," instant messages, and virtual worlds entered the mainstream of communication.

People and ideas were linked as never before. It is estimated that in the space of a decade people across more than 60 percent of the globe were connected to each other through 1 billion Internet subscriptions, 1.9 billion cell phones, and the establishment of a ubiquitous radio and television presence. In Africa and Latin America cell phone penetration is growing at 55 percent annually. With cell phones increasingly having the capacity to be small computers with access to the Internet it is estimated that most of the new growth will come in the developing world. Recently, Nokia has teamed up with the Grameen Foundation of Bangladesh to develop non-profit $40 cell phones that are durable and dust-resistant. They are relying on micro-credit to finance the growth of the personal IT market in rural areas. In Bangladesh, villagers who purchase phones have also leased out time to their neighbors. The news of this public-private partnership was announced at the Global Microcredit Summit in Halifax, Nova Scotia, in 2006. For the first time, modern communication technology is able to reach vast numbers of the rural south.[37]

The seemingly spontaneous organization of discursive communities facilitated by new ways of communicating was the crucial component of what Charles Taylor termed a "demand for recognition". The growing sphere of interactive communication revived a long-dormant interest in all things public, most importantly the public interest and public reason. The politics of recognition, as the modern preoccupation with identity and the right to be treated with dignity, heralded the rebirth of a public ideal of the individual as more than his or her instrumental rationalism. The recognitionists, from Charles Taylor to Arjun Appadurai, have filled a void in public discourse between libertarians and socialists of all stripes.

Global activists in search of Leviathan's bridle

The third narrative of globalization comes around full circle from the Keynesian welfare state, through the globalization of markets, the structural transformation of work, and the growing public anger over the unfulfilled need for community and social well-being. It tells the story of the "friction of incompleteness" and the importance of identity, belonging, and citizenship. This narrative that is still a work in progress, describes a reaction to global markets and unrestricted competitive pressures. In this most recent iteration, the attention of publics has shifted from markets to the difficult issue of global governance and the regulatory role of states.

At the heart of the globalization narrative, a great divide appeared between globalizers from above and grassroots alter-mondialization activists; the former are new economy workers wanting to hold onto what they have acquired from the first two waves of globalization and the latter are critical scholars, dispossessed workers, and political dissenters challenging the structure and system of power and seeking to redirect its dynamics. The "battle of Seattle" was the catalyst for the legitimization of the anti-globalization movement that burst onto the world's stage when thousands of activists disrupted the WTO's ministerial. They wanted inside the closed decision-making process of the world's fully realized global governance institution. Most of all they wanted accountability and transparency – in short, they wanted a responsive and truly public form of economic governance. Activists had begun to punch holes in the Hayekian vision of seamless markets and limited public intervention.

Earlier theorists of globalization were wrong in claiming that the new global order would bring convergence and uniformity across nations. They were also erroneous about the sustainability of global forms of activism. Alain Touraine, the eminent French sociologist, used to argue that global publics are actors without a system. Now millions of transnational micro-activists are engaged with its institutions and are visibly part of the system that they seek to transform. Ideologically driven assertions about "the convergent unstoppable effects of globalization" and superficial "cellular democratization" can no longer be accepted at face value.

Many other once unchallengeable hypotheses are badly outdated and have to be rethought, including:

- the flawed idea that the sovereignty of national states would be obliterated once information – elevated to a primary commodity – could move freely across national borders;[38]
- the false belief that denationalized citizens and elites would use these new tools to construct a virtual global state beyond the reach of public authority;[39]
- the misdirected notion that the state, in its employment of technology, would create a virtual citizenry based primarily in the English language and that the circuitry of culture would destroy local cultural presence;[40]
- the often crudely made assertion that only dominant political identities could survive the deluge of global media;[41]
- the highly contentious idea that policies designed to maintain an element of national identity in cultural manifestations would become entirely redundant;[42]
- the influential and erroneous claim that the only alternative to this global homogenization would be local extremism;[43] and
- the powerful but wrong-headed conviction that counterpublics are primarily cultural actors outside the political realm.[44]

In fact, the most critical idea that turned out to be false was the assertion that new information technology would only stimulate market growth and not empower individuals without waking the Leviathan longing to overcome the isolation of economics. This Lockian fantasy constructed on "a vision of economic liberalism in which [public authority] has no other end but the preservation of property" has had to be abandoned.[45] But what have we learned in two decades of intense theorization about the relationship between public "busybodies," economic determinism, and the rapidly changing narrative of globalization?

Global cultural flows: the intense movement of people and ideas

In the current iteration, it can now be seen that global cultural flows are intense transnational movements of people, media, texts, and ideas that are disjunctive to financial flows and have unpredictable streaming effects on diasporic communities and cultural diversity. They give rise to agenda-setting publics with new authority structures that are highly normative. Many countries, such as the United States, Canada, Germany, Japan, and India, effectively use global markets to produce and promote culture. However, most of the world does not have the resources to sustain the economies of scale required to compete on equal terms with Time Warner. Nevertheless, tourism, entertainment production, art, and other forms of media are vital to the gross national product (GNP) of all countries. Cultural trade in these industries is a significant portion of GNP in Western European, North American, and the highly developed Asian economies. "States are now moving toward either prioritizing cultural industries as a whole at the forefront of their development efforts or singling out priority sectors."[46] For developing countries heavily reliant on international trade, trade in cultural goods has become an essential factor in economic development strategies.[47]

Culture flows as broadly and deeply as it does today because more people can read now than at any other time in the past. Few experts have confronted the transformative potential of the rise in literacy worldwide. According to Emmanuel Todd, this may be the most significant trend of our times, transforming the poorest states from "least developed" to "developing" nations, and at the same time raising social, political, and economic expectations in the global south.[48] The growth of civil society and social movements, even in traditional societies, has been accelerated by rising educational standards and media literacy. With so many new political actors, the information age has moved from rhetoric to reality. All too frequently, a narrow economic focus on globalization misses the transformative effects of technology, liberalization, and new forms of public administration.

The most important development is that activist communities provide a sense of belonging and purpose for people looking to engage in public debates about the changes that are reshaping the way people live. The Global Citizen can be found online at Twitter, Wikipedia, and Facebook, where she uses the Internet as a tool to communicate with friends and those she has never met in person.

By the simple fact of joining a Facebook group users are making a statement about their interests and politics. It sounds corny – everyone sees who is on the Facebook profile and this means that that the Facebook citizen broadcasts to all her friends that she supports a certain political or social cause. Evidently the wired citizen does not need much to get connected. All it takes is a notepad and pencil to take notes as a citizen journalist, a digital camera to visually record important events, a computer with e-mail and instant messaging to instantly update a website and, while on the go, a cell phone with SMS to stay in touch with other citizens and organize the rabble.

Not all media are equally suited for the toolbox of the Global Citizen. To encourage public reason, a medium must be politically fluid and offer the potential to reach a large audience. Push media, like television advertising, invades your space. Pull media, like your favorite blog, sucks you in. Like the elite producers of media content, the Global Citizen uses a "broadcast model" to distribute her message. Unlike the elites, the Global Citizen is *both a producer and a consumer of media content.* The Internet is the perfect medium for the Global Citizen, because it can reach a much greater audience even with lower initial concentration. Traditional (offline) methods of information distribution only reach so far. There are not enough hours in the day to schedule broadcasts of all the information of interest to the Global Citizen. Online distribution changes the rules. Information can be broadcast on an infinite number of channels. With help from the Long Tail, and by encouraging easy content production, the Internet can facilitate public reason, and thus provide a space for the Global Citizen to operate.

The immediate consequences are that it supports information-hungry micro-activist groups, individuals working together at the local level to create an infinite variety of small-scale organizations for uniquely public ends. These loose-knit coalitions represent what Sylvia Ostry has termed a "new form of global participatory democracy."[49] They have flat organizational structures with small, permanent bureaucracies, and tens of thousands of volunteers who learn to do everything from simple administrative tasks to preparing complex policy papers.

The key asset of these dissent networks at the local through the transnational level is their expertise and savvy in using mass media to get their message across. As we will see in chapters 3 and 4, once they have developed their own set of ideas they go out and engage others from different backgrounds and join forces with kindred organizations. They operate under the radar at first, but quickly gain momentum and media attention. The media are largely indifferent to their politics of social engagement and often trivialize their politics and causes. But with a news industry hungry for content, they offer attention-grabbing headlines and give the more curious journalists the context for lively political commentary. By this circuitous route the mainstream media has inadvertently encouraged and legitimized a cycle of raising expectations that municipal, state, and national authority has to do more for ordinary people in their neighborhood, in their city, in their region.

In New Delhi, Toronto, São Paulo, and Marseilles, these active and alert micro-busybodies are standing up to school boards or hospitals who want to impose user fees. In New York, Los Angeles, and Berlin they have organized against private developers or corporations whose environmental footprint is large and dangerous to local neighborhoods. All of these on-the-ground local engagements, which take place under the radar screen and rarely make the news headlines, have had a cumulative impact. Their improvised strategy of collective action at the local level has effect and consequence. Ordinary middle of the road types are mounting audacious challenges to limpid political elites and moribund public authority. They expect different kinds of development and action of the environment. The digitally enhanced public has now become a generator of communicative power. Innis and Habermas grasped the power of interactive communication; they never predicted such open access to the interactive sphere of global communication. Each subsequent refinement of technology has made it easier for individuals to bridge the gap between self-interest and the common good, between the role of the client and the role of the citizen.

The global street corner: the poor man's couch

It is something of a truism to note that the public domain has always had many points of entry. Its norms and values are experienced in different ways depending on where you are located, who you are, and what your capacity is to master its complexities. For civil society groups and social movements, the public domain is multifaceted, imposing, and omnipresent at the local level, synonymous with the public park, the skating rink, the local library, music halls, art galleries, bus and subway routes, and the local post office. Shopping malls, theme parks, the cinema, sports events, clubs, and non-standard private/public hybrid spaces all represent significant additions to the classic ideal of the public square, playground, or commons in this postmodern age of fluid boundaries and no fixed parameters.[50] As always worldwide, every street corner functions as the ubiquitous poor man's couch.

How should these critical micro-discontinuities of the post-Washington Consensus age be theoretically understood? While the prospect of an inclusive public domain is always shaped by supporting institutions, it requires even more importantly self-directed and highly motivated participants to extend and develop it. In the information age, individuals have made a massive investment in computers, cell phones, digital cameras, and the necessary upgrading of their technical skills and abilities in order to be effective in such a complex social world. The payout has been visibly enormous.

More students are in school worldwide and digital literacy has empowered the under-thirty generation; they have access to more social networks at their fingertips – compared to a decade ago, when many people in Africa and Asia were barely visible or active participants in the global information age. Presently the remarkable fact is that the digital divide has shrunk but not disappeared as yet. People are viewing the world in terms of groups and are functioning in social networks. For Barry Wellman the fundamental difference is that the network is replacing the hierarchical command control model of society and these networked communities are far-flung, collaborative, and giving people control over their lives.[51] The interface between corporate power and popular sovereignty is edgy and tense. The WTO's agenda is deadlocked, Bush and Blair have been dethroned as iconic leaders, and the narrow focus on competitiveness of the EU is being watered down. Encouraged by these real and symbolic victories the public sphere has become self-consciously reflexive, demanding higher and more transparent levels of accountability from governments and market actors alike. Furthermore, in an age of micro-activism the barriers to recognition are breaking down. Communities of choice were once only a theoretical possibility, now they are lived reality. When the public can choose its own future, the implications for global governance are enormous.

Notes

1. Maarten Hajer and Arnold Reijndorp, *In Search of the New Public Domain* (Rotterdam: NAi Publishers, 2001).

2. Daniel Drache, "The Imperative of the Social Bond After the Triumph of Markets" in *New Socialisms: Futures beyond Globalization*, ed. Robert Albritton et al. (London: Routledge, 2004).

3. David Marquand, "The Public Conscience and the Public Domain" in *The Market or the Public Domain? Global Governance and the Asymmetry of Power*, ed. Daniel Drache (London: Routledge, 2001), p. 74.

4. Jean-Jacques Rousseau from *On the Social Contract* [1762], quoted in Jeff Weintraub and Krishan Kumar, eds, *Public and Private Thought in Practice: Perspectives on a Grand Dichotomy* (Chicago, Ill.: University of Chicago Press, 1997), p. 17.

5. Weintraub and Kumar, *Public and Private Thought in Practice*.

6. Jürgen Habermas, *The Structural Transformation of the Public Sphere: An Inquiry into a Category of Bourgeois Society* (Cambridge, Mass.: MIT Press, 1989), p. 57.

7. Michael Walzer, *Spheres of Justice: A Defense of Pluralism and Equality* (Oxford: Basil Blackwell, 1989).

8. Garret Hardin, "The Tragedy of the Commons," SCIENCE (December 13, 1968), p. 1243. For a very useful review of contemporary legal thinking on the public domain and intellectual property rights, see James Boyle, "The Opposite of Property?" *Law and Contemporary Problems* 66 (Winter/Spring 2003), pp. 1–28.

9. Harry Arthurs, "The Reconstitution of the Public Domain" in Drache, *The Market or the Public Domain*.

10. Susan Strange, *The Retreat of the State: The Diffusion of Power in the World Economy* (Cambridge, UK: Cambridge University Press, 1996).

11. John Ruggie, "Territoriality and Beyond: Problematizing Modernity in International Relations," *International Organization* 47:1 (Winter 1993).

12. Todd Sandler, *Global Challenges: An Approach to Environmental, Political, and Economic Problems* (London: Cambridge University Press, 1997).
13. Robert Putnam, "Bowling Alone: America's Declining Social Capital," *The Journal of Democracy* 6:1 (1995), pp. 65–78.
14. James Carey, *Communication as Culture: Essays on Media and Society* (Winchester, Mass.: Unwin Hyman, 1989).
15. Jeff Weintraub, "Varieties and Vicissitudes of Public Space" in *Metropolis: Centre and Symbol of Our Times*, ed. Philip Krasinitz (New York: New York University Press, 1995), pp. 280–319.
16. Habermas, *The Structural Transformation of the Public Sphere.*
17. Jürgen Habermas, *On the Pragmatics of Social Interaction: Preliminary Studies in the Theory of Communicative Action* (Cambridge, Mass.: MIT Press, 2001).
18. Darin David Barney, *Prometheus Wired: The Hope for Democracy in the Age of Network Technology* (Chicago, Ill.: University of Chicago Press, 2000).
19. Harold Adams Innis, *Empire and Communications* (Toronto: Dundurn Press, 2007).
20. Harold Adams Innis, *The Bias of Communication* (Toronto: University of Toronto Press, 1951), p. 187. For a contemporary view of Innis and his relevance to modern social thought, see *Harold Innis: Staples, Markets and Cultural Change*, ed. Daniel Drache (Toronto: University of Toronto Press, 1995).
21. Innis, *The Bias of Communication*, p. 187.
22. Innis, *The Bias of Communication.*
23. BBC Poll, "Attitudes Towards Countries," at www.globescan.com/news_archives/miller_citizen/(June 6, 2007), and at http://worldpublicopinion.org/pipa/articles/btglobalizationtradera/index.php?nid=&id=&1b=btg1.
24. Anthony Downs, "Up and Down with Ecology: The Issue-Attention Cycle," *Public Interest* 28 (Summer), pp 38–50, 1972.
25. Benedict Anderson, *Imagined Communities: Reflections on the Origin and Spread of Nationalism* (London: Verso Press, 1991).
26. Clyde Summers, "The Battle in Seattle: Free Trade, Labor Rights, and Societal Values," *University of Pennsylvania Journal of International Economic Law* 22: 1 (2001), pp. 61–90.
27. Jim Yardley, "A Hundred Cellphones Bloom, and Chinese Take to the Streets," *New York Times*, April 25, 2005.
28. International Telecommunications Union (2002), *ITU Strategy and Policy Unit News Update: Policy and Strategy Trends*, at www.itu.int/osg/spu/spunews/2002/jul-sep/jul-septrends.html.

29. Cell phone manufacturers have begun to cater to southern consumers, producing handsets for the Muslim world that point in the direction of Mecca and ring the user at prayer time. Mobile providers in India offer services for the Hindu on the go. For a nominal charge, the user can send a prayer over the wireless network to the appropriate temple. Culture plays an important role in the evolution of technology in different regions. See Lara Srivastava, "Social and Human Considerations for a More Mobile World" (paper presented to the ITU/MIC Workshop on Shaping the Future Mobile Information Society, Seoul, March 2004).

30. In a way that was unimaginable a scarce five years ago, both France and Germany are in violation of the EU Stability Pact and if the EU was stricter in the way it keeps its accounts, Portugal and Greece would have to be included in the default column as well. In November 2003, the EU voted against sanctions and did not enforce disciplinary action on Bonn and Paris for their failure to conform to the Euro-zone's fiscal framework. Instead Brussels accepted their promises voluntarily to do better.

31. Experts did not see that the Republican "values voters" were ready to abandon the Republican cause. Bush's core conservatives refused to put out the effort for the mid-term elections. The big "moral" issues for the Christian Right have lost much of their urgency and punch.

32. Doug Saunders, "The Year the Right Turned Pink," *Globe and Mail*, January 7, 2006.

33. *The Economist*, September 20, 1997.

34. Chris Giles and James Wilson, "Public Spending Bonanza – Gone North: State Largesse Brings Help and Hope but Little Change," *Financial Times*, September 20, 2006.

35. Joseph S. Nye Jr, *The Paradox of American Power: Why the World's Superpower Can't Go It Alone* (New York: Oxford University Press, 2002).

36. *Wal-Mart: The High Cost of Low Price*, directed by Robert Greenwald (USA: Brave New Films, 2005).

37. Tavia Grant, "World's Poorest Nations New Frontier for Cellphone Giants," *Globe and Mail*, November 15, 2006.

38. Thomas L. Friedman, *The Lexus and the Olive Tree* (New York: Farr, Straus and Giroux, 1999).

39. Richard Rosencrance, *The Rise of the Virtual State: Wealth and Power in the Coming Century* (New York: Basic Books, 1999).

40. Marilyn Lambert-Drache, "L'inforoute francophone et ses enjeux pour la francophonie" in *Multimédia, Internet et Études françaises*, ed.

R. Canas Marquis (Quebec: Conseil québécois de la formation à distance, 2001).

41. Zygmunt Bauman, *Globalization: The Human Consequences* (Cambridge, UK: Polity, 1999).
42. Saskia Sassen, *Globalization and Its Discontents* (New York: New Press, 1998).
43. Benjamin Barber, *Jihad vs McWorld* (New York: Random House, 1996).
44. Michael Warner, "Publics and Counterpublics," *Public Culture* 14:1 (2002), pp. 49–90.
45. Daniel Drache, "The Return of the Public Domain After the Triumph of Markets: Revisiting the Most Basic of Fundamentals" in Drache, *The Market or the Public Domain*, p. 48.
46. J. P. Singh, "Culture or Commerce? A Comparative Assessment of International Interactions and Developing Countries at UNESCO, WTO and Beyond," *International Studies Perspective* 8:1 (2007), pp. 36–53.
47. UNESCO, *World Culture Report 2000: Cultural Diversity, Conflict and Pluralism* (Paris: United Nations Educational, Scientific, and Cultural Organization, 2000).
48. Emmanuel Todd, *After the Empire: The Breakdown of American Order* (New York: Columbia University Press, 2003), p. 27.
49. Sylvia Ostry, "Global Integration: Currents and Counter-Currents" (Walter Gordon Lecture, Massey College, University of Toronto, 2001).
50. Bruno Latour, "From Realpolitik to Dingopolitik or How to Make Things Public" in *Making Things Public – Atmospheres of Democracy*, ed. Bruno Latour and Peter Weibel (Cambridge, Mass.: MIT Press, 2005).
51. Barry Wellman, "A Computer Network is a Social Network: The Rise of Personalized Networking," *International Journal of Urban and Regional Research* 25:2 (2001), pp. 227–52.

3

Digital Publics and the Culture of Dissent

Many publics and the contested terrain of ideas

Organized activist publics now position themselves as competitors or adversaries to the nation-state and its narrow defense of national sovereignty at the WTO, the UN, and the World Bank. Multilateralism from below has created its own universe of structures, coalitions, organizations, and other social forms that sustain a global culture of democratic, anti-corporate dissent.[1] Non-governmental organizations and social movements are proxy organizations for a variety of highly motivated and determined public interest advocates and defenders. Their capacity for political mobilization and their mastery of complex policy issues have transformed the "nixers" (the most radical) and the "fixers" (the more reform-minded) into quasi-permanent and highly effective global publics.[2]

In a world that is increasingly complex, rights-focused, and process-driven, citizens have a large role to play in the creation of new spheres of interaction and new ways of thinking about politics and social change. If macro-economic imperatives are no longer the best or only guide to collective need, then we have a singular unanswered question: how can global publics begin to address the issues of public interest articulation and public needs provision? This chapter provides the first part of an answer by examining the new digital universe in which publics have made themselves at home and through which they articulate their needs in surprisingly effective ways. In the Internet age, new technology and information flows offer the ordinary citizen unlimited social possibility to innovate and form discursive communities of choice around a seemingly infinite variety of issues. Joining the populist universe of public activism is effortless; there is no membership requirement as in a social movement for these communities other than to lend your voice to what you believe in. Exiting is just as simple; you quit the world of political action and go back to the world of family, work, and other fronts of private engagement.

Critical ideas, debates, and discussions are no longer ghettoized at the margins of public life. Public opinion has gone global and dissenters are no longer Cassandra-like characters that the mainstream views as curmudgeons or relentless pessimists. To borrow from Cass Sunstein, societies now realize that they need political dissent to challenge the stereotyping and self-silencing that maintains conformity within dominant intellectual traditions and political practices.[3] Healthy societies rely on dissent to encourage understanding and productive disagreement. They need new ideas to challenge accepted wisdom and social activism to renew and strengthen democratic values.

Public opinion goes global

The ease of joining and dropping membership in networked communities gives the illusion that dissent, as a movement and as a philosophy, has little staying power. But being exposed to all kinds of information, viewpoints, and ideas has had a revolutionary impact on public opinion. At first, social scientists thought that people used online information to confirm their own biases. Liberals went to alternative news sites to get a different perspective than that offered by CNN. Conservatives went online to read the newest blog entry by Newt Gingrich. But we now know that publics are not locked into hermetically sealed information echo chambers.[4] The Pew study reported that a surprising number of Democrats checked out Republican blogs and vice versa. Many users were drilling down and challenging their biases. According to the newest evidence, Internet users enter the online realm to experience new ideas and to try to understand the complex issues with which they are faced on a day-to-day basis. The Internet is not merely the next logical step towards niche and identity-based marketing and programming. While identity building is certainly one of the lures of online participation, the

Internet has grown and evolved as a communicative tool because it gives people the ability to peek over the backyard fence.

Have you ever wondered what Islamist militants or neo-fascist skinheads discuss amongst themselves? Have a look online. Do you want to know where anti-globalization activists get their up-to-the-minute information? Check out the website. The wired citizen wants news and information that is autonomous and informed. Certainly they want to be entertained as Neil Postman argued, but they also crave reliable information and not just the low intellectual bandwidth "infotainment" that passes for analysis on television.[5] Alternative news sites function like an alternative feed of information. For the first time, there is a news channel for everyone, no matter your political orientation. The message-based news format of mainstream media is designed to draw consumers to advertising and subscription-based services, but the range of alternative anti-market and anti-authority news sources that are free and participatory has exploded.

According to the Pew Survey and those of other public and private organizations that map and track changes in public opinion, it is apparent that a majority of people online do not belong to social movements, rather they self-identify as skeptics, contrarians, and doubters.[6] Furthermore, the 2007 USC-Annenberg School Digital Future Report found that, when online, people do not feel isolated or alone; instead the Internet allows them to feel connected and they use it as a powerful social tool. Facebook is a ready example of this. Since 2006, when it became available to any e-mail address in the digital universe, it has had the largest number of registered users among college-based sites with over 40 million users. But it has been adopted enthusiastically by kinder-networkers, adult trendsters, and boomer friendsters alike. From September 2006 to September 2007 its ranking soared from 60th to the 7th most visited website in the US. What makes this fact most startling is that this is simply the newest in a long line of social networking sites, the previous being the eponymous Myspace that went from cool to quaint seemingly overnight. When online adults were polled, almost two-thirds reported that their digital participation in discursive and social communities led them to all kinds of new forms of social activities.[7] Those who use the Internet primarily to build social networks are under thirty, educated, and highly diverse in their views. In many countries, the number of women is overtaking the number of men.

Many are from the boomer generation in the global north and believe that the Internet provides leverage to effect change and distribute knowledge during political campaigns. The 2004 UCLA Internet Project Study looked at poor and rich users in fourteen countries and found that 20 percent of users had low incomes. Baby boomers find the rate of low-income participation surprising because they remember vividly the time when computers were a costly luxury.

Shrinking the digital divide but not quite

As computer prices have fallen, the digital divide has shrunk. Internet growth has been fastest in the north. In G8 countries, the number of people using the Internet exploded from 7.3 million in 1993 to 297 million in 2001. Similarly, in the G20, the number of Internet users rose from 430,000 people in 1993 to more than 25 million in 2001. As of 2007, 1 billion people were online.[8]

India and China are also quickly closing the gap. During the same period, use in Asia grew from 14 million to 74.1 million people. In Africa, where telephone landlines are often a luxury, the proliferation of digital technology has faced obstacles associated with lack of infrastructure. Third generation wireless Internet technology has been slow to penetrate, and cheap modems must contend with unreliable phone lines. Nevertheless, Internet usage blossomed from approximately 40,000 people to an estimated 4.25 million in the 1990s. Experts predict that by the year 2011, 40 percent of Africans will own a cellular phone. Many of these devices will offer the same functionality as a small computer.

Broadband is the next generation of digital communication technology that is set to revolutionize the online experience. Television, movies, and even phone calls are now available through a broadband connection. In 2003, China had twice as many broadband Internet subscribers as Canada at 8.6 million compared to Canada's 3.9 million. The US leads with almost 22 million broadband subscriptions. However, nowhere in the world has broadband made faster inroads than in Korea, where 70 percent of all households are connected by broadband. In North America and Europe, price is still a key factor in broadening and deepening diffusion. As prices are expected to fall in the next five years, consumer research groups estimate that the current global market of 100 million broadband subscribers will grow to more than 300 million. Double-digit growth in broadband is projected to continue until 2010, if not longer.[9]

The production, targeted for 2007, of the $100 computer designed for Africa will extend the Internet to the one region of the world where Internet usage lags. The impact will be huge as the computer is placed in primary and secondary educational institutions. Despite the fact that economic barriers remain, discursive activism has given once isolated individuals a wealth of new networking opportunities. As a result, they feel a powerful connection to the wider world and all the opportunities and challenges that come with that new connection.[10]

The spread of mobile technology occurs unevenly at first, but the effect is often an exponential democratization of communication. The traditional left-right worldview imagines that power begets power and that new information technology empowers corporate intellectual property proprietors. Ownership of the means of communication brings wealth and the ability to control the social agenda. But with the digital communications revolution, the reverse is true. Civil society uses information and communication technologies (ICTs) to strengthen a bottom-up approach to mobilization of the sort necessary for the democratization of the information society. Now, at the dawn of the twenty-first century, digital technology has entered the mainstream of local and regional cultures alongside the other revolutionary media of mass communication – radio and television.

The unique feature of this public sphere of interactive communication is that it is composed of privately owned communications networks. Some writers believe that private ownership removes culture and communication from the public sphere, but, while many aspects of culture may be privately owned, they are always shared. The quandary facing policy makers and global governance experts is how can public authorities protect free speech, promote multicultural identities, and simultaneously recognize the property rights of corporate owners?

Meaning making: creativity and intellectual property

None of these goals triangulate easily with neo-liberal intellectual property rights. Global publics are deeply divided between two visions for the future – a global commodity chain for private economic actors or a renewed cultural pluralism for global publics. So far, there are no definitive answers, nor any consensus on how to nourish the global cultural commons.

The global cultural commons has four main features:

- *markets;*
- *intergovernmental institutions* such as the WTO, WIPO (World Intellectual Property Organization), and UNESCO;
- *norms* such as diversity, accessibility, and protection of intellectual property; and
- *citizenship practices* typified by an often porous divide between public and private.

Films, books, television, radio, and the Internet create a seemingly endless flow of cultural goods and services. These real and virtual texts create new narratives in privileged spaces about identity, diversity, distraction, and transnationality. The explosion of new information technologies has made possible the organization of many different kinds of citizen-accessed outlets and public forums at the local, national, and global levels.

David Throsby defines cultural production as involving creativity in the production process, the generation and communication of symbolic meaning, resulting in some form of intellectual property.[11] A final feature is noted by Richard Caves. Cultural products must be experienced in order to be valued. Cultural products are so valuable because they empower the consumer to make their own evaluation of the symbolic power.[12] However, just as the enclosure movement of the eighteenth century fenced off public goods and redefined the rights of investors, so intellectual property rights are primary markers of the growth and diffusion of the global cultural economy.

The Trade-Related Intellectual Property Rights Agreement formalized a formidable series of rights for property owners, particularly in the pharmaceutical and entertainment industries. But enforcement has been logistically complex and compliance remains problematic, not only in the global south, which has emerged as a network of extralegal Internet Protocol appropriation, but also in the global north, where citizens and consumers are not convinced that digital appropriation is a crime on a par with the theft of tangible goods.[13] For some trade experts market power is frequently theorized as the principal driver of cultural globalization. But it is closer to the facts to argue that although power is a central feature of the globalization phenomenon, the global cultural economy is driven by technological change towards a global, integrated, and interactive sphere of communication in which political power is inexorably moving toward the margins of international civil society.

Innis's grasp of the emancipatory potential of technology hits closer to our current reality than do Marshall McLuhan's ideas.[14] McLuhan thought that the medium of communication eclipses the message it contains, but we see today that his old aphorism, "the medium is the message," is only true for early adopters of technology in the global north for whom text messaging, for example, was a toy, rather than a communications lifeline.[15]

McLuhan believed that technology indulged the consumer's desire for distraction, passivity, and conformism. How wrong he was. In the information age, anyone, in theory, can be a social critic – no longer a detached social observer. Compared to earlier periods in history the privileged position of the specialist has been democratized, and critical commentators have had to concede genuine political space to the voices and actors in whose name key global decisions are made.

A cosmopolitan generation of public intellectuals

Cosmopolitan figures of political, social, and literary theory inspire and galvanize publics worldwide. These authorities, from Noam Chomsky to Michel Foucault, are not gatekeepers in the academic sense of controlling the canon of a discipline; rather they fulfill quite a different function. They help global publics understand the relationship between the political and intellectual maps of the world.

They help make sense of the world we live in and point towards the broader picture for "collective intervention" across the spectrum.

The great map of critical thought has changed dramatically with the end of the Cold War, the collapse of the communist bloc, the new assertiveness of the global south, the rise of US unilateralism, and the implosion of American liberalism. The demand for talking heads from all parts of the political spectrum has been driven by new media outlets and the explosion in online publishing, radio, and TV talk shows.[16] Even blogs and alternative media have fueled the demand for entertaining and expert commentary. Although the global public can be misled at times by the sheer babble of voices, one cannot underestimate the scope and extent of the technology-information grid for a culture of dissent and its opposite, the dominant culture of conformity.

Since the millennium, the social imagination of the progressive public intellectual has acquired an air of hard-won legitimacy. Edward Said was onto something important when he said that the role of the activist "is to disturb people's mental habits" – to make them think about what they do. Public intellectuals, such as George Orwell, Jean-Paul Sartre, and Susan Sontag, have long been thought of as the conscience of society, the upholders of its critical values and ideals. The intelligentsia can, in Edward Said's words, "rais[e] embarrassing questions and confront orthodoxy and dogma (rather than produce them)."[17] They have been given an elevated status as society's communicators because they have the temperament, character, and knowledge that enable them to address the non-specialist audience.

Some scholars bemoan what they see as the diminishing of the public intellectual in the digital age. Their message is frequently drowned out by the cacophony of babbling voices, acolyte competitors, and nay-saying critics. It would appear that the proliferation of information channels has flattened the realm of social discourse and allowed anyone with a big voice and narrow opinion to take the stage. Of course, this is exactly what has happened, but it is not the whole story. As intellectual life has moved out of the university, the oppositional reflex is no longer self-consciously marginal. There are new pressures to toe the line and conform to mainstream values, but there are also an incredible number of opportunities for citizens to use their reason publicly in highly innovative ways. For example, when Bush was re-elected in 2004 there was a spontaneous outpouring on the Internet of public apology by American citizens to the rest of the world. These virtual "pokes" have not diminished the role of the expert, in fact public intellectuals have moved from the salon onto the *New York Times* bestseller list, as well as the pages of *The Hindu* and *El Pais*.

The global public sphere of dissent – the expert provocateur

In a number of powerfully argued pieces James Bohman has resurrected the notion that globalization makes possible a variety of new modes of public reasoning that enable dialogue and communication to occur in the context of global public policy making. The ability of global publics and experts to dialogue and exert influence on governance issues from the environment to finance has raised the bar of accountability.[18] The newfound importance of the public intellectual, in her traditional role as expert provocateure is perhaps most influential in two realms of the public sphere: the literary realm and the world of political dissent.

People are more interested in literature than ever before, yet the newspaper book review section has all but disappeared. There used to be at least a dozen prominent review sections in city newspapers in the United States. Today there are fewer than five. Of course, the great irony of this statistic is that it was reported on Salon.com. Apparently, all is not lost as online magazines have taken up the reviewer's mantle. And this is probably accounted for by the shift in the reading habits of university-educated citizens under the age of forty, rather than by a declining interest in reading.

In *The World Republic of Letters*, Pascale Casanova brilliantly shows how public literary space has had its own internationalized rules, norms, fashions, tempos, canon, and values for more than a century. The original dependence of literature on the dominant national traditions created a geopolitical literary asymmetry of influence and power that remains today "at the heart of the inequality that structures the literary world."[19] Insiders and outsiders are identified by where they stand on the current issues, from literary theory to politics. One wonders if there is not something analogous in modernity's global republic of dissent where ideas, values, and practices about heterodoxy and publicness sustain an ethic of activism.

A current theory of the public opens new possibilities for the empowerment of ordinary people, in particular enabling them to participate in the culture of political life.[20] Michael Warner argues that our modern notions of the public and the private always constitute a psychic binary that the activist must learn to navigate. The public is open to everyone whereas the private is a closed universe; the public is the world of the impersonal while the private is intensely personal and intimate; in public we are in the presence of others; in private we are concealed and out of the "public" eye; the public is the world of state officialdom and bureaucratic rules; the private is the non-contractual world of gesellschaft. And, in the strategically important public sphere, texuality and the mass media are mediated by technology and are audience-driven; by comparison, the private world of orality and tale-telling is immediate and personal.[21]

In many striking ways the world of literature and the world of dissent are built on shared values of skepticism about the status quo, anger over injustice, and a yearning to influence the course of events. The international association of writers (PEN) has worked tirelessly to defend freedom of expression, and this form of activism, in which professional associations, rather than movements, fight to defend the values of pluralism, is not determined by the old theories of Left and Right. In this case it is driven by the writer's creed of personal responsibility and the duty of recognition. The culture of dissent, like literary culture, is triggered by our desire for what Said has described as "articulation rather than silence."[22]

Victor Hugo once remarked that:

> Without 1789 the supremacy of Paris is an enigma. Rome has more majesty . . . Venice is more beautiful, Naples more graceful, London wealthier. What then does Paris have? The Revolution . . . of all the cities of the earth, Paris is the place where the flapping of the immense, invisible sails of progress can best be heard.[23]

Of course, for the culture of dissent today, there is no one city of revolution. Every city of any G8 summit and WTO ministerial is a potential site of revolutionary disturbance, myth creation, and public reason. Seattle, Genoa, Cancún, Hong Kong, and Geneva – these are not the magical cities of our literary imagination. They are sites of conflict and struggle where the activists and dissenters can veritably hear change approaching.

Semiotic disobedience: a staple of the Information Age

At present dissenting global publics and their intellectual standard bearers are more heterogeneous and representative of the global population than at any other time in recent history. Since 1950, the number of NGOs active internationally with memberships in three or more countries has grown from 1,000 to 25,000.[24] At the local level, in both the global north and south, NGOs delivering humanitarian services and development assistance number in the hundreds of thousands.[25] The Center for Civil Society Studies at Johns Hopkins University has calculated that social movement activism, excluding religious organizations, is a $1 trillion global industry.[26] Growth of civil society and the NGO movement has exploded in the age of the network society.

Our identities of choice are part of a public discourse that is experiential, learned, constructed, and fluid. What fires the modern activist's imagination is that unlike an identity of birth, her or his identity can be reshaped, modified, and transcended through polit-ical activism. New information technologies have become a cul-turally mediated mode of expression that represents a break with previous ways of thinking and acting. What is the significance of the fact that tens of millions of people each day forward a blog, a review, an article, or report to a friend or colleague? It could be a far-reaching critique of human rights abuse or just chatter with friends or family. Your ten friends could send your counter-blast to ten others, and if properly organized the dynamics can launch a global campaign. Of course there is nothing novel in global net-working at a very basic level. This kind of pyramid networking is a direct steal from pyramid selling campaigns. But it is a strategy that can also be turned against corporate power as Nike discovered when its running shoes became the centre of a global campaign in 2001.[27]

Its products were mocked, and its advertising lifestyle slogans co-opted when a young activist recontextualized Nike's branded message. Wanting to call Nike on its sweatshop practices and human rights abuses, he ordered a customized pair of Nike shoes with the words "sweatshop" on them. Of course Nike refused and did not want to address the issue, but the story was picked up by *USA Today*, the *NBC Today Show*, and European papers. The e-mail exchange between company and potential customer was read by an estimated 10 million people. Global consumers have been changed by culture jamming, media stunts, and the subversion of corporate logos. The consumer is no longer, necessarily, a neutral spectator ignorant about the politics of the products they purchase – where they are made and how they are marketed. Global consumer movements have exploded in the new century, organizing boycotts against some of the most powerful global giants such as Coca-Cola, the GAP, and Nike, among many other producers.

Sonia Katyal, a Fordham University law professor, calls subversive action taken against corporate branding "semiotic disobedience," because it tears down carefully constructed corporate symbols and resists the market-society's consumption imperative to think less and buy more.[28] Semiotic disobedience encourages the radical reinterpretation of the prominent signs and symbols of advertising that we are bombarded with every day, focusing on consumer "talk back" to the codes of corporate advertising and communication.[29] Millions of people are now engaging in this subversive behavior. Mimicking advertising techniques that target children, the Adbusters Media Foundation popularized "culture jamming" in Canada. Creating "subvertisements," Adbusters' slick designs work to undermine the authority of brands. Its depiction of Tiger Woods with his trademark grin contorted into a Nike swoosh is particularly evocative of the mentality and ethos that inform this social activism. Other semiotic disobedience aims to deflate over-the-top corporate advertising, defy authority, and create discursive noise by digitally recreating advertising and trademarks at home rather than by sabotaging and altering existing ones covertly in the dead of night.

Semiotic resisters are united by a common vision and a shared toolbox of strategies with which to defy the larger system. These rebels are part of a global social justice movement, in which they forge a unique culture of resistance by defacing corporate trademarks or replacing them with consciousness-raising text and symbols. Such creativity produces critical illumination for a world desperately seeking to create new geographies of power, talk-back, and dissent. Some cases of in-your-face "brandalism" have led to legal action. Artist and semiotic disobedient Kieron Dwyer landed in hot water with US giant Starbucks when he created a parody of the Starbucks logo targeting rampant consumerism. Starbucks threatened a lawsuit but the attempt at legal intimidation failed since anyone can see the original lampoon of the Starbucks logo.

Corporations increasingly use legal chilling tactics such as the Strategic Lawsuit Against Public Participation to muzzle dissent but they have failed to silence their critics or opponents. In Canada the Courts rejected two significant claims designed to intimidate grassroots activists in British Columbia (2002) and the Friends of Lubicon in Ontario (1996). In the EU the European Court of Justice threw out the McLibel case when it ruled that the defendants did not receive a fair trail when McDonalds charged them with libeling the company in a leaflet. In this highly publicized case the activists were awarded £24,000 in 2005.[30] Today, acts of semiotic disobedience reflect an international cosmopolitanism drawing consumers into a world of shared, public meanings. These extend beyond "brandalism," aiming "to create dialogue where there isn't one" about important social issues.[31] It is about online networking, building cultures of resistance, and accepting the recognition that comes with successful acts of defiance. Today the hottest places to hang out and earn your progressive credentials are virtual.

Mapping the 1 billion people online

Efforts to map the Internet have been underway since the mid-1990s, with significant contributions coming from the Internet Mapping Project at Bell Labs, the Cyber-Geography Research project at the Centre for Advanced Spatial Analysis, University College, London, and the Opte Project at Prolexic Technologies in the United States. In 2002, geographers Rob Kitchin and Martin

Dodge published the first full atlas of cyberspace.[32] Many maps of
the Internet are produced from the perspective of place and build
on traditional political maps by superimposing lines of connectiv-
ity or by adding color coding or bar graphs to provide information
such as the number of Internet service providers (ISPs) or Internet
subscribers within any given territory.

To understand Internet cartography, Castells's distinction
between the "space of place" and the "space of flows" is critical.[33]
More recent Internet cartography has shifted its perspective from
representing a space of place to visualizing a space of flows. These
maps use software to represent the one-dimensional world of
cyberspace as two- and three-dimensional diagrams. They work by
converting the virtual paths that data packets take when traversing
the Internet into rendered diagrams that resemble random, non-
isomorphic, crystalline structures. These maps are visually striking,
and although they bear no resemblance to traditional territorial
maps, they are no less political in their implications.

In modernity, the enclosure of physical space was the principal
front upon which power was contested. Benedict Anderson persuasively argues that maps played a key role in the formation of nation-
states as consolidated blocs of power and authority.[34] Countries
went to war over borders, seized the land of others, and made peace
by trading territories that did not belong to them, dividing and re-
dividing the world with a passion rarely seen. European borders and
national sovereignty were established by custom, balance of power,
the modern peace treaty, and most of all, by sheer political will. The
growth of non-spatial Internet cartography indicates that the same
irreconcilable tensions of territoriality and identity formation are
underway in cyberspace. Cartography is, after all, always about con-
tests of power.[35] What cartography reveals about the digital frontier
is that it is very much rooted in existing political struggles and conflicts, most of which have an important spatial dimension and follow
quite doggedly and logically the fault lines of public and private
interest (see figure 3.1).

Mapping the e-public requires a lot of heads-up navigational
curiosity. Of course, the online universe is not another dimension
of reality. It closely mirrors our present society in many ways. It has
its share of disengaged, entertainment-oriented individuals looking

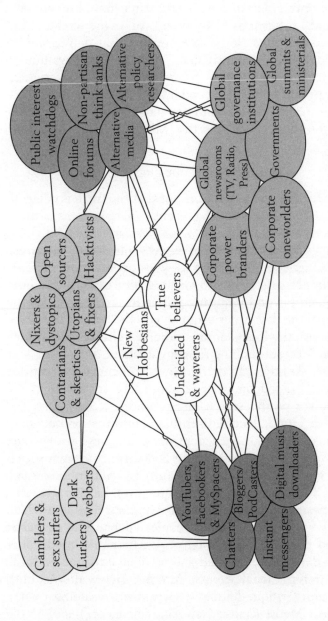

Even the huge size of the e-public understates its importance. Due to multiple linkages, growth is exponential rather than incremental.

Figure 3.1 A surfer's guide to the 1 billion-strong e-Public universe

Source: Daniel Drache, Robarts Centre, 2007

to have a good time. It has a large and growing number of "official" websites – the online portals for governments, news bureaus, and corporate brands. It has tens of thousands of "owner-created" but equally informative sites that serve innumerable demographics, ethnicities, and political constituencies. Curious and news-hungry citizens can also check out non-partisan think tanks, government websites, and public interest watchdogs, all the while downloading – for free – studies, reports, and papers from "the satanic mills" of the WTO, the World Bank, and the IMF.

Finding who is out there

The challenge for the online public is not that the truth is being filtered out, but that there is a flood. Presently there are tens of thousands of alternative media sites. Look to www.rabble.ca if you need alternative news across Canada or www.vigile.net if you are a news-hungry Quebecer. Sites such as www.opendemoncracy.net, www.counterpunch.org, or www.zmag.org similarly give the insatiable, British and beyond inquiring public its alternative take on the top stories of the day. Americans can get "the behind the news" headline stories on the Bush administration and his scandal-ridden presidency, 24/7, by subscribing to www.truthout.org.

The e-public, skeptic, activist reformer, and contrarian can log on and be fully briefed on what is happening anywhere in the world. The power of the search engine makes it easy, fast, and almost effortless. Hundreds of citizen-based information networks, in any language, can be accessed. Among the best known are: ATTAC (www.france.attac.org), World Social Forum (www.social-movements.org), Third World Network (www.twnside.org.sg), Focus on the Global South (www.focusweb.org), La via campesina (www.viacampesina.org), Committee for the Cancellation of Third World Debt (www.cadtm.org), and Peoples Global Action Against Free Trade and the WTO (www.agp.org). Alternative media sites provide up-to-the minute detailed and credible coverage on local, regional, and international events. Alternet (www.alternet.org), Acrimed (Action-Critique-Médias (www.acrimed.samizdat.net)), the Independent Media Center (www.indymedia.org), and Media Channel (www.mediachannel.org) attack and denounce the mainstream media as "weapons of mass deception." They make available films and documentaries that you cannot see in theaters or on your local television station.[36]

At the centre of this dissent matrix are alternative think tanks, social observatories, and global advocacy organizations pumping out research reports, backgrounders, foregrounders, and news analysis on the need for global governance. All of this information is part of a strategy for countering the might of global capitalism. Groups like IFI Watch Net (www.ifiwatchnet.org), Corporate Watch (www.corporatewatch.org.uk), The Public Eye on Davos (www.evb.ch), Global Trade Watch (www.citizen.org/trade), and the Halifax Initiative (www.halifaxinitiative.org) track, analyze, and monitor the shortcomings, failures, and cover-ups of the World Bank, WTO, IMF, and other multinationals. They provide reliable and free information that was at one time hard to find, and even if you do not own a computer, access is available at cafés, local libraries, and community centers.

It is estimated that over 60 percent of the world has access to global information networks on both radio and television as well as through satellite broadcasting, cell phones, and the Internet. In 2005 the number of cell phone users in the global south surpassed Internet subscribers in the global north.[37] In the highly-charged world of information and ideas, the smart citizen has to decide which media outlet is giving the big picture, which policies best reflect the e-citizen's real interests, and which are frankly those of the elite administration.

The information-hungry public can also turn to non-partisan research centers to get their queries answered. A user can jump from the margin to the mainstream depending on whatever catches their interest.

Citizen groups are organizing and working for change both globally and locally. They use the web to hatch plans, scheme, and strategize about changing the world. They are strong on critique, and despite limited resources, they are effective mobilizers virtually as well as on the ground where the net has changed the way political organizing happens. The most important innovation is that all of these oppositional and insurgent groups are "hotlinked" through their websites.[38]

The dissent matrix: its own online universe

In a "connected" world, it is no longer clear whether the distinction that once pitted global activism against local activism still has any practical meaning. The line is blurred to a degree unimaginable a decade earlier. A small sampling of advocacy initiatives reveals a rich and diverse network covering every imaginable cause: building socialism (www.socialistproject.ca), supporting the Zapatistas (www.ezlnaldf.org), resisting global capitalism (www.clac.taklc.org), enhancing political dialogue (www.ualberta.ca/parkland), fighting privatization (www.apf.org.za), exposing sweatshop abuse (www.nosweat.org.uk), and protecting cultural diversity (www.uberculture.org). The idea behind all these kinds of initiatives is to inspire more discussion and to organize "action" wherever you are. "It's the vision thing," insists Naomi Klein, where new information technologies have created a "culture of constant, loosely structured and sometimes compulsive[ly] information-swapping."[39]

In the highly-charged world of information and ideas, the smart citizen has to decide which media outlet is accurately presenting the big picture, which policies best reflect the real interests of citizens, and which are, frankly, part of the endless stream of propaganda that Paul Rutherford argues, treats the public domain as "common theatre, a site for a show" and nothing more.[40] Social networking and alternative news sites and blog-style commentaries that act as subcultural reference points for those under the age of thirty are the real focus of the online experience. In fact many of these sites have reached iconic status; think of MySpace, Facebook, the Drudge Report, and www.BoingBoing.net to name just a few. If you fancy yourself a progressive who is highly computer literate, you doubtlessly surf BoingBoing. Begun by science fiction novelist Corey Doctorow. It is a self-described "directory of wonderful things," that provides a running commentary on the movies, books, art, and public happenings likely to interest hip, engaged, urbanites from around the world.

When Michael Moore's film *Sicko* hit the theaters, BoingBoing reported a story in which a film reviewer in Texas watched the movie in a suburban multiplex.[41] The audience was a collection of bored shoppers, interested suburban wives, and their reluctant husbands. At first, the audience watched with a skeptical, conservative eye. There were a few boos as Michael Moore entered into his trademark monologues, but by the end of the film, this group of suburban film-goers were incensed with the health care industry, not Moore! They gathered together outside the theater to share e-mail addresses and discuss what they thought was wrong with the American health care system and what should be done about it.

This is the spontaneous, democratic side of the online universe. It provides a place where regular people can form the linkages necessary for changing the status quo. This incessant networking is also seen in the file-sharing and downloading participated in by tens of millions of users. The film, music, and software industries have named these people pirates and robbers, but in practice they are not a cabal of criminals so much as a massive online movement that is fundamentally reshaping property rights.

Virtual worlds require an ethic of personal responsibility and standards of appropriate conduct no less than do nations. When these global/local publics speak of "the public," it means those actions, policies, and practices that are shared by all members of the community to promote its general welfare. As such, it embodies this generation's contradictory longing for collective identity and expectation of individual fulfillment. When they cheer and fight for the integrity of their community, cultural theorists argue, they establish new citizenship practices and new ideals of pluralism.

The dark side of the net

Indeed there is a dark and very disturbing side to the net. Its exact location is context-dependent however. Free entertainment junkies threaten cultural entertainment giants, while gamblers, porn surfers, trolls, spammers, and lurkers represent the dark side of the net for mainstream society. But experts certainly agree that the Internet has facilitated the gratification of baser human impulses. Pedophilia, non-consensual sexual violence, fraud, blackmail, and the "online disinhibition effect" have contributed to a new awareness about the dangers of virtual interaction.

When the Internet was new, there was much discussion of the reasons that people took to it so enthusiastically. How could a shy individual be an outgoing or flirtatious person online? Why were people forming intense and intimate relationships with strangers they had never seen? We know now that the anonymity, invisibility, and dissociative imagination required for most forms of online inter-action are invitations for people to lose their inhibitions and recre-ate themselves online. You can be bolder, smarter, sexier, and more self-confident when your avatar is tall, blonde, and built like a body-builder, as many cyber-figures are in the popular virtual environment Second Life.[42] Everyone is the star online that they cannot be in real life.

Unquestionably there is a special kind of publicness, which comes into existence only in relation to digitally mediated repre-sentation. This is why the cultural commons is that portion of culture that remains in the public domain, where artists, as indi-viduals and citizens, exchange ideas and promote creativity. Imagination, belonging, and the relational power of networks are a potent cocktail that rouses some people to action and drives others to distraction. The dissenting public does not have "hard power," the resources of a state or a political class at its disposal; its most important resource is the capacity to write, speak, and think actively. It is exactly the phenomenon that Foucault described when he wrote: "where there is power, there is resistance."[43]

The University of Toronto's Citizen Lab is an excellent example of the way technology is enlisted in the resistance of authoritarian abuse of power and in the service of democratic dissent. As governments continue to block sites that they wish to censor and filter the flow of information to suit their own needs, Professor Ronald Deibert and his group of dedicated researchers have developed a computer program that allows Chinese dissidents to bypass the Communist Party of China's draconian censorship of the Internet. Their program, Psiphon, enables users to leap the digital blockade in a single bound, simply by logging into a computer in an uncensored country and using it to surf the net. Multinational media corporations could not be counted on to stand up to Chinese censorship; they believe that capitulation to the Communist Party's demands is the price of market access. Dissenters are those who believe that information flows are important not for their commercial value but for their polit-ical power. Professor Deibert's project is part of the OpenNet

Initiative to evade online censorship in all its guises.[44] Autocrats and dictators have always understood the political power that comes from controlling flows of information. In a digital age, dissenters are privy to the same knowledge, and they have the means to act on the strategic advantage that has come with the democratization of mass communication. The censorship of authoritarian regimes and the open defiance of dissenting groups reveal the extent to which the Internet has become a tactical weapon in the arsenal of the public.

The ethics of activism and the visceral anti-social public

Writing during the interwar years, the great German sociologist Karl Mannheim was fascinated by the aesthetic cultural sphere that he believed had a great impact on shifts in the mental climate of the public. Part of his idea was that social and cultural processes external to the nation-state triggered destabilizing movements that tore down the walls of conformity and opened up vast spaces for new ideas, social relations, and public activism.[45] The underclasses, non-conforming minorities, religious dissenters, writers, artists, working-class reading circles, literacy movements, and self-help organizations of every description were at its cutting edge.

Alternative modes of living, acting, and being "out in the public" always produce politically innovative and discursively pioneering kinds of social, personal, and sexual behaviour.[46] Nevertheless, to be out in public is never a natural act, it is a practice that is learned and acquired, and often it is threatening, precarious, risky, and demanding. You are questioned, interrogated, challenged, and often threatened by the conforming mainstream when you take a stand. This is why the educative value of books, drawings, objects, mannequins, art, poetry, photographs, and the documentary are prized; they are often used to provoke, shock, anger, and outrage public opinion.[47] Agitprop, shock art, excoriating attacks on public figures as well as public activism are seen to promote spontaneity, critical distancing, and anti-capitalist values. Official publics are by intent decorative and formal. They involve pageantry and the glamor of the nation; they celebrate the nation-building efforts of the elites, and embody the mythic idea of the people. Forward-looking and critical counterpublics challenge this way of thinking about the public sphere.

They force society and public opinion to look around and consider the world through very different eyes.

The German theorist Theodor Adorno caught the making of dissent in these terms: "The highest form of morality is not to feel at home in one's own house."[48] What he meant was that people have to feel morally compelled to challenge command-control models of power and confront the official beliefs, myths, and institutions of society. The modern global public requires images, visual and audio aids, and powerful photos that nurture the collective memory and brash ideas that change the world in new directions. The graffiti-filled wall, the improvised ever present political poster, and the ubiquitous microphone and chanting are powerful weapons of contentious dissent.[49]

These popular expressions of opposition unsettle and anger traditional bureaucracies because insurgent publics aren't willing to play by the rules. Texts and images have always framed political activism and target the public mind, working to create new knowledge about thought, morality, art, literature, and politics. Walter Benjamin, in his essay on surrealism, saw in the Surrealist Movement a "profane struggle for power with its multitudinous images flooding back and forth" where "its writing and art were concerned with experiences, not theories." What he valued above all else was the tension and psychic imagination fired up by collective and social images.[50] He believed that when images are collectively valued, they unleash stored-up human agency. "Only images in the mind motivate the will" and fire the individual imagination.

At the present, individual and collective voices have become the building blocks for a broadening of "things public." A surprisingly growing number of resource-strapped activists have been able to introduce political messages about complex issues such as the environment, trade, and weapons of mass destruction to an information-hungry public.

Many experts thought that the digital universe would become the next Disney-like playground for grown-ups of a distracted and disengaged public. And indeed this has been the outcome for many people; but online interaction has also driven our social desire for engagement, networking, and organizing. One of the most important features of the global cultural economy is its capacity to generate norms that are distinct from the norms that govern conventional commodity trade. The norms of cultural exchange include diversity, accessibility, and exclusive rights over creative output. The unintended consequence of the anonymity of online interaction has been the unraveling of the spatial limitations to human interaction. The public is once again the frame for a moral discourse about collective well-being, the protection of the sovereign individual, and the defense of the common good. In Dewey's classic definition of the public, individuals enter the public realm when their actions are no longer confined to themselves and their immediate intimates. When what they do has an impact on the wider world, that is, on people outside the private sphere, their actions enter the public domain.

But Dewey also recognized that "many private acts are social and contribute to the welfare of the community."[51] The Internet, at first blush, appears to belong in the private realm of intimate interaction. People access it from the privacy of their homes and use it in their personal time. They may be alone when they post to a blog or chat with a friend, but their words remain in cyberspace and, through a myriad of relational conduits, influence the wider world. This is especially true of political interaction online. Digital dissent has repatriated the idea of the common good and the public sphere as an indispensable element in modern political debate.

Despite the optimistic vision of the public presented here, a mountain of social research teaches us that publics have no innate essence, a DNA code for only good. Rather they are infinitely capricious, sometimes reactionary, choosing demagogues over democrats – especially in times of insecurity and upheaval. Reagan the great communicator, Nixon the arch-manipulator, Clinton the infinite master of the mass media, Mitterand the dissimulating grand figure leader of French politics – all were cheered, feared and feted by left and right publics. Public opinion has never been more powerful, yet in the information age publics frequently appear to be less certain of their goals. Globalization, market fundamentalism, unilateral militarism, and terrorism in the name of faith have shaken their vision of a more inclusive form of society. As the democratic public grows, the antisocial, xenophobic public grows alongside it. In the public domain, activists and despots, citizens and anarchists struggle to give definitive articulation to very different visions for our global future.

Notes

1. David Held, *Global Covenant: The Social Democratic Alternative to the Washington Consensus* (Cambridge: Polity, 2004).
2. Sylvia Ostry, "Global Integration: Currents and Counter-Currents" (the Walter Gordon Lecture, Massey College, University of Toronto, 2001).
3. Cass N. Sunstein, *Why Societies Need Dissent* (Cambridge, Mass.: Harvard University Press, 2003).
4. Pew Internet and American Life Project, "The Internet and Democratic Debate," at www.pewinternet.org, October 27, 2004.
5. Neil Postman, *Amusing Ourselves to Death: Public Discourse in the Age of Show Business* (New York: Penguin Books, 1985).
6. The Pew Research Center, at http://people-press.org/.
7. University of Southern California, Center for the Digital Future, "2007 Digital Future Report: Online World Important to Internet Users as Real World?" at www.digitalcenter.org.
8. Daniel Drache and David Clifton, "The Shrinking Digital Divide" (unpublished report, Robarts Center for Canadian Studies, York University, 2006).
9. Pricewaterhouse Coopers, "Global Media and Entertainment Outlook: 2004–2008," at www.pwc.com.
10. UCLA, World Internet Project 2004, "Significant Digital Gender Gap in Many Countries," but by 2007 the gap had closed and more women were online than men. The 2004 study also looked at poor and rich users in a variety of countries.
11. David Throsby, *Economics and Culture* (Cambridge, UK: Cambridge University Press, 2001).
12. Richard Caves, *The Creative Economy: How People Make Money from Ideas* (Cambridge, Mass.: Harvard University Press, 2000).
13. David Darin Barney, *Prometheus Wired: The Hope for Democracy in the Age of Network Technology* (Chicago, Ill.: University of Chicago Press, 2000).
14. H. A. Innis, *Empire and Communications* (Toronto: Dundurn Press, 2007).
15. Marshall McLuhan, *Understanding Media: The Extensions of Man* (New York: New American Library, 1964).

16. Richard Posner, *Public Intellectuals: A Study of Decline* (Cambridge, Mass.: Harvard University Press, 2001).

17. Edward Said, *Representations of the Intellectual: The 1993 Reith Lectures* (New York: Pantheon Books, 1994), p. 11.

18. Randy Germain, "Global Financial Governance and the Idea of the Public Sphere," (conference paper delivered Center for Global Political Economy, Simon Fraser University, July 14–15, 2004).

19. Pascale Casanova, *The World Republic of Letters* (Cambridge, Mass.: Harvard University Press, 2004), p. 39.

20. George Lakoff, *Moral Politics: How Liberals and Conservatives Think*, 2nd edn (Chicago, Ill.: University of Chicago Press, 2002).

21. Michael Warner, *Publics and Counterpublics* (New York: Zone Books, 2002), pp. 49–90.

22. Edward Said, "The Public Role of Writers and Intellectuals," *The Nation* 273:8 (September 17, 2001), p. 27.

23. Quoted in Casanova, *The World Republic of Letters* (trans. M. B. DeBevoise), p. 24.

24. John Ruggie, "Reconstituting the Global Public Domain: Issues, Actors, and Practices," *European Journal of International Relations*, 10:4 (2004), pp. 499–531.

25. Bas Arts, *Non-State Actors in Global Governance: Three Faces of Power* (Bonn: Max Planck Institute, 2003).

26. Ruggie, "Reconstituting the Global Public Domain."

27. Jonah Peretti (with Michele Micheletti), "The Nike Sweatshop Email: Political Consumerism, Internet and Culture Jamming" in *Politics, Products and Markets*, ed. Michelle Micheletti, Andreas Follesdel, and Dietlind Stolle (New Brunswick, N.J.: Transaction Books, 2004). Peretti's original account was published in *The Nation* (April 9, 2001), www.thenation.com/doc/20010409/peretti.

28. Sonia Katyal, "Semiotic Disobedience," *Washington University Law Review*, 84:4 (2006), pp. 489–572.

29. On the iconography of dissent, see Daniel Drache and Alex Samur, "Semiotic Disobedience: Shit-Disturbers in an Age of Image Overload," at www.yorku.ca/drache/academic/presentations/semi-otic_disobedience/player.html.

30. The Protection of Public Participation Act came into effect in British Columbia in April 2001. It was repealed in August 2001. In Ontario, the decision in *Daishowa v. Friends of the Lubicon* (see [1996] O.J. No. 3855 Ont. Ct. Gen. Div. QL) was also instructive on SLAPPs (strategic lawsuits against public participation, For the US see the SLAPP

resource centre, at www.slapps.org/. For the McLibel story, see John Vidal, *McLibel: Burger Culture on Trial* (London: Macmillan, 1997).

31. Postman, *Amusing Ourselves to Death*.

32. Rob Kitchin and Martin Dodge, *Atlas of Cyberspace* (New Jersey: Pearson Education, 2002).

33. Manuel Castells, *The Rise of the Network Society* (Cambridge, Mass.: Blackwell Publishers, 1996), pp. 453–9.

34. Benedict Anderson, *Imagined Communities: Reflections on the Origin and Spread of Nationalism* (London: Verso Press, 1991).

35. Anderson, *Imagined Communities*, pp. 163–75.

36. "Manière de voir," *Le Monde Diplomatique*, 2004.

37. Daniel Drache and David Clifton, "Access to the Global Communcations Sphere" (unpublished report, Robarts Centre for Canadian Studies, York University, 2006).

38. Ezequiel Adamovsky and Susan George, "What is the Point of Porto Alegre?" (January 21, 2003), at www.opendemocracy.net/globalization-world/article_906.jsp.

39. Naomi Klein, "The Vision Thing," *The Nation* (June 22, 2000).

40. Paul Rutherford, *Endless Propaganda: The Advertising of Public Goods* (Toronto: University of Toronto Press, 2000), p. 15.

41. *Sicko*, directed by Michael Moore (USA: Dog Eat Dog Films, 2007).

42. John Suler, "The Online Disinhibition Effect," *CyberPsychology and Behavior* 7:3 (June 2004).

43. Michel Foucault, *The History of Sexuality: An Introduction* (Toronto: Random House, 1990), p. 95.

44. Nicole O'Reilly, "Scaling the Walls of Web Censorship," *Globe and Mail* (November 30, 2006).

45. Franco Moretti, "Graphs, Maps, Trees: Abstract Models for Literary History," *New Left Review* 24 (November–December 2003), p. 83.

46. Richard Sennett, *The Fall of Public Man: On the Social Psychology of Capitalism* (New York: Vintage Books, 1978), pp. 25–6.

47. Nadeau Maurice, *The History of Surrealism* (New York: Collier Publishing, 1967), p. 209.

48. Quoted in Azar Nafisi, *Reading Lolita in Tehran: A Memoir of Books* (New York: Random House, 2003), p. 94.

49. Susan Buck-Morss, *Dreamworld and Castastrophe: The Passing of Mass Utopia in East and West* (Cambridge, Mass.: MIT Press, 2002).

50. Walter Benjamin, *Reflections* (New York: Harcourt Brace Jovanovich, 1978), pp. 177–92.

51. John Dewey, *The Public and its Problems* (New York: Henry Holt and Company, 1927), p. 13.

4

Nixers, Fixers, and the Axes of Conformity

The rise of global counterpublics

Commentators take for granted that politicians today are activists and that every activist must have a vision and policy template with which to reform their communities. In Canada, party leaders campaign on complex policy platforms that have been certified by accountants to be workable within the resources of government. In the United States, presidential candidates design complex reform strategies to fix health care and other social ills.[1] These tomes of enlightenment show voters that politicians have mastered not only the art of campaigning, but also the science of changing the world. In Europe, electoral victory is frequently presented as the art of brokerage politics combined with the science of policy formulation. In the United States, elections are a repeating test of the laws of behavioralism, and pollsters take on a divine aspect. A cynic might be prompted to observe that on some level the Europeans are absorbed with the possibilities of social engineering, and the Americans are obsessed with the inevitabilities of electoral engineering.

It used to be that the Left self-identified as activists through the Marxist concept of praxis, which is a synthesis of theory and practice. On the Right, political action was not so rigorously theorized. It was generally regarded, at worst, in the same self-interested terms as entrepreneurialism and at best as public service. The mass fascist movements of the 1930s changed this perception, and after the Second World War it was finally recognized that activism on the Left and the Right is qualitatively similar in the way that it combines political theory, social values, and the strategies of mass organizing to rally public opinion. It is a legacy of the transformative events of the civil rights movement in 1960s America that politicians and front-line political actors on both the Right and Left now tend to define themselves as activists.[2] They discuss in serious terms the potential benefits of grassroots rallies, the exigencies of face-to-face debates and door-knocking exercises, and the benefits of mass advertising and branding. They have taken to heart Walter Benjamin's exhortation to move beyond the "stage of eternal discussion," to say the least.[3]

Political activism has evolved into a Leviathan bridled by bright and educated tacticians and administrators. The best examples of the new world of activism are the worldwide concerts to raise awareness about poverty and the environment. The Live 8 concerts organized by Bob Geldof in 2005 and the Live Earth concerts organized by Al Gore in 2007 are consciousness-raising experiences to a large degree, celebrating the fact that global warming is now at the top of the public agenda. Few imagine that they can be taken at face value as a transformative political experience for audiences. Instead they are about the modern activist lifestyle, part lifestyle identity, part informed political commitment, and all about effecting change through the creation of transformative social movements.

Defiant publics want to reclaim their voices and assert their ideas in the public domain. These nagging, hectoring, persistent publics have a presence we can feel and an impact we can see. What makes them unique is that they exist "by virtue of their imagining" and their ideas are almost infinite in number. They live through texts, debate, and discursive communities. They embody civil society's predilection to be engaged when something seems to be wrong, unjust, in need of fixing – or something bolder, to destroy and build anew.

In the expanding universe of modern dissent, diversity of political identity is the rule. The choices seem infinite. There is a style and identity tool-kit for every position on the political spectrum. You no longer have to choose between an identity as a capitalist or a socialist. You can be a deep environmental paradigm shifter, a radical feminist, an anti-racist activist, a poverty eradicator, a moral crusader, a gay rights campaigner, a globalization fixer, a populist blogger, an anti-fascist agitator, a back-to-basics localist, an online "hacktivist," a union militant, a libertarian skeptic, an anarchist spoiler, an anti-war demonstrator, or a corporate culture-jammer, just to name a few of the emergent on- and offline political identities. Micro-activism thrives in this environment. If your cause is not on the list, start your own network, connect with others, organize your own community, and raise awareness.[4]

Contrast this growth with the overall decline in voting and membership in political parties across the industrialized world and one can see how consequential the shift in the political environment actually is. People are increasingly cynical about trusting mainstream political leaders and political parties that promise the world but never deliver. So with a political culture of operating on a cumulative record of broken electoral promises it is hardly surprising that distrust of political parties has reached a boiling point and can be tracked across the world in this democratic age. Voters march with their feet and don't vote, but those who do vote have plans to vote strategically. The new information economy gives people on the ground the tools to challenge elite structures and institutions. The actual word counterpublic is not yet in the *Oxford English Dictionary*, but you can find "counter-intuitive," "counter-irritant," and "counter-motion" all of which share something of the bristling qualities of the modern counterpublic. They are "counter" because they are against the grain, against conventional wisdom, against embedded conformity, and inevitably against elites and their expectations. These are the public groups that lead opinion and create the political identities whose proliferation so marks this era of globalization.

The post-modern compass of dissent

The effectiveness of counterpublics can be measured by their *performativity* or the impact of their ideas on public opinion, their *capacity* to incite anger or to force a reaction for or against a major issue, and the *resilience* of their message to inspire other groups of activists that come later. These metrics point us to examine and evaluate a new kind of political culture of opposition that is the product of the information times. The compass of dissent today is very different from the one designed by leftist intellectuals and conservative thinkers after the Second World War. In those times, left-wing activists looked to large-scale geopolitics to orient their activism and refine their theories of the revolutionary mission of the proletariat. They wanted to build mass socialist parties and seize the commanding heights of the economy. The nationalization of industry was supposed to be the best way to create a more equal set of social relations. The welfare state would replace the market as the principal mechanism for social organization.[5]

Socialist theory placed full-scale revolution at the center of the political project.[6] This worldview privileged systems and structures with the power to change collective behavior and create high levels of expectations for individuals. In social theory agency, voice, and process took a back seat to a world constructed on the ideas of functionalism and top-down collective action. Micro-activism was seen as a second-tier if not second-rate area of research. In the zeal to create an economy rooted in public plenty rather than private scarcity, socialist theorists buried important democratic concerns about identity, gender, and the value of the individual under the weighty historical mission of the proletariat. They were burdened, in the words of Milan Kundera, by the "unbearable lightness of being".

In the real world of state policy, the Left settled for the social democratic compromise. Harold Wilson, Pierre Trudeau, François Mitterand, and John F. Kennedy all made their peace with global financial markets. In the golden age of Keynesianism, the mixed economy set a high standard for market regulation and social provision in the industrialized world. Organized labor and the middle class were all the better for it.[7] But with the internationalization of markets and the idea that citizenship could only be rooted in one's singular loyalty to your community of fate, socialist theory turned out to have feet of clay.

On the Right, conservative thinkers used the realist balance of power to justify their worldview.[8] They wanted to control the intellectual agenda in the West in order to galvanize support behind Cold War policies that fitted their particular theoretical view of mutually assured destruction, containment, and the domino effect of socialist revolution. Did their jingoism protect the West from Stalinist-style authoritarianism? Scholars are divided about how much the containment of the Soviet Union helped or hurt Western prosperity. The Great Fear of "communism from within" galvanized conservative activists and spurred the political witch hunts that destroyed lives and damaged the credibility of conservatism as a bastion of the traditional values of freedom of expression and belief.[9] After the Cold War ended, conservatives gloated that the Left was rudderless, discredited, and lying in the dustbin of history. The critical point that neither the Left nor the Right anticipated was the scrambling of ideology that was to take place beyond the rubble of the Berlin Wall.[10]

The ordinals of social inclusion and citizen identity

Dissent today consists of four large, interrelated, and loosely linked clusters of engagement. The projects are guided by big ideas, soft concepts, and emerging worldviews that mark them as distinct from Cold War politics. Fixed meta-ideologies are present but take a back seat. The ordinals are points of departure and beacons for action on behalf of the vulnerable, excluded, displaced, precarious, marginalized, and victimized.

The first project on the modern compass of dissent is *social inclusion*. It is concerned chiefly with the preservation of the social bond – that difficult to define energy that draws upon the power of group identification – through economic development, poverty eradication, and the enhancement of social equality.[11] The World Social forum is at the crossroads of this powerful current. This is a huge category. It includes city activists across the globe who seek to protect the rights of the homeless in the capital cities of the world, immigration campaigners fighting for a world without borders and human rights crusaders, such as Oxfam and Save the Children, fighting for child poverty eradication. It is one that links activists in most self-described progressive movements, from the environmental movement, to labor rights networks, and even libertarian think tanks. The questions of how we can live together in a densely populated, multicultural, and increasingly complex social world absorbs the talent and time of millions of activists, analysts, and academics.

The second large ordinal is *trust and human security*. Millions who still believe that public authority is the primary means by which society defends the weak are particularly interested in the challenges of the right to human security and individual safety and the way that these rights can translate into meaningful democratic action. These activists can be called cosmo-populists – believers in the possibilities of cosmopolitan citizenship who understand the massive power potential of populism and localism. The World Social Forum attracts tens of thousands of young militants under this banner. Anti-poverty campaigners such as OneWorld, ActionAid, and the Global Development Network furious with the World Bank for their support for neo-liberal policies, are turning up the volume on governments to make good on their Millennium Development Goals. Local environmental activists are noisily pressuring their governments to honour their Kyoto commitments.

The best-known organization of this type is Médecins Sans Frontières (MSF) which now operates around the world. Founded by a group of physicians working with the Red Cross in the Nigerian civil war in Biafra in the early seventies, it is the prototype of the new cosmopolitan NGO humanitarian aid organization. Originally its founding activists criticized the techniques used by the Red Cross in Nazi Germany saying that their silence in Auschwitz was tantamount to complicity. These young and outspoken doctors created an alternative to the International Committee of the Red Cross that had required its volunteers to sign a contract of cooperation with a country's authorities. In establishing MSF their goal was to provide quick medical relief and at the same time speak out against human rights violations.[12]

All of these organizations prioritize the local but are committed to building communities on a global scale. This cluster contains human rights campaigners, crusaders against weapons of mass destruction, theorists of social capital, and even some military intelligence advocates. In a strange twist, the American neo-conservative movement draws some of its energy and legitimacy by copying the language and ethos of human security campaigners. Also, the American military has experienced in an immediate way the real effects of a breakdown of basic human rights in Iraq, and they are turning to human security advocates for help. These dissenters are focused on the Arendtian ideal of the right to have rights.[13]

The third axis is the *individual freedom* cluster. These activists privilege the libertarian aspects of liberalism at the same time that they recognize the essential role of the state in protecting minorities. Their project is one of liberal inclusion and cosmopolitan recognition. Make Aids History, ACT UP, Global Aids Alliance, and Health Global Alliance Project (GAP) are among the most successful transnational movements that have produced a new generation of activists. This group includes gay rights activists, freedom of speech defenders such as the Media Coalition, subaltern community representatives, and all manner of counterculture proponents of alternative lifestyles, from radical social experiments to fundamentalist religious sects. This cluster aims to free individuals from the bias and prejudice that deny them the opportunity to develop their capabilities and allow them to become productive members of society.[14]

Disability International is a powerful voice for those with any kind of physical or mental impairment and typifies the liberal ethos of building an inclusive world through legislative reform. Thousands of AIDS activists, medical researchers, artist collectives, and self-help groups are fighting ignorance, racism, and social exclusion in the name of individual freedom. All these kinds of projects are inspired by a powerful ideal of liberal individualism but are much more than that. They are fundamentally collectivist because they accept as true that social reform has to change the relations of power between the individual and society.

The last ordinal is the *building political community* cluster. Its project is that of the micro-activist – developing networks and enhancing the relational power of the public like Habitat for Humanity that builds homes for the homeless and low-income groups worldwide.[15] Debt relief activists like the Jubilee Debt Campaign support the goal that the people of the Third World countries cannot be held accountable for the massive indebtedness that their elites or kleptocracies incurred. Micro-activists are also organized and highly visible campaigners championing dozens of causes as different as cancelation of Third World Debt to protecting sex trade workers. In the cities of the world we can feel the presence of thousands of micro-activist organizations defending the homeless, fighting for rent controls and clean water and against the ubiquitous wrecking ball of developers in the barrios of São Paolo, the slums of New Delhi or the inner city projects of Boston.

Many of these local activists are connectors and masters of the weak social tie, as Malcolm Gladwell termed them.[16] They bridge the divide between movements and organizations of all sizes and types like the Third World Network. The human dimension of international organization fascinates them, and they are consumed with the potentiality of institution building. This group includes homelessness activists, advocates of the rights of the disabled, undocumented worker activists, networkers who aim to rebuild inner city communities, and even church groups that oppose capital punishment. Their primary goals are to oppose arbitrary state action and reinstate the procedural fairness that they perceive to be lacking in modern democratic societies. Organizations like the Polaris project to combat human trafficking and modern-day slavery aim to "empower individual survivors of trafficking while also creating long-term social change." These radicals come in a variety of forms from Jane Jacobs-type social democrats, to concerned liberals like Al Gore. The violence of heavy-handed bureaucratic responses to social problems is the catalyst for large-scale social change.

The bigtent strategy and dynamics of crossover

These broad rubrics lend themselves to a big tent buy-in strategy that is one of the foundational elements of modern public dissent. It accounts for the astonishing speed in the diffusion of dissenting ideas and mind-sets. It is this lethal combination of mind-set plus ideology that defines the particular place of every group of activists on the map of activism. And what of the orthodox Left – where is it? Of course any one of the twenty or so varieties of socialist revolution is present as part of the larger movements and culture of dissent, but they are no longer the luminous polar North Star of social activism. Marxism used to be a categorical imperative for a select set of highly influential thinkers, but the potency of classical

Marxist thought was diluted with the decline of Cold War international relations. By the turn of the twenty-first century, it had been almost fully subsumed in the pragmatic projects of progressive social movements and in the desire of activists for concrete strategies of social change.

So all in all the modern compass of dissent is ideologically fluid; it allows individuals to cross over into other movements and jump between causes and battles, from battling Bush to protecting local neighbors from private developers. The power dynamics favor those with a large capacity for technical understanding, networking ability, and a clarity of vision that convinces the cynical and wins new converts to the cause.[17] This complex and highly regionalized culture of dissent in every continent has triggered a massive cycle of political rebellion and non-conformity that cuts across the deep divides of age, class, and culture. What is the potent mix of hard to manage tensions?

Skeptics are by far the largest group of dissident and disgruntled global publics. They constantly challenge public authorities and elites about their values, priorities, and ideas. From the Greek *skeptikos*, the act of doubting is synonymous with the related notion of bearing a responsibility to dissuade others. Skeptics make common cause with persuasion and dissent. The British website opendemocracy.net is a prime example of skeptic thought, as is its American counterpart, truthout.org. They are always drilling down, searching, reading, processing the news, views, analysis, and opinion not carried by mainstream media. To get the latest behind the headline news about Burma, human rights in Iraq, pro-democracy movements in Eastern Europe, a critique of Al Gore's latest book, these sites attract tens of thousands of info-activists.

By instinct, skeptics are wary of conventional wisdom and official explanations. They like to look behind the world of appearances and beyond accepted nostrums, and for that reason, they aren't loyal subjects of a president, prime minister, or the nation writ large. They want real answers to their questions about the use and misuse of power. They are often young, well-educated, or self-taught Internet users skilled in digging for the truth. They read, research, and track issues over time. They don't let themselves be guiled by officialese and want hard evidence not sophistry in answer to their questions and worries.

Reinforcing social inclusion

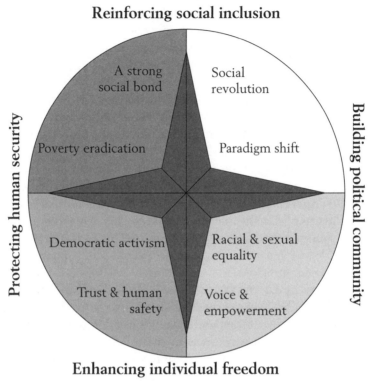

Enhancing individual freedom

Figure 4.1 The compass of post-modern dissent
Source: Daniel Drache, Robarts Centre, 2007

Skeptics are issue-focused and not necessarily joiners of social movements. They don't march in the streets and wouldn't be caught dead at the World Social Forum. They aren't anti-globalizers by temperament and see value in public security because they are middle-of-the-roaders and take a long time debating which "side" they will support. They want to weigh the arguments for and against. But they are worried and open to argument and persuasion.

Many in this category have a visceral reaction to polarizing political personalities like Vice President Dick Cheney, former prime minister Margaret Thatcher, former Italian president Silvio Berlusconi, and Russian president (now prime minister) Vladimir Putin rather than a specific boiler-plate ideology. Modern skeptics are fragmented and highly fluid bodies of opinion, wary of authority, and suspicious of the political class and the way they package their ideas. They are often drawn from the ranks of the middle class, but this categorization is not all that useful in advanced industrial countries where computer access cuts across traditional socio-economic divides. Their place-rooted pluralism sits easily with both their instinct to challenge their own national leaders as well as their voracious interest in the geopolitical universe beyond the nation-state. In a global age, they follow the global citizen's golden rule that you do not need to be a citizen of a country in order to make a judgment about it.

Skeptics militate, persuade, and argue largely under the radar screen. They may not be seen, but their ability to move public opinion is always felt. This genre of dissent builds a "democratic dam," to invoke Stuart Hall's powerful language, against conformity and the selfish individualist. Skeptical dissenters "stand apart" with others in disagreement. It is this act of dissociation from the establishment that makes the disbelieving counterpublic a force to be reckoned with in a liberal democracy. Liberal democracy as practiced is essentially about making deals and exchanging promises for votes; *strong* democracy, according to Benjamin Barber, is about choice and participation, where politics is done *by* citizens rather than *to* citizens.[18]

Low visibility often leads experts to underestimate the skeptic in an age of celebrity and fast-flowing information, but their energy and commitment has reactivated the idea of a "public of citizens."[19] This dynamic has given birth to other new sets of loyalties. They are angered by the broken promises of politicians – an anger that they feed off – and particularly by the deception, perpetrated by Bush and Blair, surrounding Weapons of Mass Destruction. They are unforgiving about being lied to and betrayed. They are angry about global warming and the indifference of governments to take effective action to limit greenhouse gas emissions. They support groups like Eco-Justice, Friends of the Earth, and thousands of grassroots environmentalist organizations.

Contrarians are by temperament and conviction tough opponents of governmental authority. Where skeptics are amateur spoilers, contrarians are professional doubters. They are pessimists par excellence who fear the worst and perceive a world falling apart.[20] Skeptics suspect that things are worse than the experts say on Iraq, on global warming, and corruption in government. Pessimistic contrarians believe that the experts are deliberately hiding the truth. They look at the world convinced that system and structure run everything; people matter but can never beat global capitalism.

The pessimists hold to the view that reform is always on offer but the political class's aim is to co-opt the opposition to put a stop to more fundamental change. Contrarians are often public intellectuals who don't trust official explanations, are chary of bureaucrats and media spin, and know how to dig in their heels to champion unpopular views. They see things from the perspective of the minority, the underdog, and the maligned. They ferret out misinformation and intend to hold the political class to account.

The contrarians represent a huge body of opinion with hard-core support among the young, the better educated, the alienated, and, particularly, the baby boomers who lived through the collapse of the golden age of Keynesianism. Many contrarians have quit electoral politics and don't vote. These anti-politician dissenters are actively reshaping political life for explicitly democratic ends. Contrarians are skeptics who have ratcheted up their criticism and now believe that their worldview is incompatible with the one presented by elites. They want more accountability for state spending, more transparency in war-making, and peace-making, and more democracy in jaded and spin-weary postindustrial societies.

Even though contrarians tend to be fatalistic about the possibilities for a better world, they are highly effective by working to limit market authority and subordinate political power to greater citizen oversight. With constant access to the World Wide Web, they don't give up on their causes easily. They are focused and committed and their attention span is far longer than that of most people. Some would call them obsessive and driven by fantasies of conspiracy and catastrophe, but in truth, contrarians like Will Hutton of *The Guardian* are always drilling down to find the nuggets of information that governments are withholding.

The iconic example of the full-blooded contrarian is Noam Chomsky, the spiritual godfather of dissent activism today. His ideas are radical and run counter to received wisdom at every turn.

In *Hegemony or Survival: America's Quest for Global Dominance* published in 2003, for instance, he presents a devastating analysis of Bush's pursuit of total domination and the catastrophic consequences of US militarism. What's more, his abrasive style and in-your-face attitude cannot be kept in check by group pressure or public sanction. Contrarians like Chomsky and his like-minded disciples defy mainstream public opinion and convention. They thrive because liberal emphasis on agreement and acceptable public opinion misses too much. Because the cold warriors ignored so many warning bells in their rush to the end of history, the contrarian has plenty of ammunition to punch through the assumptions of elites and the hypocrisy of the political class.

Radical dystopians are self-proclaimed paradigm shifters who finger the "system" as the enemy. They are operating according to their own social gestalt and include men and women of conscience, anarchists, revolutionary socialists, and radical green activists. They are the shock troops of the anti-globalization movement with their slogan "Another world is possible."[21] They have a Hegelian/Marxist belief that they can redesign society from top to bottom following a master plan of rational thought and collective imagining. Vast numbers of them are hard-core back to the earth environmentalists, international socialists, Trotskyists, Maoists, anarchists, and dystopic feminists of many different varieties. Radical dystopians have an enormous constituency in the under-thirty demographic. They also have a huge presence in the global south where their militancy finds an outlet in postcolonial struggle.

Their critique of global capitalism from a structural perspective provides a powerful vision for the angry activist who sees a linkage between racism, poverty, and globalization. Their apostolic zeal for poverty reduction and egalitarian redistribution spills over into the mainstream and often energizes less radical activists. Bono of the band U2 is an atypical example of how a mainstream superstar with his consciousness-raising feats can have a major impact on pivotal groups and individuals. Within their transnational networks, coalitions, and advocacy campaigns, the active localism of the radical dystopian has become the platform for new political initiatives on the supranational level. The World Social Forum is the "bigger than big" annual meeting place where tens of thousands of anti-poverty, anti-racist, anti-war activists worldwide assemble to develop strategies and alternative visions to global capitalism.[22]

Practical utopians are reformers who champion a system overhaul. Unlike the radical dystopians, they believe that the system can be saved, but it needs emergency surgery and a long recovery period. Practical utopians are often recognized as expert policy analysts and dedicated global actors. They are frequently hardworking, well-funded, non-governmental organizations such as Médecins Sans Frontières, Oxfam International, World Vision, Amnesty International, World Wildlife Fund, Greenpeace, and Human Rights Watch to name only a few of the best known. They attempt to cajole, shame, and persuade governments to change policies that violate international law and human rights.

Their campaigns, especially those in Europe and the global south, have become a key element in mobilizing publics and public opinion worldwide. For example, global human rights organizations, church groups, and international lawyers have worked hard to mobilize public opinion on a number of high-profile human rights issue areas such as the Land Mine Treaty, and more recently systemic prisoner abuse in the "war on terror" in Afghanistan, Iraq, and Guantanamo Bay, Cuba.

Practical utopians not only keep the pressure on governments, but they are often instrumental in providing technical, legal, and moral leadership. They have a major impact on how people think about their local and national public authority and are unrelenting in calling for democratic accountability.[23] They want to "fix" a world gone wrong – make multinational corporations answerable before the law, create accountable institutions for the world economy, and ratchet up the United Nations as the world's governing body. They are not revolutionaries; rather they are hard-nosed reformers advocating practical changes in everything from the environment, to global justice, to human rights, and beyond.

Demonstrating more and new forms of citizen engagement

Despite the sensational media coverage of post-9/11 hysteria, publics in postindustrial societies are becoming more inclusive, and they place a premium upon the values of tolerance, respect, and a humanist impulse to fight exclusion. Following the murder of Theo van Gogh in the Netherlands in 2004, Dutch voters frothed at the idea of radical Muslims in their midst, working to overthrow their moderate society. They voted in anti-immigrant politicians and adopted policy measures designed to admit "good" Muslims to the country and weed out the bad. Three years on, the hysteria has faded, and many Dutch people are sheepish about their experiment with xenophobia. They understand better the tensions of immigration, but are less inclined to abdicate their values for short-term and largely symbolic security gains.

In fact, publics across Europe are adopting the values of dissent faster than their elites and governments, and this has led to an increase in political malaise and a trend away from mass political participation. Based on data from surveys done between 1974 and 2000, Ronald Inglehart found, for example, that only about one quarter of the public had ever signed a petition in 1974. By 2000, a majority of people, about 63 percent, had signed a petition. In little more than twenty-five years, petitions had become something that a majority were familiar with and were willing to use to make their views known. The same is true of taking part in a demonstration. Only 9 percent of the people surveyed had taken part in a demonstration in 1974. By 2000, 21 percent of respondents admitted to taking part in this form of direct action.[24]

Consumer boycotts are less confrontational than direct action, yet extraordinarily, fewer people have participated in these than in demonstrations. The numbers nevertheless show a persistent rise – from 6 to 15 percent. Dissent is now a mainstream activity in which ordinary people assert their preferences. The trend in the latter half of the twentieth century has been markedly toward what Nevitte has termed "the decline of deference."[25] Significantly, Inglehart established that the decline of deference and the rise of defiance is most pronounced in Western societies. In post-communist countries, people remained more likely to defer to their elites and less likely to challenge existing power structures.

The postmodern compass of dissent reflects the ambiguities and certainties of our times. More people have access to higher levels of education, and it is not surprising that they have also become more knowledgeable about the issues that affect them at home and in the wider world. Positions on the ordinals are fluid, matching our own ambiguous relationship to identity politics. In the past, activists imagined that their identities were forged in the crucible of political struggle. Today, political positions are the product of *self-styled identity formation*. You might be a corporate culture jammer as a sociology student in college then a political contrarian when you work as a business consultant later in life. The era of Western, postwar affluence in which we assumed that dissent was primarily driven by the young, the proletarian, and the idealistic is over. This gives the compass of dissent an enormous advantage because modern activism links generations, social classes, and even ethnic solitudes in new and innovative ways. With their emphasis on being strategic, ready to form coalitions, and accommodate people with very different views is it any wonder, with so many points of entry, that activism and contrariness have come of age?

The embedded axes of conformity

Communities on the right side of the political spectrum have a strikingly different set of ideas about the social responsibility of government and the distortions flowing from enlarged markets and global competitive pressures. They are linked to each other through their social values and societal ideas. But they are a different sort of counterpublic; one that makes use of digital strategies to defend the holy trinity of patriarchy, god, and country – my country right or wrong. They believe in the transformative potential of the economically interested individual, and paradoxically, the right to indifference. Everyone has the right not to care, even if it is socially harmful, as it is when conformists use their disinterest to propagate a form of not so benign racism and exclusion.

They also support highly intrusive forms of state authority, such as those seen most recently in the breakdown of civil liberties and a transfer of power to law enforcement in America. New forms of fundamentalism, militancy, and xenophobic patriotism have emerged from the fringe to occupy a large public space of global debate and discussion. They have thousands of websites, blogs, and chatlines and Robert Kagan, David Frum, and William Kristol are but a few of the media stars and public intellectuals setting the agenda and marshaling the troops. At the core, conservatives of every stripe are conflicted about the inviolability of rights. Property rights should be expanded, but the right to privacy is something that the Arab tourist coming to the US or UK is not entitled to.

In the US, conformity is an industry unlike any other. The Hoover Institution, the National Review, the Mount Pelerine Society, the Chicago School of Economics, The Project for the New American Century, and the American Enterprise Institute have provided the US Right with its message of inspiration over the past twenty years. John Micklethwait and Adrian Wooldridge estimate that conservative think tanks spent $1 billion promoting conservative ideas in the 1990s to convince publics that conservatism is a politically and economically progressive creed:

> The American right exhibits a far deeper hostility toward the state than any other modern conservative party. How many European conservatives would display bumper stickers saying "I love my country but I hate my government?" How many would argue that we need to make government so small that it can be drowned in a bath tub?[26]

What makes every conformist movement so powerful, however, is its celebration of an ideological, knee-jerk reaction, which it terms "common sense." Thomas Paine, a giant historical figure for the American Right, would surely shudder if he knew that his public call to political consciousness would be twisted into a call to protect privilege and the prerogatives of the wealthy. In the conformist mentality, it is better to be white than black; better to be rich than poor; better to be skinny than fat; better to be Christian than Muslim – because these things single one out as separate from the herd. And once you have been culled from the herd, there is no protection from the terror of individualism. This is the great irony of neo-liberalism. Its accepted norms and practices are frequently at odds with its highest ideals and values. An aggressive belief in Western capitalism and support for the war against terrorism have created a virtual geography of conformity privileging private wealth creation, social conservatism, and laissez-faire liberalism. What are the modern ordinals of conformity?

Me individualism

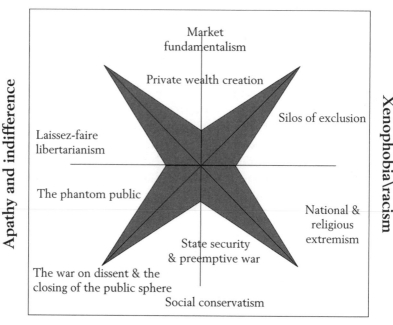

Patriarchy, God, and country

Figure 4.2 The embedded axes of conformity: me individualism
Source: Daniel Drache, Robarts Centre, 2007

Modern conformity and the culture of reaction

At one extreme of its axes is a very large group comprising the *distracted* and *disinterested*. They are not unhappy, nor are they disaffected with the status quo – quite the opposite. So long as the system takes care of their basic needs, they remain disinterested in politics, vote infrequently, and do not read newspapers. They are as likely to be professional, urban middle-class as small "c" conservative working-class. Margaret Thatcher, Jean-Marie Le Pen, Ronald Reagan, and George Bush junior and senior chalked up massive electoral victories by building highly effective, cross-class coalitions from these critical constituencies. In every industrial country, the culture of conformity has its roots in smaller, urban centres outside the major cities. They are the silent majority of Middle America, the PRI (Institutional Revolutionary Party) middle-class loyalists in Mexico, and the *pieds-noirs* from France's former colonies who feel marginalized by failed immigration policy, the fallout from globalization and the challenge of multiculturalism.

The materialism and hedonism that define conformist mentality are driven by a desire to appear too different, to not stand out – to be "normal." The suburban need to "keep up with the herd mentality of the Joneses" is the example of this mentality that is a staple of modern sociology. In this cliché, consumption is driven not by personal desire for expression, but by the neurotic need to blend in. The critical safe path is to be socially invisible, and have other people admire you for your calculated ability to stay flush in the middle of the pack.

The socially disinterested at all times see themselves as separate from the political system, and their predictable social values are those of family and work. They tend to be reflexively politically conservative, have an obsessive respect for hierarchy, and an unshakeable belief that no matter who is in charge, the basically unequal nature of wealth and privilege never changes. Frequently they may not be wealthy themselves, but they are confident and take comfort from knowing that even though things won't necessarily get better, they probably won't get a whole lot worse. The person in the driver's seat – not them – is better equipped to run the show, whether through an accident of birth or dint of training, it matters little to the disinterested, disengaged citizen.

This mind-set bias to escape into distraction is not the luxury of the few; it is the lifestyle choice of many. Conservative activists do not push traditionally-minded people to look outward beyond their local solidarities and externalize their concerns and worries. Rather, they heap praise on the common sense of the mythic everyman who recognizes that his immediate concerns are those directly at hand. In the words of Ortega y Gasset, the iconic conservative thinker, "the characteristic of the hour is that the commonplace mind, knowing itself to be commonplace, has the assurance to proclaim the rights of the commonplace and to impose them where ever they will."[27]

The disengaged citizen and traditional roles in society

The disinterested citizen's only responsibility, as far as they are concerned, is to follow their bliss, as long as it does not lead them too far from the world of home and family. They make their parochialism into a civic virtue in celebrating their inability to connect. You can see them congratulating themselves for being smart enough to recognize the deep implications of citizenship in a free society: everyone has the inviolable right to do nothing.

A large portion of this know-nothing-do-nothing attitude as much in view in New Delhi as New York must be attributed to the American-inspired culture of distraction that drives the global entertainment industries. If you do not like the world you live in, escape into the world of entertainment, personal hedonism, and Disney. The distracted and disinterested are convinced that they cannot make a difference in the world around them, and it is foolish to waste their efforts trying. Not surprisingly in many urban-dominated cultures in the capital cities of the world they slip into a lifestyle of feigned individualism and lifestyle ego-gratification.[28]

The disinterested citizen exists in the middle of the social pack and draws comfort from the fact that all the big issues and choices do not filter into their cocoon. The *undecided and waverers*, however, are aware that in the Internet age traditional roles and behaviors are declining. Business, marriage, and fatherhood are no longer defined by a single template idea. The undecided citizen accepts that perpetual disinterest is a valid political position, but they are not sure that they are willing to entirely give up all of their control over public engagement in the way that the distracted citizen has. As a result, these people are more skeptical of the paternalism of conservative pundits, but they are also turned off by the excesses of dissent.

They do not identify with values of the literary set, whom they consider to be wealthier and probably less commonsensical than themselves. Nor can they imagine for a moment marching in a political protest. American pollsters lump the soccer moms and NASCAR dads into this category. They are conventional in every sense of the term, but they always are interested in the world their children will inherit. Their self-interest in the intergenerational transfer of wealth and skills puts them into a special category that is neither non-conformist nor risk-taker. Sociologically they inhabit a sort of no man's land for a principal reason. They experienced the power of dissent in the 1970s and have the important digital skills that make a critical difference for researching the topics of the day. Often affluent, having prospered from investing in financial markets, they have benefited from more than a decade of wealth-creation. Still their curiosity about the political world around them drives the sales of bestselling summer novels and biographies of politicians. They are confident, but they do not like to commit themselves polit-ically. They prefer to maintain their views in private rather than fly them in public.

Of course, the undecided and waverers do not want to be told how to think and what to be outraged about, so they stay away from the news channels owned by Rupert Murdoch. They want to think for themselves, yet they feel that global change has impacted their lives and pulled them in new and often unwanted directions ethically. They are anxious about the inability of public authority to provide a good education for their kids and affordable health care, and are worried about rising crime rates. Ultimately, they realize that if they cannot reason through mainstream ideas and simplistic concepts offered by the political class, they are gradually forced to look elsewhere to find answers to the issues that matter the most to their strongest social values: honesty, integrity, hard work, and independence. This category of conformity is thus influ-enced less by ideology and more by ideas than other groups. They are likely to be "values voters," voting a lying politician out of office or just as likely to be swing voters in a close election. In their natural form, they are the mushy middle, but once aroused they are a potent force.

In many ways this disgruntled middle is the political phenom-enon of our times. Their numbers fuel the growth of skeptical and contrarian dissenting groups. In their respective countries, they are drawn to the tough-minded optimism of Lula (Luiz Inácio Lula da Silva) in Brazil, the magnetic personal populism of Tony Blair in the UK, the glasnost policies of Mikhail Gorbachev in Russia, and the grassroots networking of the Conservative Party in Canada.

Not everyone has the stuff to be an angry rightist. This huge sprawling body of opinion on the environment, the war in Iraq, poverty, homelessness, and corporate greed is so important that no politician can afford to ignore it. In the short run, doubters and the hesitant can be appeased and reassured by media smart and politically savvy leaders of the right, but once aroused, the undecided are extraordinarily wrathful. Waverers go one of two ways: either they allow themselves to be kept in the fold reassured by elites, or they take the next step and break with the conformist position venting their resentment at having been deceived and used by politicians.

True believers, conservative reason, and toxic extremists

At the other corner are the *true believers*. These are the hard and fast loyalists, the unapologetic defenders of hierarchy and authority, the bedrock aspirational values of the conformist belief system. In every way they are classical conservatives, inspired by Edmund Burke, always suspicious of the power exercised by the state. In every circumstance, these neo-conservatives will without hesitation choose liberty over equality. They are deep patriots rather than ideological nationalists. True believers are fundamentally committed to defending the hierarchical institutions that ensure maximum liberty with stable continuity. Like Burke, they are most distrustful and scornful of the liberal idea of the promise of progress. The Burkeian ideals of the positive benefits of social hierarchy, their much in view pessimism about the benefits of progress, and a religious-like belief in the superiority of the social value of elite-based politics are the broad organizing principles at the bedrock of conformist belief. It is not surprising to discover that the pundits of the Right are mostly earnest, serious, angry, white men who, if they do not claim expertise themselves, at least claim to know expertise when they see it.

Churchill once famously noted that the conservative "prefers the past to the present, and the present to the future."[29] In many ways, they inhabit a closed mind-set in which there is no dynamic feedback mechanism; the neo-conservative Right is always living in its closed universe self-referencing its iconic thinkers from von Hayek to a Robert Kagan or a David Frum. There is no chance the true believer will be "won over." The social Right in the US has demonstrated no temerity in exploiting all of the global Internet's possibilities for instantaneous dissemination and radical decentralization. It has thousands of informational sites, round-the-clock chat lines, and nervy, pushing-the-envelope, grassroots bloggers. Its roots can be traced back to the entrepreneurial ideal of self-reliance and hard work, but it also makes good use of the Puritan ethos of New World insecurity from the war on post-9/11 terrorism.

The irony is that anti-Semitism is a staple of conformism in Europe and conformists in America are rabidly pro-Israel. The US neo-cons attack the critical Left for having an anti-Israel bias. But intolerance of Muslims is rationalized and defended as just a "practical security consideration," not the vile prejudice that it actually is. The Christian Right is also online and fighting hard for its place in the virtual cultural wars. These are groups for whom the bias of communication is a deeply unsettling reality because as it empowers online users to think for themselves it destabilizes their privileged social position on- and offline. They sound the alarm that something must be done, and they use all of the many strategic tools at their disposal, including money, time, the organizing tactics of the progressive Left, and the Internet itself to achieve their goal of status quo stability.

Toxic e-extremists inhabit the darkest corners of the Internet. Despite their radical proselytizing and aggressive rhetoric, they are the deepest conservatives and least in touch with reality. The toxic e-extremist believes, like fascists in previous generations, that society should return to a mythical past in which races were pure, the second sex was obedient, and the Old Testament patriarch was the highest attainment of masculine perfection. Of course, this dystopic vision unites extremists from all the monotheistic belief systems. Fundamentalist Christian back-to-the-land cults and Osama bin Laden share these ideas, even if they have little else in common.

These extremists inhabit a world of conspiracy, hate, and anti-social tendencies. They include but are not limited to the Christian nationalist white supremacist movement, the radical and violent Israel for the Jews movement, and the Islamist Jihad movement. In most cases, the most violent altercations today involve one or more of these toxic extremists. These groups exploit the libertarian vision of a world without boundaries. The Internet has been a boon to them because for the first time in history, they can reach every person who was ever curious about their agenda or drawn to their hateful vision of the future. In every open system, there are evils that masquerade as individual choice. Toxic e-extremists want to destroy the social fabric and reweave it according to their own twisted visions. These anti-social elements are small compared to the larger fabric of the online universe, but they remain a significantly dangerous point on the axes of conformity.

Modernity's cultural conservatives: Their survival values

On balance what defines the modern culture of conformity? The conformist impulse always starts from a singular vantage point of looking back at the past with a nostalgic eye for inspiration and orientation. They believe that even though the past was not perfect, traditional ways are the only tried and tested road map for society – especially with the uncertainty and insecurity of the current age of globalization. Inglehart found that conformists are more likely to hold a number of what he calls "survival values."[30] These values typify many of the positions on the axes of conformity, and they are starkly at odds with the "self-expression values" that fall within the ordinals of the compass of dissent.

Conformists are more likely than dissenters to believe that father naturally knows best and a man has the ingrained qualities that make a better leader than a woman; also that a woman's preferred role and choice is to have children if she is to be fulfilled, and foreigners, homosexuals, and people with HIV/AIDS are high-risk groups and make bad neighbors. Conformists are also more likely to fall into older ways of reasoning about the defining importance of employment. They are likely to agree that hard work is one of the most important things to teach a child, that when jobs are scarce a man has more right to a job than a woman, and a university education is more important for a boy than a girl. Conformists are generally more reluctant to engage politically with other people in public. They are more likely not to have attended a meeting or signed a petition for a political cause. They believe in the need to be careful about trusting people. Overall, conformists seek predictability and security in traditional forms of gender inequality and a survivalist attitude to social relations. In seeking safety, they take refuge in a set of values that makes them feel paradoxically more vulnerable, and this feeds the conformist's mind-set and deepens her faith.

Not so long ago, the status quo used to be that governments prided themselves on their role as unifiers not dividers and their ability to speak for the nation, the national interest, and the good of the world in general. The Right has found that new technologies have expanded the possibility for identity and given new opportunities to spread the conformist message. Nevertheless, the way that new technologies have given a voice to the formerly marginalized toxic e-extremists has been counterproductive for many of the neo-conservative conformist movements trying to create mainstream cachet. After all, the conformist agenda has increasingly become a protest movement, much like that of dissent, but they are in the strange position of being a disloyal opposition. The hardline neo-conservative conformists are caught between the dissent movement and mainstream public policy. Even governments recognize that the status quo is no longer good enough. Their collective influence of rigid faith-based politics is being leached away to the centre Right, the undecided and waverers who are disillusioned by the war in Iraq, the perils of climate warming, and US-sanctioned torture. They have lost much ground to the growing effectiveness of the social movements on the compass of dissent.

Moral authority and dissent

Compared to a decade ago, the neo-liberal culture of conformity is increasingly embattled and on the defensive across the globe. Skeptics, contrarians, and whistleblowers of all kinds have a new legitimacy in a world in which conformity to the economic dogma used to be so pervasive. This confirms what social theorists have always recognized: societies need a system shock when political and economic arrangements become increasingly dysfunctional and when the rules of the game are no longer perceived by the majority as fair and even-handed. It needs a clear-cut course of action and requires a political theory to challenge conformist thinking about the possibilities of economic participation and social inclusion.

Such a theory has a necessarily pessimistic view of power. Publics have always recognized that power, if unchecked, corrupts its possessor. The relational power of publics is the power to disseminate one's ideas in ever widening political arenas. This form of power is only held vis-à-vis other activists and networks. In that particular regard it is the most decentralized sharing of power resources and is perhaps closest to resembling Nancy Fraser's concept of a public system of checks and balances, a necessary part of the process of creating alternatives. It is a maddeningly slow kind of political mobilization. Incremental change occurs through a thousand small victories (or defeats) by micro-activists at the local level and the periodic breakthroughs of transnational movements such as those that occurred at the iconic "battle in Seattle" or the signing of the international treaty outlawing landmines.

There are two phases to the big debate about "things public." The first phase, which has recently come to an end, considered whether the shrinking of the public domain worldwide was constitutive of a diminishment of democratic society. In this phase, disgruntled publics, dissenting activists, and skeptical public intellectuals won the day. Dissenters are now valuable political commentators, and their contribution adds depth to political debate. Ten years ago the currency of skeptical high-profile economists like Dani Rodrik of Harvard and Robert Hunter Wade of the London School of Economics traded at a lower level than it does today. Elites dismissed them as pessimistic gadflies who did not understand the new world order. Today, their intellectual transgression has been reinterpreted as prescient observation. Even the new conservatism is willing to embrace the non-conformist's impulse to interrogate received wisdom. In conversation with the philosopher Michel Onfray, Nicolas Sarkozy was eager to impress prospective French voters with his dissenter's credibility, stating "I believe in transgression . . . because freedom is transgression."[31] Dissent has become an essential counterpoint to the mainstream discourse of law, security, markets, and private accumulation.

The second phase, still underway, focuses on the global outcomes and possible local solutions available to democratic activists and global publics. Experts are now engaged with an in-depth analysis of the potential impacts and outcomes of the compass of dissent and the attempts by activists to "rally the public," in Michael Warner's apposite words.

Dissenters stand in sharp contrast to neo-liberal faith in the market's universalizing qualities. Nevertheless, no single group is in a position to control the public's agenda any longer. Economic determinism has had to surrender the middle ground in most jurisdictions. Normative ideas about economics and the role of the state have reappeared in public policy making. In virtual politics there is no single command and control center. The battle for public opinion is intense, fluid, and unpredictable. Gradually, the market excesses of the neo-liberal system have roused global publics from the cynicism of conformity to collective engagement. Infinite varieties of public discourse have not led to the fragmentation of politics, nor has this cacophony of voices become unintelligible to the informed listener. Dissenting publics have begun to exercise their reasoning ability and the result is a tsunami of ideas and options for fixing the relationship between publics, states, and markets. Who is listening? Everybody.

Notes

1. Theodore White, *The Making of the President: 1960* (New York: Houghton Mifflin, 1961). On the manipulative power of the executive office during the Clinton presidency, see the documentary film *The War Room*, directed by Chris Hegedus and D. A. Pennebaker (USA: McEttinger Films, 1994). See also, George Stephanopoulos, *All Too Human: A Political Education* (New York: Little Brown and Co., 1999).
2. John Micklethwait and Adrian Wooldridge, *The Right Nation: Conservative Power in America* (New York: Penguin Press, 2004).
3. Walter Benjamin, "Surrealism: The Last Snapshot of the European Intelligentsia" in *Iluminations* (New York: Harcourt Brace Jovanvich, 1978), p. 177.
4. For an examination of the politics and visual power of the iconography of dissent, see the Counterpublics Working Group reports, at www.yorku.ca/drache.

5. Eric Hobsbawm, *Age of Extremes: The Short Twentieth Century 1914–1991* (London: Michael Joseph, 1994).

6. Norberto Bobbio, *Left and Right: The Significance of Political Distinction* (London: Polity, 1996).

7. Philip Armstrong, Andrew Glyn, and John Harrison, *Capitalism Since 1945* (London: Basil Blackwell, 1991).

8. John Gray and David Willetts, *Is Conservatism Dead?* (London: Profile Books, 1997).

9. David Caute, *The Great Fear: The Anti-Communist Purge Under Truman and Eisenhower* (New York: Simon & Shuster, 1978).

10. Frank Furedi, *Where Have All the Intellectuals Gone?* 2nd edn (London: Continuum, 2006).

11. The World Social Forum is the best known global social movement with a number of transnational sites in Nairobi, India, and Porto Alegre. For information about the 2007 Nairobi meeting go to http://wsf2007.org/info/about.

12. Christine Newell, "A Working History of Médecins Sans Frontières: Changing the Face of Humanitarian Aid," Summer 2005, at www.med.uottawa.ca/medweb/hetenyi/newell.htm.

13. Seyla Benhabib, *The Rights of Others: Aliens, Residents and Citizens* (Cambridge: Cambridge University Press, 2004). Amnesty International is the most renowned trust and human security organization. See www.amnesty.org/.

14. The Canadian political theorist Charles Taylor has defined this field with his path-breaking work on the politics of recognition. See Charles Taylor, *The Politics of Recognition. Multiculturalism: Examining the Politics of Recognition*, ed. Amy Gutman (Princeton, N.J.: Princeton University Press, 1994), and "Democratic Exclusion (and its Remedies?)" in *Citizenship, Diversity and Pluralism: Canadian and Comparative Perspectives*, ed. Alain Cairns (Montreal: McGill-Queen's University Press, 1999).

15. A good example of this kind of thinking is Arjun Appadurai, *Fear of Small Numbers: An Essay on the Geography of Anger* (Durham, N.C.: Duke University Press, 2006). Jane Jacobs's work on cities and neighborhoods is rightly celebrated; Aihwa Ong, *Neoliberalism as Exception: Mutations in Citizenship and Sovereignty* (Durham, N.C.: Duke University Press, 2006).

16. Malcolm Gladwell, *The Tipping Point* (New York: Little, Brown and Company, 2000).

17. James Rosenau, "The Relocation of Authority in a Shrinking World," *Comparative Politics* 24:3 (April 1992), pp. 253–72.

18. Benjamin Barber, *Fear's Empire War: Terrorism and Democracy* (New York: Norton Publishers, 2003).
19. Michael Warner, *Publics and Counterpublics* (New York: Zone Books, 2000).
20. Scott Lucas, *The Betrayal of Dissent: Beyond Orwell, Hitchens and the New American Century* (London: Pluto Press, 2004).
21. One of the many writers from the "nixer" position is the highly regarded developmental economist, Susan George. See Susan George, *Another World Is Possible, If . . .* (London: Verso, 2004).
22. For the website of the United States Social Forum held June 27–July 1, 2007 in Atlanta, Georgia, go to www.ussf2007.org/.
23. James Rosenau, "Changing Capacities of Citizens, 1945–95" in *Issues in Global Governance: Papers Written for the Commission on Global Governance* (London: Kluwer Law International, 2003), pp. 1–58.
24. Ronald Inglehart and Christian Welzel, *Modernization, Cultural Change, and Democracy: The Human Development Sequence* (Cambridge, UK: Cambridge University Press, 2005). See in particular chapter 5, "Value Change Over Time," p. 122.
25. Neil Nevitte, *The Decline of Deference: Canadian Value Change in Comparative Perspective* (Peterborough, ON: Broadview Press, 1996).
26. John Micklethwait and Adrian Wooldridge, *The Right Nation: Conservative Power in America* (New York: Penguin Press, 2004), p. 13.
27. Ortega y Gasset, *The Revolt of the Masses* (London: Unwin, 1962, original edn 1930), p. 14.
28. Hal Niedzviecki, *Hello, I'm Special: How Individuality Became the New Conformity* (Toronto: Penguin Books, 2004), p. 9.
29. Quoted in Micklethwait and Wooldridge, *The Right Nation.* p. 13.
30. Inglehart and Welzel, *Modernization.* See in particular chapter 5, "Value Change Over Time."
31. Michael Onfray in conversation with Nicolas Sarkozy, *Philosophie Magazine* (Spring 2007).

5

Infinite Varieties of the Modern Public: Novelty, Surprise, and Uncertainty

Space, place and citizenship

The compass of dissent and the axes of conformity are the navigational devices that publics now use to chart their course over unfamiliar political terrain. New modes of communication have multiplied the dimensions of political action and made public policy much more complex. Political parties have to compete with global publics for airtime. Voters also have second thoughts about the old reflex of "blind voting" for the same party in every election. They are increasingly shopping their vote. But what has come of the great divide that separates right from left? The theological divides remain, but the middle is no longer a dead zone of swing voters and unengaged suburbanites. Arthur Schlesinger coined the term "the vital center" to describe the reformist spirit of grassroots centrism in American democracy.[1] A middle ground of public spiritedness and compromise was thought to be extinct; but the political culture of the amorphous "middle" has been reenergized with the possibility of meaningful engagement. Norberto Bobbio has identified a "composed middle" that draws on the fiscal responsibility mantra of the Right and the equality and inclusion ideas of the old Left.[2] The moderate middle may be courted by the Right and the Left, but it is also converting the old guard to a new form of populist modernism that all political parties strive to emulate. The surge of centrism goes a long way towards explaining the anti-market vote first discussed in chapter 2.

So what do we make of the public? When we speak of things public, do we mean many publics, counterpublics, and domains of the public, or is there only one public sphere to which we all belong? To speak of many publics has a fulsome ring of pluralism to it, but it also opens the door for critics to charge the unwary thinker with repackaging public choice theory. Rather than speaking of competition among many individuals, you are speaking of competition among many small groups, they will say. If we speak of the public as a single entity, we fall into the trap that many Marxists before us have fallen into. They subsumed all other projects under the command and control hegemony of the industrial proletariat. Today, Marx's vision of a monolithic, emancipatory public seems out of sync in a world that is increasingly fragmented and in which identity politics is on the rise.[3] So which is it – one public, several publics, or infinite varieties of "things public"?

Looking back over the previous two decades, it is clear that the rupture between pessimistic elites and expectant publics, who hoped that globalization would transform their lives for the better, was inevitable. It is hardly surprising that the apostles of neoliberalism obsessively fixate on the cost of the social bond – capitalists have complained about the burden of social inclusion since the first English aristocrat enclosed his fields and dispossessed his tenured workers. Economists have kept themselves at record levels of full employment by giving this venting credence.

Informed publics now see the priesthood of free-marketeers as advocating a particular ideology and policy template that has proven to be socially damaging and economically simplistic. This criticism has wounded the political establishment's pride in their capacity to alone have the sagacity needed to chart a course to economic prosperity. Just as elites in 1848 were stunned by workers rioting in the midst of plenty, so policy makers and bureaucrats in Washington, Geneva, and Brussels cannot understand what anti-globalization activists and picketing unions have to fear from free-market ideology.[4]

Focus on the supply side of the dismal science mandated that governments emphasize competitiveness, structural adjustment, export orientation, and tax breaks for businesses and entrepreneurs, not benefits for working citizens.[5] For all but a few of the most extreme xenophobes, the great fear is not of global interdependency and new forms of social and economic integration; it is fright at the excesses of corporate greed and the absence of responsible governance practices.[6] Since the divorce between publics and paternalistic experts, the explosion of innovative public agency has finally put to bed all notions that global publics only thrive when sheltered under state beneficence. Micro-activists and social movements have come a long way and now demand nothing less than equal partnership in the governance plans that are redrawing the lines of power in the international political economy. They demand devolution of power downwards and have the means to achieve it. The new activism, with its large and inclusive geography of dissent, has enormous consequences for national societies and the international system.

Diversity is always the rule, but . . .

In their agential aspect, modern defiant publics are the sum political power of many different people, whose only common goal is the public good. For sure, these people and groups are often working at odds with each other. One only has to think of the Taliban's understanding of the public good in Afghanistan and juxtapose it with the Bush administration's vision of the public good for the Middle East to see that no single group has a grasp on what is good for all of us. In fact, it is the sovereign responsibility of our elected representatives to wisely choose the best policies that will benefit most of us. Even more importantly, we count on them to implement other measures for those who are not helped and are perhaps hurt by the will of the many. Public agency has its clearest expression in democratic governance, but publics are increasingly aware that democracy is quite literally the rule of the majority, and this requires that citizens think carefully about the way their policy choices affect others both at home and abroad. It is necessary to follow the argument to the next step.

In its structural form, the spatial idea of the public is harder to grasp. Is it one domain or many? Public culture is a loosely related collection of local, regional, national, and transnational cultures. They are linked by shared memories and values. They have their own myths, heroes, villains, aspirations, and dreams and are rooted in local histories and lore.[7] Who, beyond the borders of Canada, knows the names of the rebels of Upper and Lower Canada who forced British colonial administration to develop a more responsible form of government? William Lyon Mackenzie and Louis-Hyppolite Lafontaine are public icons in a small sphere, just like thousands of other larger-than-life figures that populate the narratives of public memory.

Clearly, there are many different public domains at the national level, and they are organized and regulated according to the values and norms of their particular cultural context. They are sometimes larger, sometimes smaller. Sometimes they are inclusive and restorative of the social bond by universal education and poverty eradication, and sometimes they are exclusive, ceremonial, and authoritarian to cite only the dangerous use of war chauvinism.[8]

Will progressive states, activists, and social movements succeed in creating an inclusive domain for public interaction beyond the state? Quite possibly, the public domain beyond the state will be an inclusive global zone where an infinite number of individuals and groups will interact with each other despite their competing nationalisms. Yet as Kant foresaw, there is always danger in perpetual struggle towards an idealistic goal. World government would be what he termed 'soulless despotism' if it did away with the republics that give boundaries to the space of citizenship. It is not surprising then that the WTO's erosion of those boundaries and intrusive presence in domestic standard-setting has awakened a centuries-old fear that larger governance agglomerations will surely undermine rights and disenfranchise the most vulnerable.[9]

The private world of social preferment and global competition has a way of rewarding the fittest at the expense of the rest. The Hayekian vision of the market becomes too intrusive when private actors overtake the public interest and appropriate collective goods for private gain. Even so, national publics have never been simply creatures of the state. They arose in tandem with the sovereignist theories of the nation-state to be sure, but their genesis must be traced back to the rise of public reason, the gradual appearance of the sphere of interactive communication, and the efforts of activists and intellectuals. Nevertheless, modern public authority, with its arsenal of policy tools from monetary to social policy, must protect the social bond from corrosive pressures. It is of the utmost strategic importance that citizens in democratic societies wrap their minds around a single proposition: every society must take self-conscious measures to reinforce its public domain, whether in full-scale or piecemeal fashion.

Lineages of the modern public

For twenty-first century discerning publics the strategic questions are: what do we really know about the origins of the public domain, how can it be strengthened, and what lessons can we draw from history? In a rudimentary way the idea of a domain of public concern begins in antiquity. It emerged with the growth of cities, the delivery of early types of public goods, such as defense and food rationing, and the emergence of bureaucracy, the military, and the courts. In Lewis Mumford's words, the public emerged with

> the introduction of drains, piped drinking water, and water closets into the cities and palaces of Sumer, Crete, and Rome. Cities needed an infrastructure, roads, harbours, ports, and an administration to collect revenues, maintain order, and organize pageants and spectacles for the masses.[10]

The public was a terrain of strategic planning and engineering accomplishment. It was a practical and ingenious solution to the problems of urban densification in early settlement, much like today. It was at the center of daily life since antiquity where the formal world of politics and private interests were played out.

In his book *How to Make Things Public*, Bruno Latour asks "has the time not come to bring the *res* back to the *res publica*?"[11] The stuff of the *res publica* – "public matters", literally translated from the Latin – has never been in doubt. Things public have always been serious business for the engaged citizen because so much is at stake when we set out to develop the domain of the common good.

There is no consensus on the part of scholars about the precise origins of the boundary between public and private. Who first manned the frontier between the good of all and the privilege of the few? In Greek mythology, Prometheus is the great defender of the public; defying the gods to bring fire to humankind. In Judeo-Christian mythology, an angel with a flaming sword guards the gate to Eden and forces humanity to make common cause in suffering. Sociologists and anthropologists offer a more prosaic explanation. For Michael Mann and Charles Tilly the public interest can be traced to the need for increased public goods provision, particularly in times of war and insecurity.[12]

The military historian John Keegan reminds us that it was initially warfare and the aggressive cost of empire and not an incipient belief in welfare that built the public domain in most European countries. In the nineteenth century an effective fighting army required public authority to improve the health and living standards of the average conscript.[13] In England, parliamentary committees discovered that as much as a quarter of conscripts were too malnourished to fight for king and country.

Taxation was also initially a result of military adventurism. Income tax was introduced, in William Gladstone's words, "as an engine of gigantic power for national purpose." The rationale, he argued, was not to tax the undeserving rich, in order to use taxation to help the deserving poor.[14] But his contemporaries knew where the money for empire building actually went; the country had to pay for the glory of going to war, and this entailed massive public spending. In 1820 in the UK, 80 percent of government spending went to the military and soldiering, while only 10 percent was spent on civil society. Sixty years later, non-military spending such as on welfare and public goods had increased to a paltry 20 percent.[15]

In the passage from feudalism to capitalism, if we step back a moment and look at the dynamics of the way the public domain evolved, it is clear that the category of the public evolved through fits and starts. The entanglement of public interest and private markets was constantly in flux, and the emerging boundaries between them were inevitably contested. Earlier on, probably from the sixteenth century, the state was paradoxically a stabilizing force for societies because it reinforced class relations at the same time that it strengthened the very idea of society torn by conflict and held together by the forces of order. It is one of the great ironies of history that the egalitarian and inclusive public emerged from inauspicious beginnings in absolutism and the preening presumption of the new bourgeoisie.

In Europe, for much of the medieval and pre-modern period, there was no political language of the public good and no political culture or institutional space of the public interest in the modern sense. As Louis XIV indulgently stated, "L'État c'est moi." Public offices were bought and sold, and the landed aristocracy and upper classes, the avowed enemies of constitutional guarantees of social rights, relied on the rule of law to suppress communal interests. The modern idea of the liberal public as a freestanding and autonomous sphere began to emerge in Britain only with the closure of the commons in the seventeenth century and would take a century or more to complete its long and complex institutionalization.

Historians have shown how shifting agricultural production patterns ushered in a legal regime of private property and the abolishment of the principle of common land use.[16] The privatization of rural land placed new demographic pressures on cities, but urban public space remained restricted to the moneyed elite and later the emerging professional classes. Jürgen Habermas reminds us, in his magisterial study of the public domain, that anything we would recognize today as a robust public sphere emerged gradually and much later as part of the rule of law and the end of absolutism.[17] Fealty – loyalty to the clan, race, and family and faith – constricted the appearance of the public domain proper until the late eighteenth century. To be in the public was synonymous with bourgeois respectability, the rigid maintenance of law and order, service to the nation, and, above all, strict conformity to society's belief in sobriety and private property. So many groups, classes, and individuals were excluded from the formal world of debate and deliberation. This was hardly an auspicious beginning for our modern belief in the deliberative public sphere as a privileged place of interaction, political freedom, and citizenship.

The public domain took on a life of its own in the nineteenth century as part of the larger political project to enhance the security of elites and form a privileged site for the middle class. On the European continent, desperately needed urban reforms, such as roads and proper sanitation facilities, added public goods as a constituent part of the public in cities – although its autonomy was precarious and the spread of democratic rights of speech and assembly often in question because there was as yet no clearly articulated public interest nor legal idea of the citizen protected against the state and the private interest of property owners.

The classes without property were regarded as dangerous elements to be disciplined by the rule of law and kept in check by police magistrates. Citizenship was rudimentary and not yet a legal category with judicial clout. The authoritative idea and legacy of the French Revolution – that of "rule by the people" – would have momentous consequences on political thinking as it captured the imagination of working people across the globe. By the middle of the nineteenth century, traditional forms of being in public – the market and the fair – had been reinvented on a vast global scale, aptly called World's Fairs. The international public sphere was getting organized by the flows of ideas, people, money, and information.

The World's Fairs: new spaces of the public

We need to think a lot about this early forum of the cultural public sphere. World's Fairs were, in many ways, an antecedent to the communicative diversity that is the hallmark of online interaction today. These early attempts at the universal marketing of nationalist identities became conduits and catalysts for the movement of ideas and information worldwide. With the building of railways and improvements in national transportation systems, millions attended these showcases for the dominant ideas and novelties of the age. Between 1851 and 1900 there were over fifty World's Fairs, and the list of cities reads like Jules Vernes's *Around the World in Eighty Days*. Fairs were held in the leading cities of the day: London (1851), Paris (1855), and New York City (1853–4). They were also hosted by regional centers intent on capturing some of the cosmopolitan glamor of these events. Few remember today that World's Fairs took place in Vienna (1873), Philadelphia (1876), Calcutta (1883–4), and New Orleans (1884–5). For a brief period towards the end of the nineteenth century, there were so many cities wanting to participate that several were held in a single year. In 1897, for example, Brussels, Guatemala City, Nashville, and Stockholm all got into the act. The phenomenon lasted into the twentieth century with fairs held in Hanoi (1902), Christchurch (1906–7), and Nanking (1910).[18] Yet none of these exotic and far-flung locales rivaled the spectacle of the Parisian World's Fair.

The Exposition universelle that opened in Paris in 1889 was the most glamorous and the biggest of the World's Fairs at the end of the nineteenth century. France was at the apogee of its power and splendor, and Paris was the capital of wealth and fashion. The exposition was preceded by national industrial exhibitions and was dominated by French achievements in science, technology, education, culture, and fashion. Overseeing this extraordinary site was the massive presence of the Eiffel Tower constructed for the occasion. In London (1851), Paris (1867), and Brussels (1910), the fairs organized public expositions that introduced European publics to whole villages and peoples imported from the colonies. The scale was unprecedented – Paris had over 61,722 exhibits and paid attendance exceeded over 32 million. Chicago's World's Fair in 1893 was just as grand, attracting 27 million visitors and over 65,000 exhibitors.[19]

In the Victorian age of inter-capitalist rivalry, the fairs helped to establish and regulate the economic and political roles of different racial groups within and between countries.[20] At the 1867 World Exhibition, Victor Hugo issued his manifesto *To the Peoples of Europe*, a populist call to adopt a European identity. European people, many for the first time, confronted the cultural and linguistic diversity of the world beyond their nation-state. Importantly they came to experience mass consumption and the richness and splendor of imperial power. These "sites of pilgrimages to the commodity fetish" were not, wrote Walter Benjamin in "Grandville, or the World Exhibitions," designed to promote social justice or expand political rights.[21] They were ceremonial and celebratory spaces in which global flows of information and culture had a massive impact upon public culture. Not surprisingly the World's Fairs showcased the unbelievable trappings of material culture and ostentatious metropolitan wealth. They served another purpose, as they hid from public view the darker side of nineteenth-century public life – its repressive system of state security.

Exclusion in public

The social exclusion of millions trapped in crushing urban poverty provided a stark and constant reminder to the nine-teenth-century citizen that a public domain with rights and oblig-ations for all was a phantom. Britain, the world's leading power, provided a kind of ideational template for the emergence of an informed and properly political public in the Anglo-American world. It included a limited franchise, public parks and museums to uplift the masses, public housing, a highly constrained practice of freedom of speech, a reasonably unconstrained press, and few rights for labor unions. Freedom of association, practical liberty, and the most essential right for the working class, its collec-tive freedom to full industrial citizenship, were decades away.

Women's enfranchisement would not be complete for another long century. Instead, freedom of contract and the full panoply of social entitlements this guaranteed for the wealthy and powerful were doggedly protected by the wilful and coercive authority of the state. The place of the public in the world's pre-eminent liberal democracy continued to be small and overshadowed by the role of religious authority, the power of the monarchy, and the aristocracy. It is important to recall that in the nineteenth century, according to Roy Jenkins, half of the British Cabinet was drawn from the privileged worlds of "squierarchy and hierarchy."[22] Parliament, the much vaunted institution of British democracy, was at that time unlike anything we are familiar with today. In the mid-1860s, Parliament met sporadically and often at night out of the public's eye.

This excursion into the past is needed to establish a fundamental point about the dysfunctionality of a state top-down public sphere: limited access to public life frequently impoverished diversity in the public domain. It was a realm of vaguely and poorly defined freedom for some because the law was a potent instrument of exclusion. It is telling that in England Catholics could not hold public service jobs and Jews were effectively excluded from public life because they could not take the state and church oath if elected to Parliament. First elected in 1847, Lionel de Rothschild was elected repeatedly but faced a Parliament that refused to change the oath of office. He would have to wait until 1858 to take his seat as the first Jewish member of Parliament. While anti-Semitism operated as a high-power filter, which allowed only a few Jews to enter public life, atheists fared much worse. Charles Bradlaugh, the first atheist to be elected, was expelled from the House of Commons four times and only managed to take a seat after a decade-long battle in the 1880s.

Even education was not a public good in abundance in most countries till the end of the nineteenth century, awaiting Bismarckian reforms on the continent and the populist idea of universal education in the US before emerging as a public right and entitlement. In his magisterial biography of British prime minister William Gladstone, Roy Jenkins recounts that in the 1880s a public good such as education was available to the privileged few. Only a minority of school-age children attended state schools, and it is likely that one in three children were not schooled at all.[23] In terms of civil rights, magistrates' bills gave the police the power to arrest, detain, and imprison Irish dissidents without a hearing or anything resembling due process.[24] Few rights were guaranteed by law, and the vast majority of people were little more than subjects to be commanded and ordered about in the workplace and conscripted into the king's armies.

Was there a singular hinge moment that had enormous after-effects on the culture of dissent and enhanced the boundaries of public activism and transferred power away from the Leviathan state? It is not evident without considering the enormous contribution of the Chartists of the 1840s and how they perfected a new form of speech that historians have called "crowd activism."[25] They used the simple, flatbed printing press to rally tens of thousands through handbills and word of mouth. Word traveled fast, and these mass assemblies became a fixed and destabilizing feature of British and French politics. The art of appealing directly to the masses went far beyond the limited franchise. Their mass agitation marked a rupture with the top-down state-constructed world of the public. John Plotz argues convincingly that "Chartism laid down a pattern that virtually all American and Western European crowd activism was to follow."[26] Even by modern standards of public activism, the diversity, scale, and level of organization of the Chartists represented a high-water mark in public dissent that was not again equaled in intensity and importance until the anti-war days of rage and revolution in 1968.

The Prague Spring, the March on Washington, and Martin Luther King's "I have a dream" speech, the mass strikes in Paris in 1968, and the release of Nelson Mandela from an apartheid prison were all moments, burned into our collective memories, when acts of citizenship took on global dimensions.[27] The definitive protest song, Crosby, Stills, Nash, and Young's "Ohio," which memorialized the Kent State University shootings, has been burned into the memories of the baby boom generation:

> Gotta get down to it, soldiers are cutting us down. Should have been done long ago.
> What if you knew her and found her dead on the ground?
> How can you run when you know?[28]

Today, in a period framed by global neo-liberalism and the highly intrusive policies of the WTO the terms "public" and "citizenship" may seem to be highly ambiguous and drained of social context. Modern industrial societies are neither fully democratic nor inclusive to the extent that publics expect them to be. Nevertheless, as Hannah Arendt correctly noted, the "sharing of words and deeds" necessary for "unforced deliberation amongst diverse equals" is more of an immanent possibility today than at other times in the past.[29] When the public domain is most robust, it makes human security, strong democracy, and social diversity possible. When it is weak and ineffective, society pays in the hard currency of unilateralism, crude rent-seeking, and economic exclusion. Here is the basic truth of why the public domain's boundaries are never fixed but are shaped by the changing balance of power between social actors.

New power dynamics of the citizen

In the virtual space of the digital communicative sphere, the micro-activist finds herself in a situation where the political and ideational aspects of citizenship may be fully developed, while territorial responsibilities remain rooted at the state level. Is there a parallel to be drawn between the role played by state authority in the consolidation of "things public" and the role played by global governance in the development of the public domain beyond the state? At the international level, in place of the singular authority of the state, we see the technocratic authority of multilateral institutionalism. Obviously the parallel is only partial, and not surprisingly, the public domain beyond the state is not fully articulated, nor properly mapped.

Protection of the individual is frequently more theoretical than real, and the powerful continue to oppress the weak, even though the Internet has significantly curtailed their ability to do it behind the backs of activist publics. Furthermore, publicly-minded states continue to strengthen the mechanisms that protect and support the public domain, and governmental interventions into the formerly Hobbesian frame are striking in their breadth and depth. What is then required for the international subject to become a citizen beyond the state? It is what Arendt has called a guarantee of the right to have rights, a concept she first articulated in the aftermath of the Nuremberg Trials.

Writing in 1951 about the Holocaust and its implications for the emerging idea of fundamental human rights, Arendt says that:

> we have become aware of the existence of *a right to have rights* (and that means to live in a framework in which one is judged by one's actions and opinions) and a right to belong to some kind of organized community, only when millions of people emerge who had lost and could not regain these rights because of the new global political situation.

In a very immediate way, the horrors of Nazi slaughter brought home the realization for publics and policy makers that people deprived of rights "are deprived not of the right to freedom, but of the right to action; not of the right to think whatever they please, but of the right to opinion . . ."[30] The digital subject, a truncated citizen in its own right, at the international level has the right to action and opinion by virtue of the bias of communication. It remains, however, for a higher authority to recognize these rights and guarantee them so that they apply evenly for the affluent and the poor alike.

One example of the institutionalization of the guarantee to rights can be seen in the postwar development of a human rights regime. In ethical terms, ethnic cleansing has always been a repugnant, despicable, and cowardly solution to ethnic tension, but instrumentally rational despots consider it alongside other policy options because of its sheer finality of outcome. Today, it is an evil that only the most deranged and psychotically unhinged leaders dare contemplate. Why is this? It is not, as is usually argued, because the horror of the Holocaust galvanized public opinion against other atrocities. Memories fade. But today, genocidal politics are continuously exposed to public condemnation and the hateful face of ethnic violence is everywhere recognized as the ultimate form of inhuman nihilism.

We are not so naive as to imagine that the public can always be roused to righteous indignation in time to save the victims. Rwanda taught us the terrible cost of lethargy.[31] Nevertheless, since the end of the Second World War, internationally-minded states have initiated twenty-nine major multilateral agreements that extend the rights of the individual into the public domain beyond the state, mostly through the multilateral mechanisms available at the United Nations (see appendix). They include the Universal Declaration on Human Rights, the Convention against Torture, the International Covenants on Civil and Political Rights, and a number of conventions protecting the rights of women and children, just to name a few.

The institutionalization of authority beyond the state remains weak and incomplete. This is an observation that is true of the world's leading international financial institutions such as the World Bank and IMF, no less so than the socially progressive programs of the United Nations. Tragically, the UN is still not the force for good governance that its postwar architects hoped it would be. Powerful and self-interested states continue to flout its principles and resent its moral authority. Until such time as public authority is more concretely extended upwards into the international realm, the public domain beyond the state will be contingent upon the ongoing efforts of activists and progressively-minded governments to defend and extend it.

Whether they are aware of it or not, activists today are the inheritors of the Arendtian ethos most clearly stated when she wrote that "the right of every individual to belong to humanity should be guaranteed by humanity itself."[32] More than fifty years later, the gadflies, dissenters, and noisy agitators loudly proclaim the right to have rights and the public imperative to defend the realm of communicative action beyond the state. And so we have come full circle. Informed, articulate, and activated publics wrested governance prerogatives from the powerful class interests of nation-state in the eighteenth and nineteenth centuries and may well do the same to the international system in the future.

There is no logical reason that the relational power of activists and networks must work at cross-purposes with the structural power of states. There was always a push-pull dynamic at work between activists and public authority to be sure, but a vibrant and inclusive public domain at the national level would have been unsustainable if it was not eventually supported and nurtured by public authority. Affordable housing in the urban core and the provision of basic urban necessities such as clean water have always been provided by organized authority. The paradox has always been that governments sought to create a top-down public domain of regulated space, but with the expansion of the communicative sphere they have had to invest in public discourse and the freedoms of speech and association. Put in the starkest possible terms, the public domain is the product of both the structural power of public authority and the relational power of rabble-rousers, radicals, and educated dissenters. What is the contemporary importance of this analytical truth?

Three models of citizenship beyond the state

It used to be that globalization was measured by the exponential growth of world trade and the technological leap of the digital revolution. In a century or more, historians will also measure twenty-first century interdependence by the metrics of the Great Reversal. Hierarchical authority, centralization, and what Inglehart refers to as "bigness" are under increasing strain, burdened by the mistrust of the multitude. These sentinels of extreme economism "have reached a point of diminishing effectiveness and diminishing acceptability."

The public shift is underlined by a move away from traditional state authority and the new radical powers of the market – what Inglehart calls a shift from "scarcity values" to "security values." [33] Even so, contemporary public life is an entanglement of public and private interests. The strategic notion of the public domain as a critical space of ideational competition and collective action requires, above all, greater clarification and a more precise benchmarking of its effect upon democratic public life.

The era of global monetarism has lasted only half as long as the golden age of the Keynesian welfare state. Its fate was sealed when global publics lost confidence in elites who promised that stringency and self-help would release the market from its bonds and create unprecedented prosperity. Transnational networks rooted in the local open the possibility of new varieties of citizenship by enhancing the importance of recognition. They reveal the public as a sphere of unplanned encounter, fluid sociability among strangers, and multi-stranded public life. [34] For the foreseeable future, there are three divergent and often competing models of citizenship on offer in the global realm.

The first is the Anglo-Republican model of citizen participation. It has been aggressively promoted by the US trade representative and British and American regulators who believe that the global citizen is essentially an Anglo-American prototype of the international entrepreneur. His basic rights are guaranteed by his national passport and his standing in a national community. The other substantive entitlements he enjoys are rooted in his economic rights and the WTO's regulatory model of global governance that Michael Trebilcock has termed "negative integration." [35] Negative integration is a form of economic governance that outlines the actions that economic actors may not take. It focuses on the "thou shalt not" side of governance and remains silent about the obligation owed by economic actors to the international system. Its minimalist approach to rule making leaves a very small window of opportunity for developing substantively inclusive institutions beyond the state.

Proponents of this form of citizenship had hoped that the WTO would become a sort of economic constitution for the world. It would fulfill the same basic role that the American constitution did for the thirteen original colonies – namely laying out the basic rules for a free-market economy. Thinkers in this vein tend to believe that citizenship beyond the state can only be guaranteed by a global constitution; until such a time as the world is ready for a common set of rules, state power must stand in the place of a constitutional order. Nothing more clearly illustrates this perspective than the current issue of reform at the WTO. Its architects, rather than creating a trade organization that would deal with the substance of trade challenges, such as labor standards, created an institution that engages only with narrow legalistic issues and develops the barest framework necessary for a stable order.

Proponents of this citizenship model assume, like James Madison and the rest of the American founding fathers, that the countervailing power of liberal economic actors is the only guarantor of political freedom. The global provision of public goods, intergenerational responsibility for the environment, and the eradication of extreme poverty and illiteracy remain off its radar screen because these are challenges faced by the poor and the default template of the global citizen is a person of economic means. This model has a very weak redistributional impulse because it thrives on status quo stability, rather than innovation and the championship of change. In this worldview, the citizen is the working out of a Tocquevillian figure of voluntary association and rational individualism; he is an individual driven by economic self-interest, not collective need.

The second model of citizenship beyond the state is that which takes as its basis the European-Federalist model of governance integration. In essence, the European model advocates the construction of a new level of political authority, formally rooted in state sovereignty, and based loosely on a federal model of governance that is qualitatively more similar to the national governments of Canada and Germany than the United States, because they have very strong subnational governments which are bound together by a high-wage, high-tax, high-skill approach to citizenship and economic management. They believe that federal community is rooted in investment in the social bond. This model of a social market rests on the assumption that political integration, what experts call 'positive political integration', creates new linkages between people and territories, and these provide a stage upon which citizens may exercise their political rights. The different levels of federal authority – regional, subnational, national, and maybe even global – guarantee citizenship rights through an institutional arrangement of judicial and administrative checks and balances and international public law.

This is a progressive and analytically audacious vision of global citizenship, and its architects are convinced that it can be broadened to include a number of developing countries. In the European-Federalist model, the complex interdependencies of the market need to be managed, and market relations need to be rendered open and visible just as the activities of government bureaucracies need to be scrutinized and made transparent. It advocates a centralization of political authority that makes it possible to guarantee certain rights through governmental machinery located in Brussels, rather than London, Paris, Berlin, or Prague.

This model is intensely process-driven, and corporatist consultation is the primary mechanism by which governance change takes place.[36] It is a model in which everyone involved has a say in the outcomes, in theory, but experts point out that the flaw in European process-driven integration is that powerful business elites dominate the administrative and legislative system. Like the Anglo-Republican model, access to economic resources tend to play a significant role in who gets what, and the citizen is understood to operate in an arena of public choice.

The biggest difference between the two models is that the European citizen is far-sighted enough to see that political integration is a better guarantor of rights than is the power of the state on its own because state power has a way of waxing and waning, as the history of Europe has shown. The clearest expression of the European-Federalist model of citizenship is public space that is highly contested and social activists who are constantly multiplying their efforts to claim a larger share of federal resources for their public-interest projects. They are persistently pushing the envelope to build public domain networks from below.

The third model of citizenship that is being developed and articulated is the Developmental model of public citizenship. This template of the public is embedded in the Arendtian principle of the right to have rights. Citizenship rights are guaranteed for every person by every person; citizenship is not earned or deserved because of who you are, what you possess, or your status as a smart economic actor but instead is bestowed by virtue of common humanity. Political philosophers and policy elites alike are wary of the implications of this form of citizenship because it requires a radical rethinking of what it means to recognize another person in public, and it sets a high bar for the social responsibilities required of all of us. It would require a massive global redistribution of wealth because much of the global north's economic muscle comes from an inequitable relationship to developing countries, which have been left in a dependent position of low value-added production and service provision.

This model of citizenship is not yet fully defined or articulated and is a work in progress. But it is being developed nevertheless persistently and patiently in piecemeal fashion in the thickening bed of international institutions that are clustered around the United Nations. The developmental public is popular in the global south, where there is little prospect for a European Union style of integration because economies are not stable enough, and there are too few shared values to justify such an intrusive form of political integration. Many countries in Latin America, Africa, and Asia have been skeptical of the Anglo-Republican model of citizenship rooted in economic integration. Liberal citizenship, idealized in American political life, based on the self-starting individual is far removed from the reality of the street, the bazaar, or even the process of nation building – all of which encompass what it means to be in public in the global south.

Publics in the global south need a vocabulary and vision for protecting and expanding the public domain. They need to reconcile many different definitions of the public good and interests held in common.[37] The WTO negotiations have proven conclusively that the Anglo-Republican form of citizenship is actually corrosive for fragile and emergent forms of citizenship in the global south because it is only guaranteed by the hard power of economic superiority. The Anglo-Republican belief that the wealth of the few guarantees the rights of the many sticks in the throat of small nations who depend on American markets for their global trade, but have little say in the way that the multilateral trading system operates.

In 2000 the United Nations recognized the pressing importance of putting in place an institutional frame to address the negative externalities of economic globalization. The Millennium Development Goals are a prime example of the way in which the Developmental public builds support and cements its legitimacy amongst its many members.[38] It is well recognized by neo-conservatives and liberal reformers alike that the United Nations system is troubled and faces large hurdles in the near future. Its legitimacy rests on the fact that it is by far the most inclusive system ever created at the global level. This leaves it vulnerable from within to politicians who would undermine it, whether they are from the Bush administration or the regime of Iran's President Mahmoud Ahmadinejad. Also, its outdated processes leave it vulnerable to insider cronyism because too few states outside the G8 in the north and G24 in the south have actually mastered its diplomatic and bureaucratic complexities. But these are not reasons to weaken it further. Rather, our concern with higher order issues of institutional effectiveness suggests that the United Nations experiment has been a partial success. The job now is to retool and strengthen the mechanisms of democratic participation to make them more responsible, accountable, and transparent.

The main drawback of this model is that it rests exclusively on a Westphalian assumption of state sovereignty and therefore accords only states the prestige of full citizenship. This model has not yet fully developed an understanding of global citizenship that extends to the individual, although the growth and evolution of human rights law and the International Criminal Court are transformative movements in the right direction. The strength of this model draws from the fact that it is based on the formal equality of all nations and gives their publics equal status under international law. Pluralism and diversity are necessary prerequisites to the development of a public domain that is both open and inclusive at the global level. Addressing these challenges is part of the normal development process that slows the emergence of a sphere of global publicness. To remove them is to accelerate its progress.

Infinite varieties of the public

Leaders across the globe are beginning to realize that markets can thrive in the context of uniquely public purpose. With the slow and torturous collapse of the Doha round negotiations, there will be no forward progress in global trade liberalism, at least not for the near future. The wave of privatizations and deregulation that defined global liberalism has crested and largely subsided. This and other events have finalized the divorce between restive publics and paternalistic experts. European Union ministers are beginning to see the need to get the right balance between the public and private in the modern mixed economy. People need security, and competition is no longer the single imperative of economic policy. This major course correction by the largest trading bloc in the world will not change the direction of the EU overnight, but it is an unprecedented retreat for global neo-liberalism. It sends an unmistakable message to global publics that they do make a difference.

Ours are still pyramid societies, tiny at the apex and held together at the bottom by Hyekian economic discipline, control, threat, socialization, and the legal power vested in the dominant classes and the state. And yet due to the bias of communication, there is such a tremendous amount of power that is being concentrated and consolidated at the bottom of the pyramid that politicians are unsure if they should champion it or work to contain the threat of instability.

Text and images have always framed political activism with their timeless messages of anger, defiance, and social justice. Organized publics target the public mind while working to create new kinds of knowledge about political thought, morality, art, literature, and politics. Modern insurgent publics have never played by the rules. They are intent on establishing different rules for private actors. Ultimately the future emancipatory potential of the public is found in the threads that bind together disparate activity in the global public domain.

Like Camus's Rebel, the activist draws the line and takes her stand by declaring, "this far, and no farther will I be commanded." The digital connection is her lifeline and her line in the sand. A strong and democratic public domain is fundamental to the creation of a good life. Markets are a means to an end in the service of human society, and without the collective human good to guide them, they become weapons wielded by the powerful in the service of particularistic values and avarice. The financial disasters of Enron and World.com and the military disaster in Iraq seem to fit a common theme in the public imagination. In recent history the system of global capitalism designed for social stability has been undermined by the greed of powerful executives and war profiteers. Of course corruption is not new to capitalism; the capitalist walks a thin line between earnings and fraud.

This is the logical outcome of investors driven by the business cycle and where information is always imperfect. Citizens are perhaps not cynical about capitalism so much as they are skeptical about the claim of elites that they act in the public good. This yawning gap between economic goals and social outcomes increasingly marks global capitalism at the turn of the twenty-first century. For a half a century the Keynesian welfare state has raised public expectations about reconciling efficiency and equality. The decline of deference of the Internet age allows anyone with a modem to challenge political authority. Activists now attack the hypocrisy of the political elites and "the bloodless moralism" of American realism. Therefore, the credo of the activist, network, and social movement

is not only the slave against the master, but also man against the world of master and slave . . . Thanks to rebellion, there is something more in history than the relation between mastery and servitude. Unlimited power is not the only law.[39]

Public spaces are being created in the most unlikely places – in the mall, on the Internet, and in the millions of chance encounters in everyday life between anonymous strangers. The circle of public life seems to get larger and more complex. Infinite varieties of the public are already imagining larger and bolder changes for the international system and the global economy. Authoritarians and paternalistic politicians are justifiably frightened of the new and sophisticated forms of defiance coming up from below. The bottom of the pyramid has always been populated by "dangerous classes," who are not, in the minds of the elite, capable or trustworthy governors of their own destinies. But when communicative power is backed by political will, the reallocation of power downwards is not only possible, it is inevitable.

A Habermasian or Foucaultian public sphere?

The reallocation of power that comes with technological change is hardly a new phenomenon, but its dynamics are of singular importance to grasp. It is the case that power is always in flux, and its upward movement has vested vast power in the global corporation. With each crisis since the early 1980s, global capitalism has been able to extend its influence behind and beyond the nation-state. It is more invasive and its norm-setting capacity has utilized institutions like the WTO to enhance global governance to promote the corporate agenda. But its downward devolution is both a remarkable and persistent feature of modernity. Pessimists conveniently overlook that the industrial revolution brought with it a series of transformative social changes that culminated in the revolutions of 1848. Similarly, scientific revolutions of the twentieth century, including the invention of the birth control pill, fundamentally reorganized the power dynamics of society, freeing women from patriarchal reproductive dynamics and fueling the dissent movement of 1968. System and structure had to bend to accommodate new realities as needed.

Today, the digital communications revolution is also changing the social landscape, with the power to free millions of people from the marginalization that comes from having no voice in global affairs. These three major transfers of power, from market to state, from men to women, and from transnational elites to the global citizen, share a common theme. They have been the great levelers of class relations in the twentieth century and have redefined the power dynamics between agency and structure. None of this has occurred in the way that Marxians had hoped for. Nor does this vision conform to Foucault's complex vision of society completely dominated by disciplinary neo-liberalism. The post-structural lens has not been able to account for vibrant powerful and ultimately effective defiant global publics and the unprecedented reach of the global citizen.

In a post-9/11 world, the margin is filling up once again with the multitudes from the global south, and everywhere the political center is crowded with articulate and angry skeptics and contrarians. The bleak assessments of journalists like Naomi Klein in *The Shock Doctrine* warn us about the ways the amoral system of capitalism can be used to enrich the few at the expense of the many and provide intellectual ammunition for diverse social movements.[40] Micro-activism has exploded as a global phenomenon, and the great reversal of our age is that the list of what is shared in common is no longer shrinking. The pessimism of the neo-liberal age is challenged by the skepticism of dissenting publics and rebellious activists. In its place grows the cautious optimism of reasonable people who have begun to define for themselves the limits of liberalization and the steps required to protect the social bond from the tyranny of markets.

Democracies have the unique ability to reason publicly about which course to take in a period of crisis and change. This has meant that revolution is not the necessary end point to volatile global business cycles. Marx argued that capitalism renews itself through a flushing of the system. Similarly the networked global society has begun to regulate not only markets at home but around the world. Globalization as envisaged by neo-liberal economists frees people and capital to seek greater investment returns in foreign markets and this has unleashed an unprecedented cycle of wealth creation in the last twenty years, the likes of which has not been seen since the nineteenth century. With the globalization of wealth has come the globalization of poverty and inequality on all continents. The massive gulf between the richest and the poorest and the insouciant way elites have responded have fueled first worry and then anger in defiant publics.

Economic historians point to the relevance of other periods of globalization to have a perspective on our own times. After massive rent taking and wealth creation of elites and financial markets what comes next? The period up to the 1860s, the period before the First World War and after the Second World War each gave birth to an expansion of democratic rights at home and international law abroad. Of course the institutional weaknesses of the international order also triggered catastrophic crises. In one sense Marx was right. Periods of capitalist expansion are ultimately destructive of many things that have come before. As Schumpter has astutely noted, periods of instability are also periods of great political innovation as governments and publics fight over the best way to tame globalization. The fundamental tensions in democratic society of our era are between the compromise that crafted the status quo and the risks and rewards of leveling the hierarchy of command and control present in every society.

Fate, choice and the fully realized citizen

The agency and voice facilitated by Innisian power dynamics have fueled new citizenship practices. The democratization of political voice gives global publics the power to change state policy in fundamental ways. Habermas's idea was that citizens can change state policy through acts of assembly. "No one, as Habermas says so eloquently, can be brought to apply the results of a decision if he has not participated in the discussion that led to the decision."[41] Before the Internet era, he thought that this had to happen through face-to-face interaction. Today, digital technology has facilitated this process in a radical and decentralized way, and communities of unprecedented influence and reach are formed online. The Washington Consensus prioritized system and structure as the key drivers of public policy; Internet, satellite communications, cellular phones, text messaging, and even radio and television have turned conventional wisdom on its head. The global cultural economy is instrumental in shaping the fully realized citizen, rooted in the local, but deeply interested in, and able to influence, global issues and events by forming active communities of choice rather than disinterested communities of fate.

To be a social actor today, one needs to be patched into the worldwide digital communications network. Do-it-yourself techno-gurus, bloggers, musicians, writers, public intellectuals, social movements, counterculture activists, and even knowledge caretakers such as universities, archives, and museums contribute new ideas about what it means to be a citizen in the transnational cultural context. Benedict Anderson has argued that in the nineteenth century, print capitalism created the modern citizen and nationalism as the mainstays of the nation-state. In the twenty-first century, the most novel idea is this: hypertext is recreating the modern concept of citizenship through access to new collective identities and new ways of understanding the relationship between local and global.

Who then is going to rule the future? The bareness of liberal realism? The far Right trinity of god, family, and nation? The agential power of innovative disgruntled global publics? Global cosmo-populism? In the chaotic divorce between the economic triumphalism of elites and the activism of engaged, disgruntled global publics, what other massive transformative changes are gathering and already on the way? The times are indeed strange; be ready for anything; don't try to make things up.

Notes

1. Arthur Schlesinger Jr, *The Vital Center: The Politics of Freedom* (Cambridge, Mass.: The Riverside Press, 1962).
2. Norberto Bobbio, *Left and Right: The Significance of Political Distinction* (London: Polity,1996).
3. Zygmunt Bauman, *Globalization: The Human Consequences* (Cambridge: Polity, 1998), see chapter 5, "Global Law, Local Orders."
4. Dani Rodrick, "Goodbye Washington Consensus, Hello Washington Confusion?" *Journal of Economic Literature* (forthcoming, 2008).
5. Albert O. Hirschman, *The Rhetoric of Reaction: Perversity, Futility, Jeopardy* (Cambridge, Mass.: Harvard University Press, 1991).
6. For the survey by the German Marshall Fund, see Alan Beattie, "Job Worries Damp Public Support for Globalization," *Financial Times*, December 2006.
7. Charles Taylor, "Modern Social Imaginaries," *Public Culture* 14:1 (2002), pp. 91–124.
8. Bauman, *Globalization*.
9. Emmanuel Kant, *Perpetual Peace: First Supplement*, 1794, at www.constitution.org/kant/1stsup.htm; John Raulston Saul, *The Collapse of Globalism and the Reinvention of the World* (Toronto: Penguin, 2005).
10. Lewis Mumford, *The City in History: Its Origins, Its Transformation and Its Prospects* (New York: Harcourt Brace, 1961).
11. Bruno Latour, "Introduction: From Realpolitik to Dingopolitik or How to Make Things Public" in *Making Things Public – Atmospheres*

of Democracy, ed. Bruno Latour and Peter Weibel (Cambridge, Mass.: MIT Press, 2005), p. 24.

12. Michael Mann, *The Sources of Social Power, Vol. I: A History of Power From the Beginning to AD 1760* (Cambridge, UK: Cambridge University Press, 1986) and *The Sources of Social Power, Vol II: The Rise of Classes and Nation-States 1760–1914* (Cambridge,UK: Cambridge University Press, 1993); Charles Tilly, *Coercion, Capital and European States, AD 990–1990* (Cambridge, Mass.: Oxford: Basil Blackwell, 1990).

13. John Keegan, *The First World War* (Toronto: Vintage Canada, 2000).

14. Roy Jenkins, *Gladstone: A Biography* (London: Macmillan, 1995), p. 280.

15. Jenkins, *Gladstone*, p. 67.

16. James Boyle, "Foreword: The Public Domain the Opposite of Property?" *Law and Contemporary Problems Special Issue on the Public Domain* 66:1(Winter/Spring 2003), pp. 1–32.

17. Jürgen Habermas, *The Transformation of the Public Sphere: An Inquiry into a Category of Bourgeois Society* (Cambridge, Mass.: MIT Press,1989).

18. A fascinating full list of nineteenth-century cities that were part of the World's Fairs phenomenon is available at http://xroads.virginia.edu/~MA96/WCE/worlds_fairs.html.

19. The social impact of the Chicago World's Fair is explored in Erik Larson's stunning novel *The Devil in the White City: Murder, Magic, Madness at the Fair that Changed America* (New York: Vintage, 2003).

20. Robert Rydell and Nancy E. Gwinns, eds, *Fair Representations: World's Fairs and the Modern World* (Amsterdam: VU University Press, 1994).

21. Walter Benjamin, *Reflections* (New York: Harcourt Brace Jovanovish, 1978), pp. 151, 153.

22. Jenkins, *Gladstone*.

23. Jenkins, *Gladstone*, p. 322.

24. Jenkins, *Gladstone*.

25. George Rudé, *The Crowd in History: Study of Popular Disturbances in France and England, 1730–1848* (London: John Whiley & Sons, 1964).

26. John Plotz, *The Crowd: British Literature and Public Policies* (Berkeley, Calif.: University of California Press, 2000), p. 130.

27. Eric Hobsbawm, ed., *1968 Magnum Throughout the World* (Paris: editions Hazan, 1998). See digital reports on the politics of dissent from the counterpublics working group accessed at www.yorku.ca/drache.

28. Neil Young (lyrics), "Ohio," Atlantic Records, 1970.
29. Quoted in Dana R. Villa, "Post-Modernism and the Public Sphere," *American Political Science Review* 86:3 (September 1992), pp. 712–21.
30. Hannah Arendt quoted in Seyla Benhabib, *The Rights of Others: Aliens, Residents and Citizens* (Cambridge, UK: Cambridge University Press, 2004), p. 55.
31. Romeo Dallaire, Brent Beardsley, Samantha Power, *Shake Hands with the Devil: The Failure of Humanity in Rwanda* (Toronto: Penguin Books, 2004).
32. Arendt in Benhabib, *The Rights of Others*, p. 55.
33. Ronald Inglehardt, "Changing Values, Economic Development and Political Change", *International Social Science Journal*, 47, (1995) pp. 653–403.
34. Jane Jacobs, *The Death and Life of American Cities* (New York: Vintage, 1961); Jeff Weintraub and Krishan Kumar, eds, *Public and Private Thought in Practice: Perspectives on a Grand Dichotomy* (Chicago, Ill.: University of Chicago Press, 1997), p. 17.
35. Michael Trebilcock, *Trade Liberalization, Regulatory Diversity and Political Sovereignty* (Toronto: University of Toronto Press, 2002); Geoffrey Underhill, "States, Markets and Governance for Emerging Market Economies: Private Interests, the Public Good and the Legitimacy of the Development Process," *International Affairs* 79:4 (2003), pp. 755–81.
36. John Gerard Ruggie, "Reconstituting the Global Public Domain: Issues Actors and Practices," *European Journal of International Relations* (2004), pp. 499–531; William Wallace and Julie Smith, "Democracy or Technocracy? European Integration and the Problem of Popular Consent", *West European Politics* (1995), pp. 137–57.
37. Sarai Reader 2001:The Public Domain, at www.sarai.net/publications/readers/01-the-public (2001).
38. The 2000 Millennium Development Goals and Declaration are available at www.un.org/millenniumgoals/goals.html#.
39. Albert Camus, *The Rebel: An Essay on Man in Revolt*, originally published 1951 (New York: Alfred A. Knopf, 1956, reprinted 1961), p. 284.
40. Naomi Klein, *The Shock Doctrine: The Rise of Disaster Capitalism* (New York: Metropolitan Books, 2007).
41. Quoted in Bruno Latour, *The Politics of Nature* (Cambridge, Mass.: Harvard University Press, 2004), p. 171.

Appendix: Critical Human Rights Conventions of the Global Public Domain

June 1945 Charter of the United Nations
Details the institutional structure and purposes of the United Nations; outlines arrangements for including the UN in established international law; describes the Security Council's power to deal with disputes through investigation and mediation; establishes the Economic and Social Council, International Court of Justice, and the United Nations Secretariat.
Source: Wikipedia, http://en.wikipedia.org/wiki/United_Nations_Charter

June 1946 Commission on Human Rights
The Commission on Human Rights was set up to monitor, examine, and report to the public on major global human rights violations, or on any human rights situations in specific countries or territories.
Source: UNCHR, http://www.unchr.ch/html/menu2/2/chr.htm

December 1948 Universal Declaration of Human Rights
Asserts a wide variety of political and quality of life rights for all people and provides a common standard for all nations to that end.
Source: UN, www.un.org/rights

December 1948 Convention on the Prevention and Punishment of the Crime of Genocide
"This convention bans acts committed with the intent to destroy, in whole or in part, a national, ethnic, racial or religious group." It

makes genocide a crime that is punishable under international law, no matter whether it is committed as an act of war or during peace-time. All signators are bound to prevent and punish any acts of genocide committed within their jurisdiction.
Source: Human Rights Web, www.hrweb.org/legal/undocs.html #UDHR

August 1949 Convention for the Amelioration of the Condition of the Wounded and Sick in Armed Forces in the Field
This was the first Geneva convention, and it concentrated on setting the rights of all individuals, combatants and non-combatants, during times of war.
Source: Human Rights Web, www.hrweb.org/legal/undocs.html#UDHR

November 1950 European Convention on Human Rights (Council of Europe)
Established the European Court of Human Rights.
Source: www.echr.coe.int/ECHR/EN/Header/Basic+Texts/Basic+Texts/The+European+Convention+on+Human+Rights+and+its+Protocols/

July 1951 Convention Relating to the Status of Refugees
Defines who is a refugee and details refugee rights, and the respon-sibilities of nations who grant asylum to refugees.
Source: Wikipedia, http://en.wikipedia.org/wiki/Convention_Relating_to_the_Status_of_Refugees

December 1952 Convention on the Political Rights of Women
Establishes that all women shall be entitled to vote or run for office in all elections on equal terms with men, without discrim-ination.
Source: Human Rights Education Association, www.hrea.org

September 1954 Convention on the Status of Stateless Persons
Defines who is a stateless person and sets out minimum rights and obligations for stateless persons.
Source: Executive Committee of the High Commissioner's Program, http://rsq.oxfordjournals.org/cgi/reprint/26/1/127.pdf

September 1956 Convention Abolishing Slavery
Abolished various forms of slavery, including "debt bondage, serfdom, servile marriage, and child servitude."
Source: Wikipedia, http://en.wikipedia.org/wiki/1956_UN_Supplementary_Convention_on_the_Abolition_of_Slavery

June 1957 Convention on the Abolition of Forced Labour (ILO)
Concerned with: abolishing concentration camps, ending deportation of national minorities, ensuring fair methods of wage payment, eliminating debt bondage and serfdom, and improving worker conditions.
Source: International Labour Organization, www.ilo.org/public/english/bureau/leg/resolutions.htm

November 1962 Convention on Consent to Marriage
Establishes that no marriage is legally binding without the full and free consent of both parties. The consent given must be expressed publicly, in person, and in the presence of a competent authority as well as witnesses, "as prescribed by law."
Source: Office of the United Nations High Commissioner for Human Rights, www2.ohchr.org/english/law/convention.htm

December 1965 Convention on the Elimination of Racial Discrimination
Focuses on eliminating racial discrimination "in all its forms" and seeks to promote understanding among all races. Declares that "each State Party [will] engage in no act or practice of racial discrimination against persons, groups . . . or institutions, and [will] ensure that all public authorities and public institutions, national and local, shall act in conformity with this obligation."
Source: Office of the United Nations High Commissioner for Human Rights, www2.ohchr.org/english/law/cerd.htm

December 1966 International Covenant on Economic, Social, and Cultural Rights
"Describes the basic economic, social, and cultural rights of individuals and nations, including the right to: self-determination; wages sufficient to support a minimum standard of living; equal

pay for equal work; equal opportunity for advancement; form trade unions; strike; paid or otherwise compensated maternity leave, free primary education, and accessible education at all levels; copyright, patent, and trademark protection for intellectual property."
Source: Human Rights Web, www.hrweb.org/legal/undocs.html#UDHR

December 1966 International Covenants on Civil and Political Rights
Describes the basic civil and political rights of nations and individuals. The rights of nations include "the right to self determination; the right to own, trade, and dispose of their property freely, and not be deprived of their means of subsistence." The rights of individuals include "the right to legal recourse when their rights have been violated, even if the violator was acting in an official capacity; the right to life; the right to liberty and freedom of movement; the right to equality before the law; the right to the presumption of innocence til proven guilty; the right to appeal a conviction; the right to be recognized as a person before the law; the right to privacy and protection of that privacy by law; freedom of thought, conscience and religion; freedom of opinion and expression; freedom of assembly and association."
Source: Human Rights Web, http://hrweb.org/legal/undocs.html#UDHR

December 1966 Optional Protocol to the Covenant on Civil and Political Rights
Allows the Human Rights Commission to judge complaints of human rights violations from individuals in the signator countries and in so doing adds legal muscle to the Covenant on Civil and Political Rights.
Source: Human Rights Web, www.hrweb.org/legal/undocs.html#UDHR

November 1973 International Convention on the Suppression and Punishment of the Crime of Apartheid
Declares that Apartheid is a crime and that policies and practices of Apartheid or similar policies and practices violate international law.
Source: Human Rights Internet, www.hri.ca/uninfo/treaties/11.shtml

December 1975 Declaration on the Rights of Disabled Persons
Promotes the political, civil, and economic rights of disabled persons.
Source: Office for the High Commissioner of Human Rights, www2. ohchr.org/english/law/res3447.htm

June 1977 Protocol Additional to the Geneva Conventions
Reaffirms and develops the principles of the Geneva Conventions.
Source: International Committee of the Red Cross, www.icrc.org/ihl.nsf/ 7c4d08d9b287a42141256739003e636b/f6c8b9fee14a77fdc125641e00 52b079

December 1979 Convention on the Elimination of all Forms of Discrimination against Women
Defines discrimination against women, and sets an agenda for ending it. Is "often described as an international bill of rights for women."
Source: Human Rights Web, www.un.org/womenwatch/daw/cedaw/

December 1984 Convention Against Torture
Defines torture, and bans it under all circumstances. It "establishes the UN Committee against Torture . . . requires states to take effective legal and other measures to prevent torture . . . [and] it forbids countries to return a refugee to his country if there is reason to believe he/she will be tortured."
Source: Human Rights Web, http://hrweb.org/legal/undocs.html#UDHR

November 1989 Convention on the Rights of the Child
"A universally agreed set of non-negotiable standards and obligations." This convention set minimum entitlements and freedoms that should be respected by all nations, including individual dignity and worth regardless of "race, colour, gender, language, religion, opinions, wealth, birth status or ability."
Source: Unicef, www.unicef.org/crc/

May 1993 International Criminal Tribunal for the Former Yugoslavia (ICTY)
Worked to hold all individuals accountable for war crimes regardless of their position, and in so doing "dismantled the tradition of

impunity for war crimes and other serious violations of international law."
Source: ICTY, www.un.org/icty/glance-e/index.htm

December 1993 Convention on Biological Diversity (CBD)
Set out "commitments for maintaining the world's ecological underpinnings as we go about the business of economic development . . . establishes three main goals: the conservation of biological diversity, the sustainable use of its components, and the fair and equitable sharing of the benefits from the use of genetic resource."
Source: CBD, www.biodiv.org/convention/guide.shtml

November 1994 International Tribunal for Rwanda (ICTR)
Was created to assist in the process of national reconciliation and peacekeeping in Rwanda. Was also established for the prosecution of persons responsible for genocide and other violations of international law committed in Rwanda between January 1, 1994, and December 31, 1994.
Source: ICTR, http://69.94.11.53/default.htm

March 1999 Convention on the Prohibition of the Use, Stockpiling, Production, and Transfer of Anti-Personnel Mines and on their Destruction (Ottawa Treaty)
"The Convention aims to ban outright and mandate the destruction of anti-personnel mines in order to put an end to the suffering and casualties caused by these weapons."
Source: UN, www.un.org/millenium/law/xxvi-22.htm

July 2002 International Criminal Court (ICC)
Tries people for international crimes, including "genocide, crimes against humanity, and war crimes."
Source: ICC, www.ice-cpi.int/about.html

October 2005 Convention on the Protection and Promotion of the Diversity of Cultural Expressions (UNESCO)
Seeks to protect the cultural expressions of all countries by reaffirming the rights of states to draw up cultural policies, recognizing cultural goods and services as "vehicles of identity, values and

meaning" and strengthening international cooperation to favor international cultural expression.
Source: UNESCO, http://portal.unesco.org/culture/en/ev.php

June 2006 Declaration on the Rights of Indigenous Peoples
Asserts the political, civil, and economic rights of indigenous peoples.
Source: UN, www.un.org/News/Press/docs/2007/gal0612.doc.htm

Note: For an alphabetized topic list of "international human rights instruments," see the University of Minnesota Human Rights Library: www1.umn.edu/humanrts/instree/ainstlsa2.html

A Note on Sources

Contemporary academic literature on the public domain has experienced a well-needed renaissance. Explorations of the public sphere, public goods, public spaces and places constitute a unique interdisciplinary examination of all "things public" and its diverse corpus continues to be a rich study in scholarly innovation and intellectual originality. The great theorist of the public sphere of interactive communication is, without a doubt, Jürgen Habermas. His magisterial analysis, *The Structural Transformation of the Public Sphere*, written as his doctoral dissertation, was rejected by Theodor Adorno and Max Horkheimer, the iconic founders of the Frankfurt School, for not towing the party line on Marx and superstructural theorization. Hannah Arendt's *The Human Condition* gives us an equally compelling view of "the space of men acting together" and "where freedom can appear as civic virtue." Both Nancy Fraser in *Justice Interruptus: Critical Reflections on the "Postsocialist" Condition* and Seyla Benhabib in *Situating the Self: Gender, Community and Postmodernism in Contemporary Ethics* have forced a contemporary rethinking of the public sphere from a feminist perspective. A landmark debate on the importance of Habermas's ideas is contained in Craig Calhoun's much relied on volume, *Habermas and the Public Sphere*. John Dewey's *The Public and its Problems* and Walter Lippman's *The Phantom Public* present sharply divergent analyses of the role of public opinion and remain basic reading.

Drawing the line between the public and the private has been a central preoccupation of modern political philosophy from Hobbes to Kant through Mill, Marx, and Foucault. Jeff Weintraub and

Krishan Kumar have produced a very helpful collection, *Public and Private in Thought and Practice*. Richard Sennett's *The Fall of Public Man* is an important milestone in examining the public-private binary from an American perspective. One of the most influential books, *The Revolt of the Masses* by José Ortega y Gasset, remains a powerful statement of elite hierarchical and ornamental publics. Christopher Lasch's *The Revolt of the Elites* serves as a riposte. His is indispensable to a modern appreciation of the way elites have abandoned the public sphere in a period of ascendant global liberalism. Cass Sunstein's *Why Societies Need Dissent* is essential to understanding the virtue of dissent as a social good. Equally challenging is Michael Warner's *Publics and Counterpublics*, which examines the fragility of the modern public and its inherent bias towards the exclusion of the marginal, sexual non-conformists and disturbers of orthodoxy. Hal Niedzviecki's *Hello, I'm Special: How Individuality Became the New Conformity* is a terrific analysis of modern mass culture selling individuality to the masses. Amartya Sen's *The Argumentative Indian* examines the history of public reasoning in India and the importance of voice and heterodoxy to tolerating dissent through argument in a country facing grueling poverty, insecurity, and communal violence. Certainly his book has much relevance for democracy, not only in India, but for the growth of multicultural and diverse democracies worldwide.

Arjun Appadurai has been a pivotal figure in the examination of the contradictions and consequences of global cultural flows in an era of globalization. His earlier book *Modernity At Large: Cultural Dimensions of Globalization* is path-breaking in its theoretical originality, exploring the ways ideas, people, information, and money constitute a new phenomenon that has blurred the boundaries between the citizen and the state and created new uncertainties. His most recent book, *Fear of Small Numbers*, examines the way culturally motivated, large-scale violence has forced us to come to terms with ethnic conflict post-9/11.

Who Controls the Internet: Illusions of a Borderless World by Jack Goldsmith and Tim Wu sheds new light on the global communication sphere of the Internet and provides an important correction to the belief that sovereignty regulation and territoriality are not an integral part of the World Wide Web. Ron Deibert's "International

Plug 'n Play? Citizen Activism, the Internet, and Global Public Policy" is a useful contribution on Internet activism and the role of technology. John Downing's *Radical Media, Rebellious Communication and Social Movements* is a sophisticated examination of the way the radical media has enormous impact on shaping the thinking and values of global publics.

A very useful contemporary analysis of the public sphere and the counterpublics occupying it in a post–Cold War era is by Mike Hill and Warren Montag entitled *Masses, Classes and the Public Sphere*. Pascale Casanova's book *The World Republic of Letters* persuasively demonstrates that the diffusion of literacy norms as a global phenomenon in the nineteenth and twentieth centuries constitutes a world community of writers, translators, and publishers. Extrapolating from her work, I have been influenced to draw an analogy with the global republic of dissent as it shares many characteristics with the map of the literary globe. Richard Posner's *Public Intellectuals: A Study of Decline* is an important though ideologically-driven analysis of theorizing on the role of the modern public intellectual. With respect to the axes of conformity, *The Right Nation: Conservative Power in America* by John Micklethwait and Adrian Wooldridge contains much information about the American social conservative movement's ability to capture the US public agenda. In terms of the economic aspect of the public domain, Michel Albert's *Capitalism vs Capitalism* remains one of the best introductory treatments on the role of collective goods in Anglo-American, German, and social-democratic economies. Inge Kaul's edited collection *Global Public Goods* provides the reader with a strong theoretical introduction to public goods, as well as expanding the definition in innovative ways. She and her contributors argue that public goods not only require international cooperation, but the public has to play an active role in shaping the global public domain and its constitutive elements.

The irrepressible Jagdish Baghwati, the reigning Anglo-American king of contemporary free-trade theory, provides a lucid critique of one of the foundation pillars of classical economics in *Free Trade Today*. A. Claire Cutler's *Private Power and Global Authority* provides an important corrective to modern liberal orthodoxy. *Production Power and the World Order: Social Forces in the Making of History* by Robert Cox is a seminal engagement with the dynamics, structures, and processes of the modern world economy.

Michael Walzer's *Spheres of Justice: A Defense of Pluralism and Equality* is an important theorization of the modern public domain as an instrument of governance. David Marquand is another original theorist of the contemporary public domain; see his *The Decline of the Public*. Maarten Hajer and Arnold Reijndorp *In Search of the New Public Domain* is probably the best study of the reconfigured public domain in the modern European city. *The Market or the Public Domain: Global Governance and the Asymmetry of Power* edited by Daniel Drache explores the concepts, policies, and practices of new instruments of governance at a time of growing skepticism in civil society that the existing global order can survive without major reforms. James Bohman has written extensively on the globalization of the public sphere and new norms of publicity. See for instance "Cosmopolitan Republicans, Citizenship, Freedom, and Global Public Authority." Engin Isin's *Being Political* is an important contribution to modern citizenship practice.

Much scholarship has been focused on the toxic impacts of global neo-liberalism on all aspects of the public. Aihwa Ong's *Neo-Liberalism as Exception: Mutations in Citizenship and Sovereignty* examines the way an interactive mode of citizenship is able to organize people both within the nation-state and globally. David Held's *Global Covenant: The Social Democratic Alternative to the Washington Consensus* contextualizes the anti-globalization movement and global counterpublics in their turn towards the cosmopolitanism, global governance, and transnational citizenship practices.

Branko Milanovic's *Worlds Apart: Measuring International and Global Inequality* is a fundamental text on the challenges of measurement and on understanding why far too little progress has been made in eradicating human misery and exclusion. The United Nations 2006 Human Development Report *Beyond Scarcity: Power, Poverty and the Global Water Crisis* is a chilling document in its detail and accuracy. It demonstrates again the failure of the global trading system to make significant inroads in the provision of the public services so necessary for human progress. For contemporary analysis of the social impacts of the WTO and its dispute resolution mechanism see my studies and reports at www.yorku.ca/drache.

Select Bibliography

Albert, Michel (1993). *Capitalism vs Capitalism*. New York: Four Walls Eight Winds.

Appadurai, Arjun (1996). *Modernity at Large: Cultural Dimensions of Globalization*. Minneapolis, Minn.: University of Minnesota Press.

— (2006). *Fear of Small Numbers*. Durham, N.C.: Duke University Press.

Arendt, Hannah (1998). *The Human Condition*. Chicago, Ill.: University of Chicago Press.

Baghwati, Jagdish (2002). *Free Trade Today*. Princeton, N.J.: Princeton University Press.

Benhabib, Seyla (1992). *Situating the Self: Gender, Community and Postmodernism in Contemporary Ethics*. New York: Routledge.

Bohman, James (2001). "Cosmopolitan Republicanism: Citizenship, Freedom and Global Political Authority," *The Monist* 84:1: 3–21.

Calhoun, Craig ed. (1992). *Habermas and the Public Sphere*. Cambridge, Mass.: MIT Press.

Casanova, Pascale (1999). *The World Republic of Letters*. Cambridge, Mass.: Harvard University Press.

Cox, Robert (1989). *Production Power and the World Order: Social Forces in the Making of History*. New York: Columbia University Press.

Cutler, A. Claire (2003). *Private Power and Global Authority*. Cambridge, UK: Cambridge University Press.

Dewey, John (1954). *The Public and Its Problems*. Athens, Ohio: Swallow Press.

Deibert, Ron (2000). "International Plug n' Play? Citizen Activism, the Internet, and Global Public Policy," *International Studies Perspectives* 1:3: 255–72.

Downing, John (2001). *Radical Media, Rebellious Communication and Social Movements*. Thousand Oaks, Calif.: Sage.

Drache, Daniel (ed.) (2001). *The Market or the Public Domain: Global Governance and the Asymmetry of Power.* London: Routledge.

Fraser, Nancy (1997). *Justice Interruptus: Critical Reflections on the "Postsocialist" Condition.* New York: Routledge.

Goldsmith, Jack, and Wu, Tim (2006). *Who Controls the Internet: Illusions of a Borderless World.* New York: Oxford University Press.

Habermas, Jürgen (1989). *The Structural Transformation of the Public Sphere.* Cambridge, Mass.: MIT Press.

Hajer, Maarten, and Reijndorp, Arnold (2002). *In Search of the New Public Domain.* Rotterdam: NAi Publishers.

Held, David (2004). *Global Covenant: The Social Democratic Alternative to the Washington Consensus.* Cambridge, UK: Polity.

Hill, Mike, and Montag, Warren (2000). *Masses, Classes and the Public Sphere.* New York: Verso.

Isin, Engin (2002). *Being Political.* Minneapolis, Minn.: University of Minnesota Press.

Kaul, Inge, Grunberg, Isabelle, and Stern, Marc A. (1999). *Global Public Goods: International Cooperation in the 21st Century.* New York: Oxford University Press.

Lasch, Christopher (1995). *The Revolt of the Elites and The Betrayal of Democracy.* New York: W. W. Norton & Company.

Lippman, Walter (1925). *The Phantom Public.* New York: Harcourt Brace.

Marquand, David (2004). *The Decline of the Public: The Hollowing Out of Citizenship.* Cambridge, UK: Polity.

Micklethwait, John, and Wooldridge, Adrian (2004). *The Right Nation: Conservative Power in America.* New York: Penguin.

Milanovic, Branko (2007). *Worlds Apart: Measuring International and Global Inequality.* Princeton, N.J.: Princeton University Press.

Niedzviecki, Hal (2004). *Hello, I'm Special: How Individuality became the New Conformity.* New York: Penguin.

Ong, Aihwa (2006). *Neo-Liberalism as Exception: Mutations in Citizenship and Sovereignty.* Durham, N.C.: Duke University Press.

Ortega y Gasset, José (1932). *The Revolt of the Masses.* New York: New American Library.

Posner, Richard (2001). *Public Intellectuals: A Study of Decline.* Cambridge, Mass.: Harvard University Press.

Sen, Amartya (2005). *The Argumentative Indian.* New York: Penguin.

Sennett, Richard (1974). *The Fall of Public Man.* New York: W. W. Norton & Company.

Sunstein, Cass (2003). *Why Societies Need Dissent*. Cambridge, Mass.: Harvard University Press.

United Nations (2006). *Beyond Scarcity: Power, Poverty and the Global Water Crisis*, at http://hdr.undp.org/en/reports/global/hdr2006/.

Walzer, Michael (1983). *Spheres of Justice: A Defense of Pluralism and Equality*. New York: Basic Books.

Warner, Michael (2002). *Publics and Counterpublics*. Cambridge, Mass.: Zone Books.

Weintraub, Jeff, and Kumar, Krishan (1997). *Public and Private in Thought and Practice*. Chicago, Ill.: University of Chicago Press.

Index

abortion 68
Abu Graib 4, 44
accountability 3, 26, 55, 79, 84, 97, 126, 128
Acrimed 104
ActionAid 120
activism ix, 6, 7, 16, 20, 45, 47, 48, 61, 64,
    79, 90, 93, 98, 99, 100, 106, 109, 110,
    115, 116, 118, 122, 124, 126, 130, 146,
    154, 164, 169, 181, 184
activism beyond state boundaries 45
acts of assembly 13
ACT UP 121
Adbusters Media Foundation 100
Adorno, Theodor 61, 110, 179
advertising 82, 91, 100, 114, 116
aesthetic cultural dphere 109
Africa 2,33, 38, 62, 63, 78, 84, 92, 93, 162
Ahmadinejad, Mahmoud 163
alternative media 96, 104
alternative news sites 90, 91, 106
Alternet 104
American Enterprise Institute, the 131
American founding fathers 12, 160
American neo-conservative movement 2,
    120, 136
Amnesty International 128, 142,
anarchists 49, 50, 112, 117, 127
anarchy 25, 50
Anderson, Benedict 15, 23, 62, 86, 102, 114,
    168
Anglo-American legal tradition 25, 32, 153,
    159,
Anglo-Republican model of citizen
    participation 159, 161, 162
anti-corporate dissent 89
anti-globalization activists 75, 91
anti-globalization movement 66, 127, 182
anti-Japan demonstrations of 2005 63
anti-market politics 70, 75, 91
anti-market vote vii, 64
anti-war movement 20, 62, 73, 128, 155
Appadurai, Arjun 9, 10, 22, 23, 43, 52, 78,
    142, 180, 184

arena of activism 16
arena of 'competing claims' 31
arena of conflict 11
arena of public choice 161
Arent, Hannah ix, 9, 10, 13, 22, 26, 60, 121,
    155, 156, 157, 161, 171, 179, 184
Argentina 4, 17, 61, 64, 72
Arthurs, Harry viii, 56, 85
articulation ix, 89, 98, 112
Asia 3, 7, 35, 39, 58, 60, 62, 63, 81, 84, 92,
    162, 166
atlas of cyberspace 102, 114
ATTAC 45, 104
Auschwitz 120
autonomy, individual 27
autonomy, state 75,
axes of conformity, the v, vii, 115, 130, 132,
    138, 144, 181

baby boomers 92, 126, 155
battle in Seattle 20, 62, 86, 140
Bangladesh 78
Barber, Benjamin 88, 125, 143
behavioralism 115
Beijing 63
Bell Labs 101
belonging 24, 29, 47, 48, 79, 81, 108
Benhabib, Seyla 46, 53, 142, 171, 179, 184
Benjamin, Walter ix, 88, 110, 114, 116, 125,
    141, 143, 152, 170
Berger, Peter 47, 53
Berlin Wall 1, 119
Berlusconi, Silvio 65, 67, 124
Bhagwati, Jagdish 37, 51
bias of communication, The 14, 58, 60, 86,
    164
bigness 158
Bin Laden, Osama 137
BlackBerry 76
Blair, Tony vii, 4, 5, 42, 67, 72, 125, 135
blind voting 144
blog 58, 82, 90, 99, 106, 111, 130
blogger 62, 117, 137, 168

blogging 8, 61
blood and belonging 24
Bobbio, Norberto 142, 144, 169
Bohman, James 22, 97, 182, 184
BoingBoing 106
Bono 127
boomer generation 11, 91, 92
borders ii, 36, 80, 102, 119, 146
bottom-up approach 44, 63, 93
boundary disputes 57, 148
Bradlaugh, Charles 154
brandalism 101
branding 31, 100, 116
Brazil 2, 3, 4, 17, 28, 29, 38, 42, 61, 64, 70,
    135
broadband 63, 92, 93
broadcast model 82
British Columbia 101, 147
British politics 147, 153, 154
building political community 121
Bull, Hedley 25, 50
bureaucratic interests 11, 35, 72
bureaucrats 27, 126, 145
bureaucracy 32, 148
Burke, Edmund 136
Bush, George 132
Bush, George W. vii, 3, 4, 5, 22, 28, 36, 41,
    42, 48, 49, 68, 69, 71, 84, 87, 97, 104,
    123, 125, 127, 132, 146, 163
business cycle 38, 65, 167
Byers, Michael 48, 53
Byrd amendment 36
Byrd, Robert 36

Calderon, Felipe 65
Camus's Rebel 164, 171
capitalism 2, 15, 20, 21, 23, 54, 56, 62, 105,
    106, 114, 126, 127, 128, 131, 142, 149,
    165, 166, 167, 168, 171, 181, 184
Canada ii, 4, 21, 35, 56, 58, 64, 67, 76, 81,
    92, 100, 101, 104, 115, 135, 146, 147,
    160, 170
Cancun Ministerial 44, 51, 99
Canclini, Nestor 31, 51
cartography 102
Casanova, Pascale 97, 113, 181, 184
Castells, Manuel 10, 15, 22, 23, 61, 102, 114
Catholics 153
Caves, Richard 94, 112
cellular democratization 79
cellular phones 60, 63, 78, 82, 84, 86, 87, 92,
    105, 168,
Centre for Advanced Spatial Analysis 101
Centre for American Values in Public Life 68
Centre for Civil Society Studies 99
centrist voters 68, 71
Chartists 154
Cheney, Dick 69, 124
Chicago School of Economics, The 131
Chile 4, 72
China 17, 29, 38, 40, 42, 61, 63, 77, 92, 108

Chomsky, Noam 95, 126, 127
Christian Nationalist Movement 137
Christian Right, the 87, 137
Churchill, Winston 136
circuitry of culture 80
citizen iii, ix, 1, 3, 4, 5, 6, 7, 8, 9, 10, 11, 13,
    14, 15, 16, 20, 21, 24, 27, 35, 38, 41,
    43, 44, 45, 46, 48, 49, 51, 52, 53, 57,
    58, 60, 61, 62, 65, 68, 75, 80, 81, 82,
    86, 89, 91, 95, 97, 104, 105, 106, 112,
    125, 126, 133, 134, 142, 143, 145, 146,
    148, 153, 155, 156, 159, 160, 161, 162,
    163, 166, 168, 171, 180, 182, 184, 185
citizen engagement 20, 128
citizen identity 119, 151
Citizen Lab 108
citizenship 1, 10, 15, 16, 21, 23, 24, 43, 45,
    46, 47, 55, 57, 60, 62, 79, 94, 107, 118,
    120, 134, 142, 144, 147, 150, 151, 153,
    155, 158, 159, 160, 161, 162, 163, 168,
    169, 182, 184, 185
citizenship practices 15, 94, 107
citizenship rights 1, 16, 55, 161
citoyens sans culottes 12
CIVICUS 45
civil rights movement 116
civil society 16, 20, 22, 24, 30, 35, 63, 81,
    84, 95, 99, 116, 149, 182
civil society activists 30
Clinton, Bill 111, 141
Clinton, Hillary 3, 42, 69
CNN 77, 90
Coca-Cola 100
Cold War 2, 73, 96, 118, 119, 123, 127
collapse of the communist bloc 96
collapse of the Doha round 18, 32, 50, 164,
    169
collapse of Keynesianism 126
collapse of the US Subprime housing market
    3
collapses of Enron, Worldcom and Hollinger
    14
collective action 1, 13, 14, 64, 118, 159
collective bargaining 37
collective goods 181
collective intervention 96
collective social interest 55
collective voice 110
command and control 2, 14, 20, 84, 141,
    145, 168
Committee for the Cancellation of Third
    World Debt 104
commodity fetish 152
commodity trade 111
communication technology 8, 11, 58, 60
communicative action 11, 13, 14, 86, 91,
    158, 166
communicative diversity 151, 158
community 6, 8, 9, 10, 15, 19, 32, 39, 47, 49,
    57, 62, 63, 79, 105, 107, 111, 117, 118,
    121, 156, 159, 160, 179, 181, 184

Communist Party of China 108
communities of choice 10, 48, 85 89, 168
communities of fate 168
compass of dissent vii, 117, 118, 119, 123,
    129, 130, 138, 144
competition ii, 18, 29, 32, 37, 38, 51, 145,
    147, 159, 164
composed middle, the 144
computers 43, 63, 78, 82, 84, 88, 92, 93,
    105, 106, 108, 125
conforming publics 73, 109
conformity v, vii 20, 66, 90, 96, 109, 115,
    117, 119, 121, 123, 125, 127, 129, 130,
    131, 132, 133, 135, 137, 138, 139, 141,
    143, 144, 150, 174, 180, 181, 185
conservation (environment) 57, 177
Conservative Party in Canada 135
Conservatives 2, 12, 14, 59, 67, 68, 87, 90,
    113, 118, 119, 120, 131, 133, 135, 136,
    137, 138, 139, 141, 143, 163, 181, 185
constitution(s) 18, 24, 32, 47, 55, 85, 150,
    159, 160, 169
contrarians 91, 125, 126, 127, 139
consumers 31, 32, 51, 62, 82, 91, 94, 95,
    100, 101
consumer boycotts 129
Continued Dumping and Subside Offset Act
    of 2000 (*see* Byrd Amendment) 36
Convention Against Torture 176
convergence 60, 72, 79
copyright 32, 37, 61, 120, 175
corporate agenda 30, 31, 32, 84
corporate branding 31, 100, 104
Corporate European Observatory, the 45
corporate trademarks 101
corporate watch 44, 105
corporatist consultation 161
corporations 15, 17, 31, 33, 61, 74, 83, 101,
    108, 128
cosmopolitan(s) 10, 22, 23, 24, 41, 45, 48,
    52, 95, 101, 120, 121, 182, 184
cosmo-populists 120, 169
counterpublics 66, 80, 88, 104, 113, 115,
    117, 125, 130, 141, 143, 144, 170, 180,
    181, 182, 186
counterculture 62, 121, 168
creative class 35, 76, 112
Crosby, Stills, Nash and Young 155
crowd activism 12, 154, 170
culture 7, 9, 20, 22, 23, 31, 32, 41, 51, 52,
    54, 60, 62, 63, 67, 70, 80, 81, 86, 87,
    88, 89, 93, 96, 98, 101, 106, 108, 112,
    113, 114, 117, 122, 123, 130, 134, 144,
    146, 150, 152, 169, 180
culture jamming 100, 113, 117
culture of conformity 96, 133, 138, 139
culture of dissent v, ix, 89, 96, 98, 123,
    154
culture of opposition 117
cultural activists 59, 80
cultural cohesiveness 29

cultural diversity 31, 88
cultural flows 43, 80, 180
cultural goods and services 31, 81, 94, 177
cultural industries 81
cultural protection 31, 94, 109, 150
culture of entitlement 1, 42, 67, 72, 77, 131,
    153, 154, 159, 173, 176, 181
cyberspace 102, 114
Cyber-Geography Research Project 101
cycle of wealth creation 167

dangerous classes 165
Darwinian Individualism 44
decentralization 7, 58, 60, 137, 140, 168
decision making (economic) 34
decline in deference, The 5, 42, 61, 117
defiance 44, 101, 109, 129, 164, 165
defiant publics i, iii, viii, 44, 101, 109, 129,
    164, 165
Deibert, Ronald 108, 180, 184
democracy 4, 12, 18, 22, 23, 29, 56, 86, 88,
    112, 114, 123, 125, 126, 143, 144, 146,
    153, 155, 170, 171, 180, 185
democrats 3, 49, 68, 90, 122
democratic action 27
democratic rights 9, 151, 167
democratic values 26, 56, 90
democratization 63, 72, 79, 93, 109, 168
denationalized citizens 80
deregulation 2, 14, 17, 20, 25, 31, 36, 47, 48,
    55, 57, 70, 74, 76, 91, 96, 100, 102,
    125, 140, 154, 161, 164
de Rothschild, Lionel 153
developing countries 18, 28, 66, 81, 88, 161,
    162
developing nations 44
developmental model, The 161
Dialectic of Enlightenment 61
diasporic communities 45, 81
digerati 76
digital appropriation 95
digital dissent 111
digital divide 43, 63, 84, 92, 112
digital literacy 84
digital participation 91
digital publics v, 89
digital technology 7, 15, 62, 63, 92, 93
digital universe 89, 91, 110
disability international 121
discursive activism 20, 93, 100
discursive communities 10, 58, 78, 89, 116
disgruntled middle 135
disgruntled publics 4, 56, 70, 123, 140
disloyal opposition 139
dissemination 58, 59, 137
dissent 8, 16, 17, 35, 45, 59, 73, 82, 89, 90,
    91, 93, 95, 96, 97, 98, 99, 101, 105,
    106, 107, 109, 110, 111, 112, 113, 117,
    118, 119, 123, 124, 125, 126, 129, 130,
    132, 135, 139, 140, 141, 144, 154, 166,
    170, 180, 181

dissenting publics 73, 99, 108, 122, 135, 140, 141, 167
dissidents 108, 154
distracted and disinterested, the, 134
distraction 56, 62, 94, 95, 108, 133, 134
diversity 21, 31, 32, 50, 68, 81, 88, 94, 106, 111, 116, 142, 146, 151, 152, 153, 154, 155, 163, 171, 177
Dobbs, Lou 77
Doctorow, Corey 106
Dodge, Martin 102, 114
Doha round 18, 28, 32, 50, 51, 164
domain beyond the state 16, 32, 45, 47, 48, 49, 147, 156, 157
domestic governance 29, 37, 56
doubters 91, 125, 136
downward devolution 14, 146, 166
Doyle, James 25, 50
Drudge Report, the 106
Durkheim, Emile 56
Dwyer, Kieron 101
dynamics of power ix, 6, 7, 26, 35, 61, 155, 166

eco-justice 125
economic activity 57, 160, 162
economic determinism 17, 80
economic development strategies 35, 81, 119, 171, 177
economic goals 165
economic globalization 41
economic integration 8, 21, 54, 145, 162
economic liberalism 12, 14, 80
economic theory 9, 12, 29
economies of scale 81
Economist, The 29, 87
education 11, 135, 138, 141, 147, 154, 173, 175
educational standards 81
elites 1, 2, 3, 4, 5, 11, 17, 20, 24, 27, 41, 54, 59, 60, 61, 72, 80, 83, 117, 121, 123, 127, 129, 140, 145, 150, 159, 161, 162, 165, 166, 167, 180, 185
El Pais 97
emergent forms of citizenship 15, 162
engagement 7, 15, 20, 57, 58, 83, 128, 134, 182
Englehart 61
Enron 14, 165
entertainment industries 30, 60, 95, 134
e-public vii, 102, 104, 171
essay on surrealism 110
ethic of activism 9, 98
Europe 7, 29, 35, 62, 67, 68, 71, 72, 93, 115, 123, 129, 137, 150, 152, 161, 173
European 18, 28, 30, 34, 38, 45, 66,71, 72, 73, 81, 100, 102, 113, 115, 128, 131, 141, 149, 150, 152, 154, 160, 161, 162, 164, 170, 171, 173, 182
European Court of Justice 101
European-Federalist model 160, 161

European Union (EU) 18, 28, 32, 34, 63, 71, 72, 73, 84, 87, 101, 162, 164
European Commission 38, 73
European-Federal model of governance integration 160
European framework 66
exclusion 9, 56, 121, 129, 130, 132, 142, 153, 155, 180, 182
exposition Universelle 152
externalities 38

Facebook 81, 82, 91, 106
family x, 5, 11, 12, 37, 44, 48, 61, 73, 90, 99, 133, 134, 150, 169
federal community 160
fertility rates 44
feudalism 149
feudalization 60
financial globalization 19, 28, 74, 77, 118, 157, 167
financial flows 81
Financial Times, The 14, 23, 50, 51, 87, 169
fixers v, 89, 115
flows, capital 14, 74, 81, 151
flows, information 15, 20, 43, 44, 76, 89, 108, 109, 151, 152
flows, media 31
fluid boundaries 70, 82, 84
focus on the global south 104
Fordham University 100
Fordist (economy) 76
foreign investment 76
Foucault, Michel 4, 21, 95, 108, 114, 166, 179
France viii, 17, 18, 63, 64, 71, 72, 87, 104, 133, 152, 170
Fraser, Nancy ix, 140, 179, 185
freedom of association 153, 175,
freedom of expression 98, 119, 175
freedom of speech 121, 153,
free market ideology 76, 145
free trade 2, 35, 36, 37, 51, 86, 104, 181, 184
French Revolution 151
Friedman, Thomas 33, 51, 75, 87
Friends of Lubicon 101
Friends of the Earth 125
Frum, David 130, 136
Fukuyama, Francis 2, 21, 75
fundamentalist Christian 137

G7 42
G8 countries 92, 163
G8 summit 50, 71, 98
G20 92
G24 163
GAP, the 100
gay marriage 68
gay rights 117, 121
GDP 17, 40, 71, 72
Geldof, Bob 116
gender 44, 47, 70, 112, 1188, 139, 176, 179, 184

General Agreement for Trade in Services 30
General Agreement on Tariffs and Trade
    (GATT) 33, 50, 51
genocidal politics 157
geopolitics 118
Germany 4, 17, 61, 64, 71, 72, 81, 87, 120
gesellschaft 98
Gingrich, Newt 90
Gladstone, William 149, 154, 170
Gladwell, Malcolm 122, 142
Global Aids Alliance 121
global capitalism 2, 26, 105, 126, 127, 128,
    165, 166
global citizen iii, ix, 15, 24, 61, 62, 81, 82,
    125, 160, 163, 166
global competetive pressures 29, 51, 74, 130,
    147
global consumer movements 100
global counterpublics 115, 182
globalization ii, viii, ix, 2, 6, 7, 14, 15, 18, 19,
    21, 26, 27, 33, 34, 36, 38, 41, 42, 49,
    51, 52, 53, 54, 61, 65, 66, 68, 72, 74,
    75, 76, 77, 79, 80, 81, 85, 86, 88, 91,
    95, 97, 111,114, 117, 127, 138, 145,
    158, 163, 167, 168, 169, 180, 182, 184
global cultural flows 43, 80, 180
global cultural economy 30, 31, 110
global development 33, 120
global development network, The 120
global economic community 32
global financial corporations 14
global free trade 2, 37
global governance 23, 30, 50, 52, 79, 85, 93,
    105, 113, 143, 156, 159, 166, 182, 185
global information networks 104, 105
global institutions 15, 16, 19, 26, 27, 28, 34,
    45, 61, 79, 94, 157, 162, 166
Global Microcredit Summit in Halifax 2006
    78
global neo-liberalism 2, 3, 18, 66, 69, 155,
    164, 182
global north 36, 43, 46, 77, 92, 95, 99, 105,
    162
global polis 58
global public domain 44, 47, 113, 113, 164,
    171, 172, 181
global public opinion 43, 49, 60, 61, 90
global participatory democracy 82
global provision of public goods 160
global republic of dissent 98, 181
global public interest 26, 27
global social justice movement 101
global south 29, 30, 37, 43, 62, 81, 95, 96,
    104, 105, 127, 162, 167
global trade 19, 105, 162, 164, 182
global trade liberalism 164
globaltTrade watch 105
global warming 66, 116, 125, 126
globalization of poverty 167
Globescan 42, 52, 86
Goldstein, Judith 33, 35

Gorbachev, Mikhail 135
Gore, Al 116, 122, 123
government 1, 2, 3, 4, 5, 6, 9, 11, 13, 15, 18,
    20, 27, 29, 31, 33, 34, 36, 37, 38, 41,
    42, 44, 46, 47, 55, 56, 57, 61, 66, 67,
    68, 69, 71, 72, 73, 74, 75, 76, 84, 89,
    94, 104, 108, 115, 120, 125, 126, 128,
    129, 130, 131, 139, 145, 147, 149, 156,
    157, 158, 160, 161, 168
governance issues 97
Grameen Foundation 78
grassroots 8, 52, 59, 64, 72, 79, 101, 116,
    125, 135, 137, 144
great reversal, the 14, 167
Greenpeace 45, 128
Greenwald, Robert 77, 87
gross national product (GNP) 81
Guantanamo 49, 128
Guardian, The 126

Habermas, Jurgen ix, 11, 13, 26, 35, 55, 58,
    60, 72, 83, 85, 86, 150, 166, 168, 170,
    179, 184, 185
Habitat for Humanity 121
Halifax Initiative, the 105
Hall, Stuart 125
hard power 27, 47, 108, 113, 162, 181
Hardt, Michael 10, 22
Harvard 41
Hayek 136
Hayekian 79, 147
Health Global Alliance Project (GAP) 121
Held, David vii, 9, 10, 22, 23, 52, 112, 182,
    185
Hegel 2, 127
*Hegemony or Survival: America's Quest for
    Global Dominance* 127
Hindu, The 97
HIV/AIDS 6, 110, 121, 138
Hobbes, Thomas 25, 55, 156, 179
Hollinger 14
homogenization 80
Hoover Institution, The 131
Horkheimer, Max 61, 179
hot money 74
How To Make Things Public 148, 169
Hugo, Victor 98, 152
Human Development Index 38
human rights v, ix, 6, 9, 46, 49, 63, 99, 100,
    119, 120, 123, 128, 156, 157, 163, 172,
    173, 175, 176, 178
human rights watch 128
human security 26, 55, 120, 121, 142
humanitarianism 33, 99, 120, 142
hypertext 15, 20, 62, 169

idealist institutionalism 25
identity 6, 8, 10, 15, 23, 29, 31, 44, 48, 75,
    78, 79, 80, 90, 94, 99, 102, 107, 116,
    118, 119, 130, 139, 145, 152, 177
identity and territory 8

ideologies 26, 119
ideology 28, 56, 67, 119, 122, 124, 135, 145
identity-based marketing 90
identity building 90
identity politics 130, 145
IFI Watch Net 105
Ignatieff, Michael 24
"I have a dream" 155
imagination 1, 46, 52, 96, 99, 108, 110, 151, 165
imperial power 3, 152
individual freedom 121, 124
industrial proletariat 145
informed publics 38, 116, 145
India 17, 23, 28, 29, 38, 40, 42, 61, 63, 64, 70, 77, 81, 87, 92, 142, 180, 185
individualism 13, 14, 41, 76, 121, 131, 132, 134
individuals 8, 9, 12, 14, 15, 16, 24, 32, 35, 40, 46, 47, 56, 60, 75, 76, 80, 82, 83, 84, 93, 102, 111, 118, 121, 123, 127, 145, 147, 150, 173, 175, 176
industrial citizenship 153
information 7, 9, 14, 15, 34, 43, 49, 55, 59, 61, 62, 63, 73, 74, 75, 76, 78, 80, 81, 82, 84, 87, 89, 90, 91, 94, 95, 96, 99, 102, 104, 105, 106, 108, 109, 111, 117, 118, 125, 126, 142 151, 152, 165, 180, 181
information age 49, 81, 84, 95, 99, 111
information and communication technologies (ICTs) 63, 93
information age publics *see* publics, information age
information flows *see* flows, information
information processing 34
information production 15
information revolution 73, 74
information technologies 9, 76, 94, 99
informed publics *see* publics, informed
"infotainment" 91
Inglehart, Ronald 6, 7, 22, 129, 138, 143, 158, 159
inhuman nihilism 157
Innis, Harold ii, 8, 14, 22, 58, 59, 60, 67, 83, 86, 95, 112, 168
insurgent publics 105, 110, 164
instant messaging 78, 82
intellectual ammunition 167
intellectual divide 44
intellectual property 28, 30, 33, 50, 51, 63, 85, 94, 175
intellectual property rights 30, 33, 85
intellectuals 19, 35, 95, 96, 97, 113, 118, 130, 140, 142, 147, 168, 181, 185
interdependence 8, 25, 28, 158
interdependencies of the market 161
interdependency 25, 37, 46, 47, 76
interests held in common 162
independent media centre 104
intergovernmental regulation 31, 46, 94

intermediary institutions 74
international association of writers (PEN) 98
international criminal court 163, 176, 177
international community 8,9,19
international covenants on civil and political rights 175
international diplomacy 48
international financial markets 74
international human rights laws 9, 46, 178
international market conditions 37
international markets 59
International Monetary Fund (IMF) 52, 72, 104, 105, 157
international realm 24, 157
international trade 28, 29, 33, 34, 36, 50, 81
International Trade Commission 36
Internet, the 15, 58, 63, 74, 77, 78, 81, 82, 89, 90, 91, 92, 93, 94, 97, 101, 102, 105, 107, 111, 112, 134, 137, 138, 156, 165, 180, 181
Internet age ix, 89, 134, 165
Internet Mapping Project 101
Internet service providers (ISPs) 102,
Internet subscribers 105
Internet users 92, 123
inviolability of rights 131
invisible hand, the 41
Iraq, invasion of 4, 5, 42, 48, 63, 68, 71, 120, 123, 126, 128, 136, 139, 165
Islamist Jihad movement 137
Islamist militants 97
Israel for the Jews movement 137
IT (digital or information) revolution 43, 63, 73, 74, 76, 93, 158, 166

Japan 34, 63, 71, 73, 81
Jenkins, Roy 153, 154, 170
Johns Hopkins University 99
Jubilee Debt Campaign 121

Kagan, Robert 130, 136
Kant, Immanuel 22, 50, 147, 169, 179
Katyal, Sonia 100, 113
Keegan, John 149, 170
Kennedy, John F. 118
Kent State University 155
Keohane, Robert 29
Keynesian welfare state 12, 79, 159, 165
Keynesianism 68, 118, 126
King, Martin Luther 155
Kitchin, Rob 101, 114
Klein, Naomi 106, 114, 167, 171
Kristol, William 130
Kundera, Milan 118
Kyoto 120

LaFontaine, Louis-Hyppolite 147
laptop computer 43
Latin America 39, 68, 78, 162
Latour, Bruno 88, 148, 169, 170, 171
la via campesina 104

Lazarsfeld, Paul 7, 22
Lefebvre, Henri 27, 50
legitimacy 6, 16, 17, 24, 46, 56, 64, 96, 120,
    139, 163, 171
Lexus 51, 75, 87
liberals 12, 90, 113, 122
liberal citizenship 162
liberal democracy 1, 125, 153
liberal institutionalism 28, 46
liberalism 2, 3, 11, 12, 14, 18, 21, 24, 27, 38,
    39, 42, 65, 66, 69, 71, 80, 96, 121, 131,
    142, 145, 155, 164, 166, 180, 182, 185
liberalization 18, 19, 29, 30, 32, 33, 37, 51,
    54, 81, 167 171
lifestyle identity 116
lineages of the modern public 148
Lippman, Walter 20, 23, 179, 185
literacy 43, 44, 58, 65, 81, 84, 109, 160, 181
Live Earth concerts 116
Live 8 concerts 116
localism 120, 127
Locke, John 55
London School of Economics 140
Long Tail, tThe 82
Louis XIV 150
Lula da Silva, Luiz Inacio 135

Mackenzie, William Lyon 147
Madison, James 12, 160
Make Aids History 121
Malthusian markets 41
Mandela, Nelson 155
Mannheim, Karl 109
Mann, Michael 149, 170
Manuel Lopez Obrador, Andres 65
march on Washington, the 155
market(s) ii, v, vii, 1, 3, 8, 11, 14, 17, 19, 22,
    28, 36, 37, 38, 41, 42, 43, 49, 50, 54,
    56, 57, 59, 66, 74, 75, 76, 79, 81, 85,
    86, 88, 94, 113, 118, 130, 135, 140,
    141, 149, 162, 164, 167, 171
market growth 80
market failure 37
market fundamentalism v, 2, 18, 28, 38, 49,
    54, 55, 57, 59, 61, 63, 65, 67, 69, 71,
    73, 75, 77, 79, 81, 83, 85, 87, 111
market actors 17, 24, 57, 85
marketization of Western capitalist
    democracies 41
market stabilization 38
Marquand, David 23, 55, 85, 182, 185
Marseilles 83
Marxian dependency theory 29
Marxism 14, 122
mass communication 63, 109
mass consumption 37, 152
mass culture 20
mass media 7, 61, 82, 111
McCain, John 3
McDonalds 101
McLibel 101

McLuhan, Marshall 15, 95, 112
media activism ix, 100-106, 181
media channel 104
media coalition 121
media conglomerates 32
media literacy 81
Médicins Sans Frontières 45, 120, 128, 142
medium is the message, the 95
Merton, Robert 7, 22
Merckel, Angela 4, 65
meta-ideologies 119
Mexico 3, 38, 63, 65, 133
micro-activist(s) 2,6, 16, 19, 44, 48, 73, 79,
    82, 121, 122, 140, 146
micro-activism ix, 6, 15, 19, 20, 44, 64, 85,
    117, 118, 167
Microsoft 45
middle class, the 29, 77, 125, 150
Middle East, The 39, 75, 146
Micklethwait, John 131, 141, 143, 181, 185
Milanovic, Branko 38, 39, 50, 52, 182, 185
millennium development goals 52, 120, 171
misrecognition 10
Mitterand, Francois 67, 111, 118
mixed economy 18, 164
mobile technology 63
moderate middle 144
modern industrial societies 155
modern sovereignty, paradox of 75
monopolies 14, 33, 37, 59
monopolies of communication 59
Moore, Michael 106, 107 114
moral authority 139, 157
Mount Pelerine Society, the 131
multiculturalism 22, 42, 133, 142
multilateralism 32, 36, 48, 51, 89
multilateral institutionalism 156
multilateral trade governance 28, 32, 162
multinational corporations 17, 128
Mumford, Lewis 148, 169
MySpace 91, 106

narcotizing disfunctionality 7
national identity 29, 80
National Review, the 131
national sovereignty 15, 89, 102
nation-state 15, 17, 52, 62, 69, 74, 89, 109,
    125, 147, 152, 158, 166, 169, 170, 182
Nazi Germany 120, 156
NBC Today Show 100
negative integration 159
Negri, Antonio 10
neo-conservatives 2, 120, 136, 137, 139, 163
neo-liberal economic theory 29, 167
neo-liberal trade model 29
Neo-liberalism 2, 3, 18, 65, 66, 69, 71, 131,
    155, 164, 166, 182, 185
neo-liberal model 3, 12, 17, 18, 29, 35, 48,
    66, 68, 70, 71, 72, 94, 120, 139, 141,
    167
Netherlands, the 64, 129

networked activism 15, 47
networked communities 7, 84, 90, 167
networked global society 167
networks 2, 11, 31, 45, 57, 58, 60, 73, 82,
    84, 92, 93, 104, 105, 108, 119, 121,
    140, 158 159, 161
network society 10, 15, 22, 23, 99, 114
Nevitte, Neil 5, 22, 129, 143
new citizenship practices 1, 15, 107
New Delhi 23, 40, 83, 122, 134
new information technologies 9, 76, 99
New York Times, the 5, 53, 86
niche marketing 90
Nigerian civil war 120
Nike 99, 100, 113
9/11 5, 44, 128, 137, 167, 180
nineteenth-century press 59
nixers v, 89, 115, 117, 119, 121, 123, 125,
    127, 129, 131, 133, 135, 137, 139, 141,
    143
Nixon, Richard 73, 111
Nokia 78
non-conforming publics 55
non-governmental actors 15, 47,
non-governmental organizations (NGOs) 3,
    6, 31, 44, 45, 84, 88, 99, 120, 128
non-market life 57
North America ii, 29, 35, 63, 69, 77, 81, 93
Northern Europe 67
northern governments 18
Nuremburg Trials, the 156
Nye, Joseph 52, 76, 87

Obama, Barak 3, 69
OECD countries 23, 29, 40, 72, 73
official publics 109
offshoring 76, 77
olive tree 51, 75, 87
online (going online) 7, 62, 63, 76, 81, 82,
    90, 91, 92, 96, 97, 101, 102, 104, 106,
    107, 108, 109, 110, 111, 112, 114, 117,
    137, 138, 151, 168
one laptop per child program ($100
    computer) 63, 93
OneWorld 120
Onfray, Michel 140, 143
online disinhibition effect 107 114
online participation 90
open markets 36, 37, 41
oppositional publics 2, 105
Opte Project 101
organized hypocrisy 36
organized labour 118
Ortega y Gasset, José 133, 143, 180, 185
Orwell, George 96, 143
Ostry, Sylvia 34, 35, 50, 51, 52, 82, 88, 112
ownership 59, 63, 93
Oxfam 119, 128
Oxford English Dictionary 117

Paine, Thomas 131

Peoples Global Action Against Free Trade 104
Pew Survey 90, 91, 112
Plotz, John 154, 170
pluralism 1, 9, 29, 31, 85, 88, 94, 98, 107,
    125, 142, 145, 163, 182, 186
Polaris project 122
Polanyi, Karl 19, 23, 54
politics 1, 2, 3, 5, 21, 22, 27, 43, 49, 50, 51,
    52, 58, 60, 61, 64, 66, 67, 68, 69, 70,
    76, 78, 82, 83, 89, 97, 100, 110, 111,
    113, 115, 118, 119, 125, 126, 130, 132,
    136, 139, 141, 142, 145, 148, 154, 157,
    164, 169, 170, 171
political actors 116
political activism 7, 116, 164
political elites 83, 165
political and intellectual maps 95
political integration 160
political malaise 129
political participation 129
political power 8, 17, 60, 95, 109, 126
political refugees 48
political resistance 70
political semiotics 60
political struggle 48, 102, 130
popular dissent 59
populism 18, 120, 135, 169
Postman, Neil 91, 112, 114
postwar period 26
postwar development 1, 37, 46, 48, 77, 130
poverty 6, 8, 38, 40, 43, 116, 119, 120, 124,
    127, 128, 136, 147, 153, 160, 167, 180,
    182, 186
practical liberty 153
practical utopians 128
Prague 155, 161
Prague Spring 155
praxis 115
print capitalism 15, 62, 168
printing press 15, 58, 59, 64, 154
private 8, 11, 12, 16, 18, 19, 25, 26, 27, 40,
    42, 47, 50, 55, 56, 57, 66, 73, 77, 78,
    83, 84, 85, 90, 91, 93, 94, 98, 102, 111,
    118, 123, 131, 132, 135, 140, 147, 148,
    149, 150, 151, 159, 164, 171, 179, 180,
    181, 184, 186
private markets 149
private ownership 93
private property 26, 57, 150
private sphere 57, 73, 111
private interest 8, 19, 26, 55, 148, 151, 159,
    171
privatization 17, 18, 30, 40, 70, 74, 106, 150,
    164
privatization of health care 40
privatization of public services 30
production of information *see* information
    production
Prodi, Romano 65, 67
progressive 3, 30, 58, 96, 101, 106, 119, 131,
    137, 147, 157, 161

proletariat 118, 130, 145
prolexic technologies 101
Project for the New American Century, The
 131
Prometheus 86, 112, 148
property rights 2, 27, 30, 33, 55, 56, 74, 85,
 94, 107
protect me globalization 42
protectionism 42
protection of the individual 156
Psiphon 108
public action 15
public activism 90, 109, 154
public acts 13
public agency 146
public agenda 66, 116, 181
public authority 7, 11, 17, 18, 27, 37, 39, 45,
 57, 67, 80, 83, 120, 128, 135, 149, 157,
 158, 182
public citizen 44
public citizenship 161
public communication 58, 59
public culture 88, 146, 152, 169
public debate 13, 81
public discourse 8, 11, 78, 99, 112, 141, 158
public dissent 2, 59, 122, 154
public domain v, viii, 1, 5, 8, 9, 11, 16, 17,
 18, 19, 21, 23, 25, 26, 27, 29, 32, 39,
 40, 44, 45, 46, 47, 48, 49, 50, 54, 55,
 56, 57, 58, 60, 61, 76, 77, 83, 84, 85,
 88, 106, 108, 111, 113, 116, 140, 147,
 148, 149, 150, 153, 155, 156, 157, 158,
 159, 161, 162, 163, 164, 170, 171, 172,
 179, 181, 182, 185
public endeavor 57
Public Eye on Davos, The 105
public good 19, 42, 146, 150, 146, 154, 162,
 165, 171
public goods 9, 12, 25, 36, 51, 57, 71, 114,
 148, 149, 150, 160, 179, 181
public health 40
public imagination 165
public information 73
public infrastructure 36
public institutions 27, 174
public intellectual(s) 19, 95, 96, 97, 113,
 126, 130, 140, 168, 185
public interest vii, 2, 16, 26, 27, 35, 55, 72,
 73, 76, 78, 86, 89, 104, 147, 149, 150,
 151
public life 44, 68, 90, 152, 153, 154, 159
public matters 148
public mind 110
public reason ix, 5, 8, 9, 12, 17, 35, 58, 65,
 78, 82, 97, 99, 147, 180
public regulatory authority 57
public of citizens 126
public opinion 4, 11, 13, 23, 35, 42, 43, 49,
 58, 59, 60, 61, 65, 90, 91, 109, 110,
 111, 116, 117, 127, 157, 179
public organization 46

public participation 77, 101, 113
public policy 17, 19, 29, 30, 39, 43, 66, 68,
 97, 139, 141, 184
public power 26
public sector 9, 12, 18, 40, 57, 71
public services 30, 115, 183
public space ix, 12, 27, 31, 57, 75, 86, 130,
 150, 161, 165, 179
public spending 17, 68, 71, 72, 87, 149
public sphere v, 11, 13, 16, 18, 24, 25, 27,
 29, 31, 33, 35, 37, 39, 41, 43, 45, 47,
 48, 49, 51, 53, 56, 60, 61, 66, 72, 73,
 74, 85, 86, 93, 97, 109, 111, 113, 132,
 145, 150, 151, 153, 166, 170, 179, 180,
 181, 182, 184
public sphere of interactive communication
 93
public values 30
publics, informed 7, 16, 21, 38, 62, 145, 153
publics, information age 111
publics, skeptical 140
pull media 82
push media 82
Putin, Vladmir 124
Putnam, Robert 7, 58, 86
pyramid 43, 62, 99, 164, 165
pyramid networking 99
pyramid societies 164

Quebec's provincial election 67

radical dystopian(s) 127
radical ideas 8, 58
radical media 181, 184
radio 7, 63, 78, 93, 94, 96, 105, 168
rally 26, 30, 39, 47, 77, 99, 110, 115, 116,
 138, 141, 146, 148, 154, 180
rally the public 141
rational individualism 160
Reagan, Ronald 42, 73, 111, 132
Reaganomics 42
reallocation of power 166
reason (public) *see* public reason
recognition 9, 10, 13, 22, 47, 78, 85, 98, 101,
 121, 142, 159
Red Cross 120
redistribution 44, 70, 127, 160, 162
redistributive social policies 39, 41
refeudalization of the public sphere 11, 72
regulation 1, 2, 17, 27, 28, 31, 34, 37, 39, 42,
 74, 76, 118, 164, 180
relational power 26, 47, 108, 121, 140, 158
republic 97, 98, 113, 181, 184
Republican 68, 69, 87, 90, 159, 161, 162,
 182, 184
Research In Motion 76
resource dependency 35
res publica 25, 148
restructuring 77
Rifkin, Jeremy 76
rights-based discourse 9

right to have rights, the 10, 121, 156, 158, 161
right to indifference 130
Rio 40
Rodrik, Dani 52, 140, 169
Roman law 25
Rousseau, Jean-Jacques 55, 85
Ruggie, John 8, 22, 85, 113, 171
Rule By The People 151
rural poor 43
Rutherford, Paul 106, 114

Said, Edward 96, 98, 113
salon.com 97
Sao Paulo 83
Sarkozy, Nicolas 3, 18, 66, 140, 143
Sartre, Jean-Paul 96
Saunders, Doug 71, 87
Save the Children 119
scarcity 12, 118, 159, 182, 186
Schumpter 168
Schumpterian 16
skeptical publics *see* publics, skeptical
skeptics viii, 76, 91, 123, 124, 125, 126, 139, 167
Schlesinger, Arthur 144, 169
Schwab, Susan 32, 51
Schroeder, Gerhard 65, 67
seamless markets 79
Second World War *see WWII*
second globalization story 76
security values 159
self-expression values 138
self-interest 12, 25, 46, 49, 54, 83, 115, 134, 157, 160
self-organizing publics 2
semiotic disobedience ix, 99, 100, 101, 113
semiotic sesisters 100
Sen, Amartya 17, 40
sex trade workers 121
Shanghai 40, 63
Shell Oil 45
shock doctrine 167, 171
sicko 106, 114
silence 98, 101, 120
SMIG 72
social action 15
social agenda 93
social activists 24, 57, 61, 90, 91, 100, 122, 161
social belonging 29
social bond 26, 31, 36, 42, 85, 119, 124, 145, 147, 160, 167
social change 2, 7, 8, 9, 89, 122, 123, 166
social conservatives 12, 131, 132
social discourse 96
social diversity 21, 155
social engagement 48, 83
social Europe 71
social inclusion vii, 119, 124, 140, 144, 145
social movement activism 5, 99

social movements 2, 5, 8, 17, 81, 84, 89, 90, 91, 99, 123, 139, 142, 147, 165, 168, 181, 184
social networks 60, 78, 84, 88, 91, 92
social programs 17, 41
social relations 4, 48, 109, 118, 139
social research 49, 111
social responsibility 130, 162
social movements 2, 5, 8, 17, 81, 84, 89, 90, 91, 99, 123, 139, 142, 147, 165, 168, 181, 184
social welfare 71
social network(s) 60, 78, 84, 88, 91, 92
social networking 78, 91
social stability 165
socialist movements 59
social values x, 41, 73, 116, 130, 133, 135
society 2, 5, 7, 10, 11, 12, 13, 15, 16, 20, 22, 23, 24, 27, 30, 32, 35, 49, 50, 53, 57, 61, 63, 64, 65, 67, 73, 81, 84, 85, 86, 87, 93, 95, 96, 99, 100, 102, 107, 110, 111, 114, 116, 120, 121, 127, 129, 131, 134, 137, 138, 140, 148, 149, 150, 155, 165, 166, 167, 168, 170, 182
Sontag, Susan 96
soulless despotism 147
southern hemisphere 72
Smith, Adam 55
space, place, and citizenship 144
space of flows 102
space of place 102
sphere of interactive communication 2, 19, 43, 78, 147
spheres of political interaction (spheres of interaction) 10, 89
squierachy and hierarchy 153
Stanford University 33
Starbucks 76, 101
state enterprises 18, 27, 74
state policy ii, 118
state sovereignty 24, 46, 74, 75, 163
Stiglitz, Joseph 34, 35, 51
Strange, Susan 47, 50, 53, 85
strategic lawsuit against public participation 101
strategic planning 148
strategic voting 117
status quo 98, 107, 132, 137, 139, 160 168
status quo stability 137, 160
structural power 47, 158
structures of modernity 47
Sunstein, Cass 90, 112, 180, 186
survival values 138
Sweden 4, 17, 64, 68
swing voters 4, 6, 20, 65, 69, 135, 144
systems and structures 118
systemic interdependency 46

Taliban 146
talk back 100
Tarrow, Sidney 45, 53